CW01509426

Salaam Bollywood

Salaam Bollywood

THE PAIN AND THE PASSION

Bhawana Somaaya

SPANTECH & LANCER
1999

First published, 1999

ISBN 1 897829 54 X

Published by
Spantech & Lancer
Spantech House
Lagham Road
South Godstone
Surrey RH9 8HB, England
Fax 44 1342 892584
E-mail books@spantech.demon.co.uk

Spantech USA
3986 Ernst Road
Hartford WI 53027, USA
Fax 1 414 6739064

Spantech & Lancer
119 Stratton Cres. S.W.
Calgary, Alberta,
Canada T3H 1T7
Fax 1 403 2492477

Distributed in India by
Seagull Bookstore Private Ltd.
31 A Shyama Prasad Mukherjee Road
Calcutta 700 025
Tel 91 33 4765865; Fax 91 33 2805143
E-mail seagull@giascl01.vsnl.net.in

Printed at
Print Perfect, New Delhi

TO

MY PARENTS

WHO INCULCATED IN ME

THE RIGHT VALUES OF LIFE

Foreword

Introspective journalism seldom brings more economic benefit than one that is sensational.

One always remembers or goes straight to the gossip page rather than the 'editors note.'

I admire journalists. I admire them because their job is difficult and tough. It's tough being part of a human real-life experience, without the thought crossing the mind that it could make a terrific copy.

It's like acting. Rarely does an actor not be a part of a real-life experience, without the thought crossing his mind, how wonderful and effective it would be if he could recreate it, in front of the camera.

Attitudes of the acting and journalistic professions have similarities. One recreates what one observes or experiences on film, the other on paper. A judgement of the calibre comes when one views the sincerity of the reproduction. Actors may not necessarily be in a position to have first-hand experiences. Journalists most of the time do. Or at least, readers expect that the integrity of their profession or their code of conduct, will coerce them to do so. And this is where the dilemma comes in.

Film journalism has thrived on personalised reportage. The actor, quite obviously, is the saleable commodity—the human, the individual, the celebrity, the personality. But the journalist is an individual and a human too.

When and where does he stop being one and becoming the other?

Every evening, or whenever it is, they sit to write their

column, a journalist will make decisions. Decisions which will invariably be tough and difficult.

As humans, they will desire normal human relationships— most of the time with the subject of their profession.

They will be privy to episodes and attitudes hitherto unknown, to the ever-so-hungry-and-starved-for-information, reader. So, how far do you go? Do you protect the trust and sincerity of your association or do you fearlessly exhibit the loyalty that your profession demands?

Is all that you will read in the pages that follow, all that Bhawana Somaaya was privy to? Did she retain the sincerity of her relationship? Or was she loyal to the profession? If there is a balance, what yardstick did she use? And more importantly, who can and who will judge the measure!!

Either which way, the pleasure will be entirely the readers. That's what this book will profess to do.

And are we not in the midst of a dichotomy right here— an actor passing word on a journalist? Which is why—I admire journalists. I admire them because their is difficult and tough.

AMITABH BACHCHAN

Preface

CHRONICLING THE incidents with specific dates would have been difficult. I have relied on my memory and some clippings to recall the encounters. The excerpts reproduced with relevant alterations are from articles contributed to various journals and publications—*Cinema Journal, Super, Movie, Sunday* and *g*. There's a possibility that there are some lapses, but I have tried my best.

This book wouldn't have been possible without Edna Sundaresan, my coordinator whose speed and precision in typing remains unmatched. Her patience and involvement till the very end remained undiminished. Edna is precious for her original and fearless feedback.

Without the unflinching support of Monica Motwani, who walked into my life out of the blue and proved a permanent and a selfless sounding board.

And to *g* (Chitralekha) for providing the relevant pictures.

BHAWANA SOMAAYA

Prologue

I STAND ON THE road waiting for my car feeling perfectly happy. Suddenly, the feeling disappears. There is a tautness within the belly. Without warning, an ache is coming on. I feel cheated. Only a few minutes ago, I was complimenting the weather, wondering if I could go picking dry leaves. Things seemed perfectly in control, without a shadow of stress. The car pulls up and halts by my side. As I get inside the vehicle I'm aware of a weariness. Maybe I'm getting melodramatic, like the actress I interviewed yesterday. My profession has strong, operative influences. Hopping from studio to studio, make-up room to make-up room, getting involved in the experiences of so many stars, is not healthy.

For distraction, I reach for the book I'm reading. It says: 'Today we visited the home where Charles Dickens wrote my beloved *David Copperfield*. I remember weeping as I read it. And today, standing by his desk, I felt sure he wept writing it.' The lines move me and sure enough the weariness abates. When stars quote similar thoughts in my interviews, I'm judgemental.

I remember director Mahesh Bhatt yelling, 'look exposed' from behind the camera as the trolley moves towards Shabana Azmi. Her face cracks with unleashed emotions and what follows is a spillover of pent up tears. Dwelling in a world of heightened consciousness, the stars, in their violent outpouring of emotions for the camera, quite often lose grip on reality. They have enacted so many scenes, displayed so many emotions and mouthed so many lines that they feel out of 'quota', that they ought to restrict themselves from demonstrating any further. They become so sensitive to their own situations that everytime they feel like an outburst, they hold themselves back. 'This looks like a film scene. . . . That sounds like a film dialogue,' they say. What is real, is suppressed for the fear that it might appear false. But the pent up emotions must find release.

They do. While enacting a serious scene. The director says, 'Wow! what a good shot.' The artiste is himself surprised, little realising that there is so much seething within, that all it needs is a trigger. Such ingenuous control over feelings that the functioning itself is frightening. Insecurity is an overwhelming emotion in any creative profession. In the film industry, more so. There are more emotional wrecks here than any other place. Aren't they selling emotions? Some are better manipulators—they play games. Some are better fighters—they survive. Some take to the bottle—the escapists. Some find release in involvements—the weak ones, who need live crutches to help them out.

When the influences become overpowering, I throw up my hands and say, 'No more!' It is a day when all possibilities get exhausted. I have heard so many secrets, read so many scandals that my soul feels soaked to the skin. The outpourings resulting in a person who gradually stops reacting. With time comes distance and a certain detachment. From the participant, I become the spectator. But the feeling doesn't last. Despite the shame and the scandals, the deprivation and the degradation, the exhibitionism and the eccentricity, there is an energy, a fatal attraction about the world of cinema that is obsessive. Once you've been a part of it you feel incomplete without it.

This book is my homage to the film world.

The memories are an essential part of my growing up. Some hurt even now. Some soothe me—they are reminders of destiny being kind to me. I'm convinced that no other profession could have been as enriching. I owe many lessons of life to the film fraternity.

1

THERE WAS A madness about that summer. When things are going to change, you can sense it in your surroundings. My parents, who had never left my sister and me alone for a night, had confirmed a three-month long vacation with my brother in Canada. This was our first experience of freedom and we were too excited to conceal it. The exhiliration was apparent as we stood at the airport waving them goodbye. My brother-in-law, watching our gleeful faces remarked, 'You girls don't look like someone whose parents are going away for a month.' Perhaps my parents sensed this too. Watching them from a distance, I felt my father suddenly looked tired and my mother distressed. She had been giving us instructions until our eyes could meet no longer.

We began our celebrations the very next day. Everyday we would bring home a bunch of friends from college. A major part of the afternoon was spent cooking food and later eating it. Those days enjoyment meant simple things like listening to music and chatting. It was during this absolutely languorous phase that a college friend suggested that I join her at her new job. She was assisting a neighbour who had recently got into the publishing business. For a few weeks, the friend and I would travel everyday from Churchgate to Colaba after college. The magazine was called *Superstar*. And the office, if you please, functioned from a garage in the friend's building. A broken desk and two shaky chairs served as furniture. The editor, Mr. Gomes was a curly-haired, bushy moustached, big built man. Gomes asked me no questions and confirmed me on a monthly salary of Rs.100.

My first thought was, 'What will I do with so much money?' Prior to this I had been assisting a solicitor, who helped Swedish parents adopt Indian children. It was a dignified but boring job. In comparison the new job was a picnic. My friend and I would sit all afternoon in Gomes' office and listen to him wax eloquent. 'It will be a dream magazine . . .' he would say, his eyes full of stars.

Gomes resembled and spoke like the late comedian Keshto Mukherjee. 'Stars will walk into this place and pester you guys to write about them.' When he said that I'd stare at the harsh sunlight streaming into the room, the chipped teacup in my hand and the shaky legs of the desk resting on bricks and wonder why anyone would want to come to a hole like this. My friend was equally amused but more sympathetic towards her neighbour. I couldn't be as sympathetic because Gomes made so many faces while talking that I would be in splits. A favourite subject of Gomes that I can't forget even after all these years is his discussion of bribes by stars. 'They may try to tempt you, make you offers under the table.' That was the first time I'd heard the phrase and naively ducked to check what exactly he meant. 'How much do you think they will offer?' I asked innocently. Gomes shrugged. 'Anything. . . . It can be just about anything.' Silly as it may now seem, but anyone offering a sum bigger than Rs.100 at that time was unimaginable. Over the years, I read and was told about corruption in journalism, about power-drunk producers buying over reviewers, but unfortunately, nothing so adventurous ever happened to me. Perhaps bribe givers recognise their potential clients.

A week after getting our first salary, my friend and I arrived one afternoon, to find our boss crestfallen, holding his head in both his hands. 'So many dreams. . . . And now it is all over. There is a financial crisis. We have to fold up the magazine. But we'll meet again . . .,' he said shaking my hand. 'We will,' I said knowing fully well that I'd never bump into Gomes ever again.

For a while I forgot all about journalism, until one fine day I saw an advertisement in a paper which said, 'Wanted college students with a flair for writing.' After my one month stint at Gomes' garage, I felt I was a deserving candidate, never mind that I hadn't written a single sentence during the forty-day tenure. It was a monsoon morning and I'd borrowed a purple saree from my sister for, in those days appearing for an interview in any other dress was unthinkable. I slipped on my platform heels and took a BEST bus to an address I had only heard about, never visited. Hotel Taj, Apollo Bunder.

My father worked for the Burma-Shell and five-star culture wasn't a part of our lifestyle. Twice a month we were taken to the movies but only after father approved of the review in the papers. On weekends, on moonlit nights he'd walk us down and buy us creamy pastries from the local Irani restaurant. Flamboyance wasn't part of our growing up. So a distinct feeling of fear overcame me as the strong draft of the air-conditioner filled my nostrils. Even today, I associate the smell with that old memory. A sea of faces in the long passage outside the ballroom blocked my vision. A few volunteers distributing application forms were guiding candidates into a walk-in interview. I was surprised. I didn't know for one, that so many people read newspapers. Two, that so many people were jobless and three, most important, so many people fantasised of themselves as writers. So after the initial fear, I let the crowd mentality take over. There is comfort in being a commoner. Suddenly, it didn't matter how I fared in the interview. It didn't matter that everyone, except me, was accompanied by an escort. Unknowingly, I had followed the first rule of journalism. Unless confirmed, never let anyone into a secret.

Looking back, I think that it was the most professionally conducted interview I ever went through. Beginning with the filling of a detailed application form, one was put through a gruelling question-answer session by a panel of four intimidating judges. As I waited for my turn, I wondered what I was doing in a strange place with strange people. I thought of my parents and shuddered to think of their reaction. Money was never in excess at home, but working was never made out to be a necessity. The emphasis was always on education. Strangely, for me, the process of finding a job was far more exciting than getting the job. There was no doubt in my mind that I didn't want the job. That I wasn't writer material. My self-image was that of a hardworking, sincere and moderately talented person. My brother thought otherwise. Once, he happened to read a college tutorial that I had left on the desk and said, 'Do you know you can write? Actually write?' I didn't take his compliment seriously.

My mind clouded with all these thoughts, I walked into the sparsely furnished room for my share of interrogation. A long table covered with a white cloth, a few flower baskets and some unfriendly faces stared at me from behind the desk. Two of them didn't speak a word, the third, a turbaned gentleman dug his teeth into a *tandoori* chicken. This was my first exposure to undisguised non-vegetarian food and I felt nauseous. The fourth, the spokesman (a grey-eyed man) looked at me icily and said, 'I'm Mohan Bawa.' I drew a blank. 'I'm a senior journalist,' he continued, 'Don't you read film magazines?' I shook my head. 'Then what are you doing here? We're hiring film journalists for a new magazine.' I knew this wasn't going to be easy. Scared as I was, I told grey-eyed Bawa that I knew nothing about film magazines. Had never seen or read one and nobody in the family was even remotely connected to any kind of journalism. Only a daily newspaper, *Readers Digest* and *Life* magazine came home because my older siblings read them. Attached to KEM hospital as medical social workers, my choice in reading and films was influenced by them. An old friend in school purchased *Stardust* regularly and once or twice tried to educate me about their saucy style of writing but because I wasn't a regular reader I couldn't follow the bites and the barbs. I guess I wasn't sufficiently interested. Considering the limited pocket-money one was given, indulging in film magazines wasn't a priority.

Bawa wasn't impressed and there was an awkward silence as I picked up my bag to leave. I was almost at the door when on second thoughts he asked me to come back. He suggested that I sit in the adjoining room and list out ten questions I'd like to ask my favourite star. I did what I was told. Next, he asked me to jot down imaginary answers to the questions. Looking back I feel it was a dangerous precedent to set to debutant journalist. That's when the rot sets in. The unsuspecting fresher surrenders to the technique and over the years, nurses less and less guilt about spicing up dull copy. My second lesson in journalism was: Don't succumb to rules you don't believe in. With time, I learnt that different editors had different methods of hiring staff. When I became one myself, I relied on my instincts! How did they introduce themselves, their body language and eye contact, what books had they read. . . . It always helps when applicants carry clippings of their writings.

When I handed my answer sheet to Bawa, he had one look at it and said, 'You are hired on a salary of Rs. 500 a month.' I quickly calculated that this was a far better deal than the sunlit garage with broken cups, but better sense prevailed and I said, 'No, I don't want to be a film journalist.' By now Bawa had had enough of my tantrums. 'Don't want to be a film journalist?' Then what the hell are you doing here wasting everybody's time?' Shocked at him hollering, the turbaned gentleman, who had by now finished with his *tandoori* chicken, rose to my defence. 'Maybe you should think about it and get back to us tomorrow,' he said gently. The tone was reassuring even if it was a face I didn't completely trust. I didn't get back to them, in fact, forgot all about it until the following day when they phoned. The voice introduced himself as 'Kohli', said that he was leaving for Delhi the following week and needed to confirm their Mumbai representative. He wanted to know if I had made up my mind. I had. I didn't want the job.

They persisted all the same. Said I didn't have to be accountable to anybody because they didn't have an office in the city, which meant that I could continue with my college undisturbed. A salary hike was promised within six months. I was still contemplating an adequate answer, when Kohli added that they were holding a launch party the same evening and wanted me to be present on the occasion. 'Since you are to be our representative, what better opportunity to introduce you?' Completely unaware of the reputation Delhi film magazines had those days (they were notorious for the semi-pornographic articles on stars), I had walked into a trap!

My first question, silly as it now sounds was, 'All the way to the Taj? How will I get back home?' 'You can take a taxi,' he said distractedly. 'Not so late, I get scared,' I argued. 'And I won't come alone either.' 'Okay bring someone with you. We'll organise your return transport,' he said, slightly exasperated. So at 8 p.m., taking my sister and her friend along I arrived at the Taj Hotel, full of trepidation. Nothing in our wildest imagination could have prepared us for what was to unfold that evening. . . . An uneasy feeling, a premonition that I had made a mistake sunk into me the minute I walked into the room. A handful of people sat on sofas. The hosts were busy at the bar. After a few awkward moments of hanging around we moved to the balcony. And that's where we stayed all through the evening.

As hours progressed and moods soared, we felt safer staring at the lonely street from the balcony. My sister and her friend edged me to leave the party, 'Ask him about the return transport,' they urged. I couldn't, simply because the two men refused to pay me any heed. Too busy fussing over other guests, they brushed me off everytime I approached them. We stood in a corner like bumpkins, clutching each others' hands as we witnessed open flirtations, superficial behaviour. It was a bizarre evening and a strange fear gripped me in the pit of my stomach as midnight drew closer. Mustering courage, I finally interrupted their conversation and inquired about the car which was to drop us home. Too drunk to concentrate on my query, one of them dismissed me with, 'The driver was tired so I sent him off,' and shifted his attention to a screeching Reena Roy and her giggly sister, Barkha. The other guests included Zahira,

Nazneen, Premnath and Kamini Kaushal. . . .

Eventually, it was Kohli who organised the return journey. He requested Zahira to drop us girls home. She was too polite to refuse and agreed half-heartedly. We were waiting outside the Taj lobby looking rather pathetic. Taking pity on us, Zahira took us in the car, but halfway home announced that she was taking the straight road and we would have to take a cab. 'I'm frightened,' I pleaded. For a minute, it looked as if she would change her mind. But escort Mohan Bawa, seated beside Zahira, who seemed to have made it a habit of hollering at me raised his eyebrows condescendingly and said, 'What kind of a journalist will you make if you are going to get so scared?' I was too wrapped up in my pain to appreciate the humour in the situation. Overprotected and shielded, I was shattered by the ugly episode. There was no way I was going to take up this job and a week later, when my parents got back from their trip, it was curtains to my midsummer madness! Or so I thought.

A month later, R.R. Chopra phoned again. He said that *Stargazer* had closed down and he was launching his own magazine *Star Gloss*. By now I had begun to find all this funny. In my three-month stint with journalism, every magazine I touched had closed down! Chopra said that he had split with his partner Kohli and was willing to pay me a salary of Rs. 750 a month. I was convinced that the man had gone mad. They were chasing me like I was the last talent in the country. This, when I hadn't written a single line or conducted a single interview.

Chopra went back to Delhi and for a while the chapter was closed. Every few weeks, however, his office phoned to find out if I had changed my mind. That's when I spoke about the job offer to my parents. My father rejected the idea outright. My mother was more accommodating, her main concern being, 'What will the community say?' She was a bit nervous about my interviewing deadly looking villains. 'Would you also have to meet Gabbar Singh?' she inquired. Even though the subject evoked a lot of curiosity, it was clear that the job offer was not taken seriously by the family. One of the reasons also being that my parents believed that this could affect my value in the marriage market. Secretly relieved, the next time Chopra's office phoned me I informed them about my decision. This time, it was their charming assistant editor, Rama Luthra, who was put on the line. A woman with unusual convincing powers, she broke my defences and made me commit myself to a job I wasn't mentally prepared for.

The commitment led to volatile discussions at home. From the very beginning my father had encouraged us to express our opinions. He inspired us children to channelise our energies into constructive activities. Many years ago he had made me give up classical dancing because he was sure I wouldn't pursue it as a profession. 'If you are sure that you will, I will not object.' If not, I'd rather you concentrate on getting better grades in school.' This time too, he was ready to support me, provided I was sure of my decision. The trouble was, I wasn't but I didn't want to say so. Father found it difficult to digest that writing could be a source of livelihood. Still, he was ready to trust my judgement. Both mother and he were confident that I'd outgrow the passion in a couple of years—by that time I'd have graduated and they'd have settled me down. I didn't sense any anxiety in them. Or maybe they didn't reveal it to me. They never discussed my job once they had laid down the ground rules. My mother extracted three promises from me which were quite similar to Mahatma Gandhi's before his South Africa trip. No matter what the pressures, I would not attend a party. No matter how important, I would not stay out beyond 7 p.m. and finally, travelling out of Mumbai, even if it was for a day, would not be allowed.

The job, I realised, was more of a excursion since they had no office in Mumbai. The Delhi office sent me regular work briefs and whenever it wasn't convenient or I was busy with my terminal exams, I'd call them back and say that the star was out of town. Sometimes I was caught and pulled up for it. If I bunked assignments, it wasn't because I was lazy or negligent, but because I had no guidance. Simple things like star directories didn't exist those days. Or at least, I didn't possess one. I didn't know how to locate the addresses of stars I had to meet, but managed somehow. I did not particularly look forward to Chopra's visits to Bombay either. Something about him didn't give me a good feeling. Like I wasn't in the right place.

Chopra put up at the Taj Hotel and usually stayed for about four days. The purpose of his visit was mainly to purchase pictures from freelance photographers and meet advertisers. I was expected to accompany him during these official visits. How I hated those four days. We'd travel by a local taxi from Colaba to Andheri and all through the journey Chopra would deliver a non-stop monologue. He had a nasal tone that put me off and to switch off I'd stare out of the window enjoying the breeze. He had a peculiar manner of talking. Whenever the breeze got too much, the 40-plus man would caress his balding head and say, 'Khidki upar kar do, meri zulfein bikhar jayengi.' One afternoon, after a crucial meeting with our advertisers, as I was taking leave to go home he mentioned that the new issue had arrived and I could collect a copy from his room. Innocent as I was, I didn't realise it was a pass.

Now, when I reflect upon it, I feel strange that nobody had warned me against the dangers of visiting a stranger in a hotel room. Everything happened so quickly that when I go over it in my memory, I tell myself I must have been hallucinating. Chopra was sitting in the arm chair, bending over his files. When I stretched my hand to pick up the copy from the table, he pulled my hand. . . . I shuddered and jumped. I think I screamed so loudly that he got alarmed. I threw the files on the floor and charged towards the door leaving my bag behind. He looked frightened himself and began accusing me, saying that I had not done my work right and that his trip had been wasted because I was negligent. I didn't hear what he was saying. Standing by the door, too stunned to move, I began trembling. Tears threatened, but I controlled them. With great difficulty I found my voice and said I was leaving. 'As you wish,' he said, sulking. My purse and portfolio were lying on the table beside his chair. 'I want my stuff,' I said, faltering, hoping he'd stretch his hand and give them to me from a distance. 'Take it,' he said authoritatively. I don't think I can ever forget that ten-step walk from the door to the table. I don't know why I went back for the purse, perhaps out of confusion. When I came close to his chair, I grabbed the purse and ran out of the room rushing into the elevator without realising it was ascending, not descending. Seconds later, the lift door opened on the third floor and who should walk in but Chopra. My heart stopped beating. I had been lucky enough to escape once, but now I felt my luck was running out. I held my breath and refused to look up, shrivelling in a corner of the cubicle. When we reached the lobby, I raced out of the hotel to catch the first taxi I found on the road. I wept all the way home. . . .

For years after that I could never enter the Taj lobby without my heart sinking. Next morning at breakfast I told my parents I had left the job. No questions were asked. And no confidences were exchanged. If I didn't confide in anyone it's because I wasn't willing to accept that something so ugly had happened to me. We were reared to hold ourselves precious where wounds were not allowed to fester. I buried the incident until many months later. . . . The first time I articulated my feelings was to a complete stranger I met on a train journey. Perhaps it was something about her face, or the way she initiated a conversation, but a chord had been touched. We were standing at the exit passage, breeze lashing our faces. I didn't even know her name. I've never been able to analyse the whys and hows, but I unburdened my secret to her. Ever since, I've believed that solace comes from sources least expected. When the train stopped at the following station I alighted, but I didn't look back. I didn't want witnesses. Not even in my memory.

2

'C AN YOU PRETEND to smoke for a while?' Simi Garewal said pushing the ashtray in my direction. We were sitting at Simi's elegant penthouse 'Pavlova' on Little Gibbs Road, downtown. She was reminiscing about her childhood memories. . . . Of the time Pandit Jawaharlal Nehru wrote her a letter at school in England and she misplaced it amongst her books. 'My classmates would just not believe me when I said that I had received a letter from the Prime Minister. They accused me of cooking up tales because their Queen never wrote to them. I was heartbroken, and to regain their trust, wrote another letter to the Prime Minister that same night requesting him to write to me again or my friends would never believe me.' A few days later, another letter arrived and her classmates' faith in Simi was restored. 'He actually wrote to me again. And it was such a sensitive letter.'

There was a sparkle in Simi's eyes as she recreated those moments. We were sitting on the low sofas in her living-room. Her long, silky Rapunzel hair falling on the floral cushions, she looked as pretty as a painting, as she elaborated her feelings using her long, delicate fingers. . . . The glass doors leading to the terrace were open and one could hear the sparrows chirping. 'I love the stillness of the afternoon,' she said looking out into the open. 'It's my favourite hour of the day.' Then, lowering her voice whispered, 'I'm going to smoke a cigarette.' The tender expression in the eye was a signal to not mention it in print. I concentrated on my scribble pad.

She must have barely taken a few puffs when the servant

informed us that there were visitors at the door. 'Now?' she said startled. Then looking at me remarked, 'How can anybody just land up without an appointment?' She wasn't in a mood to be disturbed. Not until she had relished her cigarette. She was still contemplating a suitable answer when another servant walked in with the visitors names. 'They are my new producers and have come for dates. I'll have to see them . . . ,' Simi said reluctantly. 'If only I could have finished this . . . ,' she said, looking at the unfinished cigarette. She asked the servant to let in the visitors pushing the unextinguished cigarette in my direction. She was confident that the visitors would leave soon. But the guests stayed longer than Simi intended.

We made a comic sight. A group of people sitting around the table with a lit cigarette on the ashtray. Now when I recall, I think it was prudish and unsporting of me to not support Simi in an embarrassing situation. Too serious and sensitive, I took everything to heart. The details of the incident could have made a hilarious article but sense of humour isn't all that common when you are unsure and unconfident. No wonder scoops just slipped from under my nose.

It was late evening and I had been waiting outside Dharmendra's make-up room at Natraj Studio, Andheri, for over an hour. He had seen me when his car drove into the studio.

He appeared lazy and promised to call me for an interview in the next ten minutes. Thirty minutes passed, but there were no summons from Mr Deol. Slaves rushed in and out of his room carrying snacks, ice-buckets, soda, etc., but his Man Friday, insisted, that 'Saab was resting.' An hour later as it started getting dark outside, I got restless. I had to file my story the same evening and was debating whether to knock at his door when the door opened. A sleepy Dharmendra slowly walked out of the room as if in a trance.

'Let's keep our appointment for tomorrow,' he said distractedly, then very slowly walked down the staircase to the sets. . . .

As I stood there watching the actor disappear with his henchmen, an elderly gentleman accompanying Dharmendra, probably the writer of the film, came back half-way. 'Don't you understand anything?' he yelled at me. 'Can't you see it? Or will you risk anything for the sake of an interview?' Even though I could sense that his hollering was more out of concern than authority, I was outraged. These were serious pointers to which I had no answer. The enormity of such words would sink in much later, but the feeling that this was a strange world was slowly creeping in. The only way I could deal with the unknown was with silence. The star insinuations, in the meanwhile, had begun already. Suspicion and distrust, I soon realised, were recurring emotions stars traded with journalists. . . .

Natraj Studio again. It was the lavish *mahurat* of Ramanand Sagar's Jeetendra-Hema Malini starrer, *Hum Tere Aashiq Hain*.

Decorated in marigold flowers the studio resembled a wedding *mandap*. The set was packed with people and when the camera rolled everyone craned their necks for a *dekko*. Loud music followed the rise of the curtain. The set was for a dream sequence. Trees stuck with stars, fog, a moon and a beautiful Hema Malini who looked lovingly at Jeetendra, blushed and lowered her eyes. . . . 'Cut'. The shot had been okayed. Innumerable people rushed to congratulate the pair. So did the photographers. *Pedas* and Gold Spot bottles made the rounds and guests who missed them, asked for them loudly. A few even fought for them. Getting out of the set was more difficult than getting into it because at every step someone was hugging or shaking hands.

After great difficulty I found my way out. My editor had warned me to not come back without fixing a photosession with Hema Malini and I was afraid that I was going to miss the opportunity. Fortunately, she hadn't left as yet. Surrounded by a number of people, she was walking towards her van, when I pushed my way through to give her the editor's message. She gave me an icy stare. It was a look that could freeze anyone. Only I didn't know the reason behind such extreme hostility.

In the same week, at Mohan Studio, Andheri, I interviewed Shashi Kapoor on a flamboyant topic—women and wine. 'The first thing that attracts me to a woman is her eyes, then boobs, back and finally the brains.' A sensational quote but one that had me blushing. Half-way through the interview, he went for the shot and forgot all about me. I stuck around for some time unsure if I should follow him onto the set, or go home. After a great dilemma, I decided to hang around. An hour later, when Shashi walked into the room accompanied by four other men, he was completely unprepared and somewhat embarrassed to find me sitting in a dark room. I hadn't switched on the lights because I felt I had no authority to do so. 'Light, *kyon nahin jalayi?*' Shashi asked more as a plea, lest his friends misunderstand his motives. Then in a slightly exasperated tone said, 'We'll have to postpone the interview for another time.' It was a clear signal for me to leave. I did.

Every encounter was a clear indicator that I wasn't cut out for the profession. There was rejection, awkwardness, discomfort, a feeling of uneasiness. It wasn't even as if I was particularly driven by a craving to write. I stuck on, I think, because of my singleminded drive. Discipline was an integral part of my growing up. We were taught to not give up things half-way, whether it was the unwanted food in the plate or the incomplete homework. And that is why I couldn't just break off and continued with film journalism. To make things easier for myself, though I worked out a method in the madness. I learnt by trial and error how to lower star defences. It wasn't easy. To begin with, I had to introduce myself a hundred times, before they would register my face. Then, I would sometimes discuss costumes, sometimes the weather, sometimes zodiac signs, numerology or palmistry. . . . Each time it was a different technique I used to break the ice with the superstars.

Making small talk, smiling, being social, didn't come naturally to me. But that was the only way to do it. Always, the responsibility of initiating a conversation rests with the journalist. From the watchman outside the studio right up to the star it was a long journey of heartbreaks. Suspicion and distress were the key emotions. Often mistaken for a star-struck fan, one was rudely pushed around. The only way to get through the iron gates was with bravado. A preoccupied expression on my face and handbag flung on the shoulder, I would walk up the pathway without making eye contact—like I owned the place. The worst and the most painful was the taxi ride! The minute you gave a studio address, the first thing the taxi-driver did was to adjust the rear view mirror to have a closer look at you. I dreaded the eye contact. As the destination drew closer, so did his curiosity and nine out of ten couldn't resist asking personal questions. 'Filmon mein kaam karte ho?' Silence. 'Kaunsi film ki shooting hai?' Silence. 'Aur kaun actor hoga udhar?' Silence. With time, I learnt to handle these intrusions with smartness. I wouldn't give him the address until we were almost at the studio gate. This resulted in a different set of problems. When you asked him to drive inside the forbidding gate he looked outraged, 'koi lafdewali baat to nahin hain?'

Moments of warmth came just as spontaneously, when you least expected them. One afternoon, I walked into Ranjit Studio at Dadar and spotted an overweight Rekha with bleached eyebrows and in a green puff-sleeved kaftan talking to somebody near the reception. She was inquiring where the phone was. . . . Even though I was visiting the studio specifically to interview Rekha, I couldn't get myself to approach her—at least not in public. Something told me that the timing wasn't appropriate. She looked preoccupied. In her absence, somehow, I felt more confident knocking on her make-up room door. Her hairdresser, Sheila let me in. A warm, elderly, Chinese woman, she offered me tea and said that madam would be back soon.

By the time Rekha returned a rapport had been established between the hairdresser and me. The truth was that within the privacy of her make-up room, I could accept her rejection but not in front of an audience. The vanity of film journalists, Shabana Azmi once remarked, depends on how a star treats them in public, but very few acknowledge this! Ten minutes later, Rekha returned to the room, chirpy and bouncy. She had one look at me and said, 'Weren't you outside a little while ago?' I nodded. 'I have to do my make-up and my hair,' she said after a pause. 'Will you wait?' For the next forty-five minutes I sat glued to my chair. I watched the pinks and the blues being applied smoothly and expertly on her face. The short hair getting pinned up, the long wig being attached. A couple of braids and finally it was all coiled into a big round bun. I watched as the fingers, ears, nose were adorned with rings.

This was the first time I was witnessing a star getting ready and both as a journalist and as a woman, I was fascinated. There was a knock on the door. It was Amitabh Bachchan, her co-star in Dulal Guha's, *Do Anjaane*. He was on his way to the sets and wanted to check how long she'd take to get ready. Standing at the door he said, '*Amma . . . bahut mote ho gaye ho aap.*' Rekha stared at him through the reflection in the mirror and without turning to greet him, continued with her make-up. A while later, after he had left, she retorted, 'So what if I'm fat? My weight is a sign of prosperity. The producers are free to sign thinner heroines. Why do they run after me?' Changed into a pink and grey *gadhwal* saree worn in the Bengali style, she sat decorously. Tiny silver bells adorning her *jooda* made music as she, from time to time, shook her head while emphasizing a point. 'You are looking very attractive,' I complimented her. She smiled, probably unused to compliments from my tribe. Amidst sips of *nariyal paani* served in a steel glass, she answered my questions.

Who is the best looking man in the industry?
Shashi Kapoor.
Who has the best voice?
Amitabh Bachchan.
Who is an ideal co-star?
Randhir Kapoor. I'm most comfortable working with him. Even my fans like us best together.
Who is the best human being?
Vinod Mehra.
What does Hema Malini have that you don't?
Dharamji.
What else?
Hema has a beautiful smile. I have an okay smile.
And?
Hema looks beautiful when she cries. It's very important for an actress to look beautiful when she cries. I don't. I cry like a baby. I spoil my eye make-up.
What is it that you have that Hema Malini doesn't?
Hmm . . . ask Hema. I don't know.

The assistant came to say that the shot was ready. It was time for me to say goodbye.

I met Zeenat Aman on the sets of Manmohan Desai's *Dharamveer*. Dressed as a princess, she looked weighed down by her elaborate costume. 'I can't wait to get out of

this,' she said to co-star Indrani Mukherjee, playing *Rajmata*
and was dressed in a similar costume. The scene involved
over five-thousand junior artistes scattered around the ground.
It was a huge fort-like set and the shooting had been going
on non-stop since morning. . . . At about 5 p.m. the
assistant came and told Zeenat that they required to shoot
with her on the following day as well. 'But it's a Sunday and
I don't shoot on Sundays.' 'We have to demolish the set on
Monday,' argued the assistant. Zeenat sighed. 'Madam, we'll
relieve you in two hours,' he persisted. 'In that case, why
don't you complete my work today. I don't mind waiting,
but putting on make-up and driving all the way from
Napean Sea Road for a few hours of work is not worth it,'
pleaded Zeenat. The argument continued for some time.
The assistant went to and fro a couple of times, then finally
returned with, 'It's okay—no extension today and holiday
tomorrow. The director says we'll demolish the set on
Tuesday.' 'Thank you, thank you very much. I truly appreciate this,' gushed Zeenat. Twenty minutes later, changed and
greasepaint scrubbed off her face, Zeenat was unrecognisable
in jeans and T-shirt as she waited for Tukaram, her driver, to
roll in the Mercedes. I stood self-consciously beside her and
smiled.

After the way Hema Malini had rebuffed me, I wasn't
sure about the right time to ask a star for an interview. I still
don't. The nervousness must have shown. Actors are good
judges of people. They see through you, even if they don't
admit it. When Zeenat consented to an interview, I couldn't
sleep all night. I went to meet her wearing clog shoes and a
short jersey top. I even put on green eye-shadow because I
thought that was the way to dress when meeting a glamorous babe. I must have looked horrendous, but zany Zeenat,
even if slightly amused, didn't make it apparent.

Today, when I'm an editor myself and recruit new staff, I
often notice how inappropriately some of them are dressed.
The girls wear dangling ear-rings, dark lipstick and gaudy
colours. The guys use too much aftershave and shiny foot-

wear. With every visit to the studio and meeting with stars, they pick up grooming tips on their own. There is a perceptible improvement in their wardrobes. In an industry so predominantly appearance conscious, everyone is hooked on to glamour and beauty is an obsession. The effect is bound to rub off on you sometime. With economic independence come changes in taste and temperament.

Unknowingly, Rekha played an important role in my grooming. The first to make me feel I had the potential to look attractive, she made it a point to comment on my sarees and bangles every time we met. Sharp and observant, her eyes missed nothing. Obsessed with aesthetics, she gave tips unsolicited. . . . What colours to wear, what to avoid, what food to eat and what was injurious to health. How to maintain one's hair and skin. I had a lot of pimples those days. She put me on a 'Rekha diet', made me abstain from oily and spicy food. When I'd ask her the technique of make-up, she'd admonish me with, 'Not for you. You are fine as you are, with *bindi* and *kajal*.' She instilled confidence in me and in my simplicity, said I was a natural and had to be myself. Her gestures were spontaneous. When I pierced my ears, she removed the silver bells from her own lobes, at the shooting of Anil Ganguly's *Aanchal* and fixed them onto mine. On another occasion, when shooting a dance sequence, she offered me strings of jasmine flowers for my hair. They were touching gestures.

There was constant wear and tear of emotions. It was like being a yo-yo. Star moods swing like a pendulum—now on, now off. And with every swing in the mood, the self-image gets distorted. My friends at college sensed my anxiety but couldn't identify with it. Because I could never articulate my inner conflict, a feeling of restlessness prevailed. To not alienate them completely, I shared with them the lighter side of my job. The car Zeenat Aman used, the jokes Shashi Kapoor cracked, the lipstick and nail polish shades Reena Roy wore. Together, we had a good laugh at them and worked out our own list of who was hep and who wasn't.

My friends took my glamour world in their stride and became accustomed to my disappearance act between lectures. This wasn't my first job. I'd started earning my own money in the very first year of college.

It all began when our neighbour asked me to teach her children English, followed by a brief stint with the Indian Market Research Bureau (IMRB). Next, I assisted an advocate who helped Swedish parents adopt orphaned children and finally came film journalism though I never looked upon journalism as a serious career. I thought I would write for a while and then move on to something else. There were conflicting moments when I couldn't fathom peculiar star attitudes. In a mysterious way, that cannot be explained, only experienced, stars breed more complexes in people who came in contact with them than they realise. It happens subconsciously because of the halo around them. . . .

Vinod Khanna, looking devastatingly handsome in his Rajneesh *chola*, had one look at me and said, 'Why do you have so much acne and why aren't you doing something about it?' Even if it was well-intended, it was taking liberties with a young girl's vulnerability. I was crestfallen. At times like this, I relied on the support of my four friends. Even if they weren't always right, at least their reactions were pure and unbiased. They meant well and their objectivity prevented me from judging stars too harshly. Strangely, none of my friends ever expressed any desire or curiosity to meet the stars or accompany me to the shootings. Only once and that too out of sheer coincidence because we had to visit a common friend who had delivered her first baby at a neighbouring hospital, did one accompany me to an appointment with director Sultan Ahmed.

When I knocked on his make-up room, the film-maker was lying on the couch facing the door—one foot on top of the other. His spotboy announced my arrival. The name didn't ring a bell, so he widened his feet in to a 'V' formation to have a closer look at my face. Lying in the same position and chewing *paan*, he asked, '*Tum akhbarwali ho na?*' I nodded, still standing at the doorway. '*Main bahut thak gaya hoon*, is it okay if I conduct this interview lying down?' Stunned beyond words, I looked at my friend. She had rage in her eyes. After being fed on the chivalry of our boyfriends in the college who always opened doors, pulled chairs and stood up when we entered a room, this was nauseating! I don't know from where I got the confidence, but looking directly into his eyes, I said, 'I do mind it Mr. Ahmed. Maybe we can do the interview another time, when you are not so tired.'

My friend and I drove to the hospital in complete silence. The episode reflected my new job in poor taste and I felt exposed. The incident became a crucial yardstick in their assessment of the film fraternity and even though in the two decades that followed, they did brush shoulders with many well-mannered dream merchants, somehow the old memory persisted. . . . I guess that's how images are formed.

Mehboob Studio, Bandra. Make-up room again. It was lunch break and I was in the middle of an interview with actress Raakhee, who was coming back to films after a break of marriage and baby with *Tapasya*, in the middle of a sentence choked. . . . Tears threatened and after a while the dam burst. I stiffened. There was no one else in the room. Her staff had gone for lunch and the rest of the studio seemed deserted.

I couldn't figure out what was it about my questions that had triggered this outburst but the tears didn't stop. So I shut my notebook and sat quietly, listening. And I guess that's what she wanted me to do. To listen and to understand. When the tears dried and her staff returned, I excused myself and left. We've met on several occasions since, talked about various things but never mentioned this incident. Even today, I don't know the reason for her outburst. Or why she chose to bare herself to me. Was it just a coincidence? Some pent up pressure that needed a release and it was the perfect moment?

Or the safety of exposing yourself to a complete stranger? I'm not sure but after the incident of my own outburst with the stranger on the train, I believed it was possible. I've never underestimated the intensity of an impulse ever since! Feelings don't respect protocol.

3

'IS WHAT YOU HAVE written really true?' editor Rauf Ahmed of *Cinema Journal*, film supplement to the *Free Press Journal*, phoned to ask one late evening at home. After my traumatic encounter with *Star Gloss*, I had made up my mind not to have anything to do with the film world. My elder brother however talked me into sending postcards to publications offering my services as a freelancer. The response was positive and within a month's time I was doing assignments for *The Bulletin*, *Film World*, *Current*, *Cine Advance* and *Picture Post*. I also joined *Cinema Journal* as a retainer. Committed to one story and a few snippets every week, the only time I attended office was to submit my articles.

On the afternoon I stopped by to give in the Sachin-Sarika break-up story, the editor was not in his seat. In the evening, he phoned to inquire about my source of information. The subject was too controversial to be relied upon a junior reporter. His non-confidence in me was understandable. Ignorant of the repurcussions such an expose could involve, I answered, 'I wrote what she spoke.' The enormity of the story dawned on me two days later as I walked out of Churchgate station to my college. Sarika's sensational headline, 'I was never in love with Sachin' stared at me from the news stands.

Problems between the two began when Sachin's father, in the wake of Rajshri Productions musical hit, *Geet Gaata Chal*, wanted to cash in the pair's success. A project starring Sachin, Sarika and two more heroines was announced. Sarika's mother, Kamala Thakur, declined on the grounds that Sarika would have little to do in a film that had two other girls. The issue became a bone of contention between the two families. Looking back, the break-up was more of an ego conflict between the parents, rather than a lovers' tiff. It was sad that it ended the way it did. Sachin and Sarika fought through film magazines and destroyed what could have made history. The decision affected both their careers adversely but both were too busy mourning the debris of a dream to look ahead. The outburst was initiated by Kamala Thakur, Sarika's mother, but the pain was her own. Her confession was full of minute details, the kind only a jealous lover can impart.

'I was never in love with Sachin!'

'He told me he wouldn't be celebrating his birthday this year because they were holding the *mahurat* of their film that morning. On the eve of 16 August, he said, he had an important meeting with producer Dev Sharma, so celebrations were ruled out. Since I wasn't in the film, I didn't attend the *mahurat*. I thought it best not to. His family had been upset about my opting out of the project. Later in the day, though, my mother and I went across to wish him at his home. We were greeted coldly by his family. Sachin looked embarrassed and kept quiet. After a 20-minute awkward silence, we left. . . . Then, through sheer coincidence, we happened to meet Dev Sharma. I inquired about his meeting with Sachin, he was surprised. He said he hadn't met Sachin in a long, long time. That's when I learnt that Sachin had been lying to me. He wanted to celebrate his birthday eve with his co-star Bhavna Bhatt at her home, so used Dev Sharma as a cover-up. He thought I'd feel bad because I wasn't invited to the party. As if I care. What hurt me were his lies. How could he do this to me? When I confronted him with the truth, he said that Bhavna had not the slightest idea that it was his birthday. That she only got to know of it at midnight, when half-way during the dinner, everyone began to wish him. Can this be possible, when Bhavna and Sachin are such old friends? He wore a purple *lungi kurta* which had been specially tailored for the occasion and he still expects me to believe him that it was an impromptu party. He said in an interview that he phoned me from Bhavna's residence at midnight because he wanted me to be the first to wish him. If he did, how come I never received the call . . .? There are too many contradictions. To one paper he claimed that he celebrated his birthday a day early because he was flying out the next morning. How could he when he had the *mahurat* the next day? Sanjeev Kumar was confirmed to give the clap and Subodh Mukherjee to switch on the camera. Would he have cancelled dates with such important people? They celebrated the birthday on 16 October because it was not him but Bhavna who was going out of town on the 17th.

'I can go on and on about the details. I don't want to. What about the dozens of bouquets? The photographer? Which florist is open at midnight? And the photographer, did they wake him up from sleep? As for Bhavna Bhatt, she is causing me a lot of tension. She keeps changing statements in all her interviews. Sometimes she says that the party was at a friend's home, sometimes at her own home. Then she says that the rift between her and me has been cleared. What rift is she talking about? How can I fight with someone I have never met? The girl has the cheek to tell a journalist that she isn't inclined towards Sachin because she knows he was involved with me. I want to put on record that there is nothing between Sachin and me. We are good friends but all these rumours of my forbidding him to drink or smoke are baseless. I am not Mahatma Gandhi to stop the world from drinking. He smokes because he enjoys it. He says smoking makes his voice sexy.

'In all this fight, what has hurt me the most is him accusing me of flinging paper cuttings of his party at his face. How could he say these things? How could he stoop so low? He knows very well that the last time I went to his house was to wish him on his birthday. I've not met or spoken to him ever since. That was the last time I climbed the staircase of his house.'

Cinema Journal, Friday, 12 November 1976

A few months later I met Sarika again on the sets of Basu Bhattacharya's *Madhu Malati*. Shooting at some college near Jogeshwari, she was sitting under the shade of a tree, spectacles on her nose, reading a book. At a little distance

Sachin, her co-star, was sitting with a group of people, laughing loudly trying to attract Sarika's attention. From time to time he looked in our direction and a few minutes later, when director Basu Bhattacharya joined us for tea, he joined us too. Kamala Thakur, Sarika's mother, who was somewhere in the background, noticed this and dashed in our direction. There was much tension in the atmosphere and even though Sachin and Sarika didn't exchange a single word, their eyes followed each other all the time. . . .

I wasn't able to get the interview that afternoon, so a few days later met Sarika again. This time at her home, Havana, in Versova. It was Sunday morning and she was preparing custard in the kitchen. When she finished, we retired to the bedroom. Mrs Kamala Thakur made sure that we were not disturbed because the topic was sensitive. '*Sab theek tarah se samjha do . . . Samjha do ke* Sachin *ke saath koi pyar ka chakkar nahin . . . ,*' the mother warned the daughter. Kamala Thakur had decided what had to be said in the interview. And Sarika said it.

The interview was a turning point in my career for two reasons. One, it became the foundation for a long and cherished friendship with Sarika, and two, gradually I was getting drawn to the magic of my new environment. And more important, enjoying it. Rauf Ahmed had titled one of my columns 'Casually Speaking' modelled on the famous Devyani Chaubal's immortal 'Frankly Speaking'. The column was noticeable because it appeared on the same page as Bikram Vohra's (*Khaleej Times*, Dubai), widely read humour piece. Working with Rauf was a completely different experience after working with the unprofessional Delhi group. I knew instinctively that I was in the right surroundings.

The frequent byline boosted my confidence. I was getting tougher in my interaction with stars. My days were divided between attending college and making the rounds of the studios. I visited editors only when I had to collect my cheques or discuss a story idea. T. Ramachandran, editor of

Filmworld was a kind, old man who made it a point to order *idli sambar* for me every time I went to his office. 'Health is wealth,' he would say, 'You take care of your health and the wealth will follow.'

Call it irony, but in his last days Ramachandran suffered immensely. All journalists he groomed and launched were present at his funeral. I met him a few months before his condition became critical. He had dropped by at my office to collect a colour transparency of Amitabh Bachchan. When I told him that I'd send it across to his house, he refused. 'I cannot ask for a favour and expect to be pampered.' I've remembered that. Coughing incessantly, he said he suffered from a weak stomach. 'The long hours at office . . . the endless rounds of tea . . . the pressures of deadlines are finally catching up.'

And film jargon was catching up with me. When the stars mentioned, 'lunch break' it was universally understood as 1 to 2 p.m. Make-up men were uniformly addressed as *dada*, whereas hairdressers usually had a pet name given by the star. The personal spot boys addressed the traditional heroines as *didi* and the bohemian ones as 'Madam'. The driver was the usual confidant. Whenever an escort accompanied the star to make an urgent phone call, it was a cover-up to summon the lover on the line. When they shared tiffins, when they didn't, when they spent more time on the sets, when they kept aloof in their own rooms was all reflective of the stage at which the relationship was at that moment. At dubbings they were better dressed than for the shootings and they came without paraphernalia. Stars travelled in imported cars, technicians in Indian vehicles, visitors in taxis, journalists in rickshaws and photographers, despite their heavy load, by local trains. You could tell a struggler from his swagger. The brand of sunglasses, ice buckets, cigarettes and mirrors they used were an indicator of their rise in status. For me, too, life was definitely easier working as a retainer rather than as a freelancer. The most heart-breaking thing about freelancing is the inability to belong. There is no security about the job.

Getting attached to a magazine is like acquiring a surname. It's an end to the innumerable introductions, an end to the identity crisis.

About six months later I learnt that Rauf Ahmed was leaving *Free Press Journal* to launch a new magazine to be brought out by the then Law Minister, H.R. Gokhale's dynamic son Rajiv and his wife Namita Gokhale, author of *Paro*. The magazine was called *Super* and after a month of settling down, Rauf absorbed sub-editor Elfreda Martis and me as part of his new team. Initially, there was some conflict about the title. *Super* was an unusual name for a film magazine but after the first few issues, it was readily accepted. The common reaction was, '*Super* is really super'.

Days ran into months and years and I continued to explore the film world with new assignments. Analysing Rajesh Khanna's failure in March, celebrating Holi at R.K. Studio in April, listening to Neetu Singh's romantic musings in September and trailing her mysterious secretary at a remand home in December.

Will Rajesh Khanna make it to the top again?

Directors Shakti Samanta, Hrishikesh Mukherji, Asit Sen and Basu Chatterji analyse Rajesh Khanna's chances of a comeback. . . .

Rajesh Khanna has the uncanny knack of being constantly in the news. If it's not by being 'in', it's by being 'out'. The question uppermost in the minds of Rajesh-watchers at the moment is: Will he or will he not survive the current bad patch? It's interesting how four of our leading directors, Shakti Samanta (who skyrocketed Rajesh to fame in *Aradhana*), Hrishikesh Mukherji (who took Rajesh to the heart of millions in *Anand*), Asit Sen (who gave him a serious style in *Safar*) and Basu Chatterji (Rajesh's latest director) feel about his present box-office position. . . .

SHAKTI SAMANTA: After working with Shammi Kapoor, a total extrovert, working with Rajesh Khanna was a change for me.

Rajesh's strongest point is his ability to do emotional scenes. He is excellent when you make him underplay a role. His minus point is his 'good man' face. He is too goody goody. Rough and tough roles don't suit him. If you ask me, he should not do crime films. His personality is not cut out for action. The rising popularity of action films is the cause of Rajesh's low phase. It is fallacious to say that Rajesh Khanna is finished. It is just that he's going through a bad time. When he became a superstar, he was still immature. Success came to him too early and too easily. Success like this is momentary. His current low phase doesn't mean the end. Rajesh Khanna's problem is that he's too much of an enigma. He is too reserved. This reserve often becomes a negative point in a man's personality as it leads to a lot of misunderstanding. *Mehbooba* did belie people's expectations. Yes, it did let Rajesh down very badly. But then, this business is so unpredictable. Maybe *Anurodh* will do for Rajesh what nobody expects it to. . . .

HRISHIKESH MUKHERJI: When Rajesh Khanna came to me he was a very big star. Before agreeing to work with him, I asked him a simple question, 'When was the last time you saw a sunset?' He was dumbfounded. 'I cannot remember,' he replied. 'Go and watch it someday. Try to be a normal man, do not work like a machine. And maybe then we will work together.' Of the four films (*Anand, Namak Haram, Bawarchi* and *Naukri*) we did together, *Naukri* was the only one to run into trouble. There was a lot of friction and undue delay. Unlike *Anand*, which got every free moment of Rajesh Khanna's, *Naukri* had to constantly put up with his latecoming. All the same, I maintain that whatever strain there was, was merely professional. If he had any problems, it was with the producer not with me. On a personal level, Rajesh and I are still good friends.

Personally, I have always been a little sceptical of youngsters achieving instant success and becoming over-ambitious. I wish success had waited for Rajesh instead of chasing him. It is terribly humiliating to fall after a resounding rise. According to me, success should come steadily and failure gracefully. I have no doubts that Rajesh will come back. An artiste is never over. Like everything that goes up must come down, everything that goes down must come up. That's the rule of the game. Remember Amitabh? They called him a flash in the pan and said *Anand* was a big fluke. Remember Sunil Dutt? They used to refer to him as 'a has-been'.

RAJESH KHANNA

Success came to Khanna too early

ASIT SEN: When I first met Rajesh he was a thoroughly frustrated man. He was so unhappy about his career that he used to say, '*Dada*, I think I will never make it.' When I started *Khamoshi* he was under contract with the United Producers and so our first choice for the role. Of course, he suited the role. As an artiste, he is okay, just *theek hai*. As a person, he is moody and very unpredictable, but not bad at heart. I am no authority on the causes of his setback but I don't like the way some people say that his directors are responsible for his failure. When he was a superstar nobody gave credit to his directors. Nobody said that we made him. So now that he is fading, why blame us? In a nutshell, I was surprised at his success and shocked at his failure. Will he come back? Well, I am not his horoscope.

BASU CHATTERJEE: It *is* true that Rajesh tends to come late for shootings and leave early. But I do not hold it against him, because the amount of work I get out of the others (Vidya Sinha, Zarina Wahab, Amol Palekar) in eight hours, Kaka (Khanna) does in only *two*. In fact, for *Chakravyuh* he has been so cooperative that we will finish the film in eight months. Before I start work on the script, I have an image of the character. If the artiste lives up to that image, I'm satisfied. In *Chakravyuh*, Kaka has interpreted his role beautifully. I will say this much. If the film flops, the blame will be solely mine. And vice versa!

I have heard that he tampers with scripts and interferes with the director's work, but he has not tried it with me—nor would I allow it. I can't comment on why his films have begun to flop suddenly. He is bound to come back again because talent can never die. I cannot comment on his earlier success because I have not seen most of his films. But I have seen *Aavishkar* which didn't run, while *Premnagar*, a mediocre performance, was a super hit.

Super, March 1977

R.K. celebrates Holi . . .

The RK Holi celebration is famous for being one of the Showman's biggest 'shows'. It is the time when not only the Kapoor clan but the whole industry is on parade.

Preparations are on a grand scale. The studio is decorated with strings of marigold. Chairs are arranged in neat rows on the lawn. Musicans play old RK hits and the *Satyam Shivam Sundaram* banner is stretched out and fluttering in the breeze. When Raj Kapoor strolls into the lawns at 1 p.m. the *shehnai* starts to wail, *tablas* begin to boom and crowds appear from nowhere.

An Australian unit shooting a documentary, has come to cover the function. As they set up their equipment, one of them asks, 'What's happening? Why are they pushing?' I tell them that's their idea of having a great time. The fun begins once the stars arrive. Asha Sachdev and her mother are the first to enter. They join the ladies of the house who sit in a corner. Krishna Kapoor looks glamorous in a printed white georgette saree and lipstick. Babita is more pragmatic. She wears a simple, white organdie saree, hair tied in a pony tail.

The star to get the most attention is Shatrughan Sinha. The Showman embraces him, says, '*Ab ke aaye ho?* I've been waiting for you all morning!' They dump him in the tub. Sitara Devi holds Shatru around the waist and forces him to join the dance. The way she pulls him seems more like an assault than an invitation for a jive. For a change, it's Shatrughan Sinha who is blushing. He tries to wriggle out of Sitara's grasp, she clasps him closer to her and teases, '*Sharmao mat bachhe.*' The crowd wickedly adds to Shatru's discomfiture by chanting, '*Naach meri jaan phata phat!*'

Around 3 p.m. when everyone has had their fill of playing Holi, Shammi Kapoor arrives with wife and children. He shepherds Neela Devi to where the Kapoor women are seated. It's a hot afternoon and Neela Devi fans herself vigorously. '*Tauba kitni garmi hain. . . .*' Someone offers her a glass of *thandai*. From a distance one spots Rima Kapoor, the younger daughter of RK, make an entry with a bunch of rowdy college friends. She is about to greet the older ladies in the family when she catches sight of Babita. '*Bhabhi!*' she screams and hugs Babita. '*Sukhi raho aur jaldi jaldi beta paida karo*' Babita blesses her. It's nice to see Babita play the role of the elder for a change. She spent the entire afternoon touching the feet of one or the other Kapoor. The price one pays for being an RK *bahu*.

Around 4 p.m. the guests of honour—the *hijras* arrive. The music becomes louder and livelier, the crowd cheers and claps, the *hijras* swing to the beat in obscene poses, make vulgar gestures. There are cheap thrills and the onlookers roar for more. The extra drum-beats signify the arrival of someone special. By the time Amitabh and Jaya arrive, the ladies have gone for lunch and the men are shamelessly high. Amitabh Bachchan is in equally high spirits. He throws colour, dances the lusty *bhangra*, gulps down several glasses of *bhang* and beer and generally has a good time. Jaya sits demurely with the women, keeping a close eye on her husband.

At about 5 p.m. I decide to leave. I am at the gate when the Australian crew waves out to me. 'Are you leaving?' one of them asks. 'Yes,' I reply. 'But after I've said goodbye to Raj Kapoor.' 'Which of them is he?' she asks looking at the crowd. Jee-sus, I think to myself. Can there be anyone who doesn't know Raj Kapoor?

Super, April 1977

Love is . . . missing him

It is a bright afternoon, but at Worli Seaface it is raining cats and dogs. Basu Chatterjee is shooting a clingy rain sequence with Neetu Singh for his film *Priyatama*. A large crowd waits on the pavement to watch the shooting. As they linger, the crowd discusses Neetu Singh with interest. They debate whether Rishi Kapoor (Chintu) will eventually marry her and who was lucky to get whom. Some of them are disappointed that Ms. Singh has chosen to travel in a *desi* Fiat instead of an imported car. Others are relieved that she is not as fat as she seems in real life. Some are curious to know if the Chinese girl sitting with Neetu (her hairdresser Shirley) is Helen or one of her relatives.

The crowd is getting thicker by the minute. Passers-by who stop merely to have a look find themselves included in the babble of spectators. Cars which have to slow down due to the heavy traffic linger a while longer than necessary. And in the midst of all the confusion there is this stern looking *havaldar*. Up and down he walks in his half pants. Everytime someone steps out of the invisible line he has marked out, he thumps his *danda* on the ground and grunts, 'Peeche, peeche hato . . .' Neetu is wearing white trousers, a short red top and a sexy black poncho. Her make-up is pale—after all, it's a rain scene. The moment she spots me she lets out a shriek, 'Ooooh—I envy all of you because you are nice and dry while I have to get soaked in the rain. How can you be so selfish? I am going to drag you in with me and drench you as well.' 'Where is Chintu?' I try to distract her, for she already has a firm grasp on my arm.

'Chintu?' Neetu repeats sadly. 'His Highness has gone to London for a holiday. What a life! While he has a super time abroad I have to do these terrible rain scenes. . . .

'Aw . . . I am surely going to catch a cold. I can't tell you how much I miss him. Of course he calls up every day, but what's a phone call? The trouble with us is that we spend too much time together. We are shooting all day long and after that he rings up in the night. We are together sooo much that when he leaves for an outdoor shooting, I cannot bear it. I miss him terribly. He is going to be away for sixteen days! And, her voice rises, 'Today is only the third!'

Did that mean that Chintu will make sixteen calls from London?

'Maybe even more,' Neetu blushes. 'It is very expensive I know, but what can we do? Both of us have to speak to each other. It is only when he's not in town that I realise how lonely I am without him. I feel absolutely lost.' Just then they call Neetu for her shot. The artificial rain pours down on everybody. The crowd steps back to avoid the shower and I snuggle inside Neetu's car for shelter. From behind the glass window, I watch Neetu dance, sing, and splash in the rain. Basu Chatterjee is more than pleased with the way she performs. 'She is excellent,' he says. 'So far she hasn't been given the chance to prove her talent. I am giving it to her.' 'Which according to you is your best film?' I ask Basuda. He smiles. 'All of them are good but because *Rajnigandha* gave me recognition, I guess I'm more partial towards it.' 'What about the heroines?' I ask. 'Which of them are you partial towards?' 'None! Each one was chosen to suit the character, and so they all did well. The newcomers work harder, the established ones are sharper. Take Neetu, for instance. I just have to explain the scene once and she says '*Hanji*'. This kind of quick understanding saves a lot of time.'

Priyatama, I gather from the director is a typical Basuda film. Like the others, it is a Boy meets Girl—Boy loses Girl—Boy gets Girl story. But unlike *Rajnigandha*, *Chhoti Si Baat*, *Chit Chor* and *Swami*, *Priyatama* does not have a triangle. There is just Neetu-Jeetu to make love, fight and spilt and live happily ever after.

Suddenly it starts raining. This time it's real rain. The heavens open up and down comes a brisk shower. Everybody is confused. '*Arre sachchi barish ho rahi hai,*' says Munni (Neetu's right hand-cum-confidante-cum everything). 'Oh! I adore getting wet, but I like changing into dry clothes right away,' says Neetu's hairdresser Shirley. The Production Manager is excited. 'My God!' he screams. 'All the cheques have got wet and now everyone's payment will get delayed.' Only the onlookers are unmoved. They stand in a row, under black umbrellas and wait to see what happens next.

Neetu comes running to the car followed by a group of fans clamouring for autographs. 'I have spoilt my poncho. Look at the way the colour is running,' she moans. 'I'm not bothered as long as I can snatch some time to fly to London.' She accepts the pen and paper offered by an eager fan. 'I have changed my autograph,' she announces with as much importance as if the Prime Minister had changed the Cabinet. 'Previously I used to write—regards, now I write—smile always'—and as if to prove it, she signs autographs by the dozen.

Inside the car, everybody is talking at the same time. Munni says, 'Muslims don't wear *bindis*. That is why my forehead is bare.' Neetu says, 'Our conversation on the phone is very brief. He says, 'Hello. How are you?' I say, 'I am fine.' He says, 'How was your day?' I tell him about it. He says, 'Any problems?' '*Bas* . . . I miss him.' The rain scene they are shooting today is Neetu Singh's entry scene in the film. 'I am waiting at home for Jeetu and he does not turn up, I go to meet him and on the way it starts raining.' 'So you start singing and dancing?' I say, 'How romantic!' 'Yes,' she smiles back. 'But how impossible! If such things happened in real life I would be on the streets of London.' I did not tell her so, but she was wrong. If such things happened in real life, Chintu would be on the streets of Mumbai.

Super, September 1977

Neetu Singh's mysterious secretary

The girl is 16, speaks fluent Hindi and passable English. She is well-informed about our film stars, their films, and the studios they work in. And she is clever. She decides to skim off some of the cream floating around in filmland. And in the tradition of all con-men, she begins her game. She shops at the best of Bombay's boutiques and asks for the bills to be made out in the names of some of the leading heroines. She visits big producers and direc-tors, travels only by taxi and tells them to pay the massive fare. 'Put it on the heroine's account,' she orders. To people who are suspicious of her, or reluctant to foot the bills, she arrogantly introduces herself as the film star's 'sister', or 'secretary'. And many *filmwallas* have fallen for the ploy.

Sulakshana Pandit is the first victim. A couple of months later, she realises that she's being asked to pay bills for things she had never bought. Concerned about money as she is, Sulu decides to investigate and comes up with the first clue to identifying the mysterious 'secretary sister'. She discoveres that a look-alike is going around introducing herself as one of the Pandit sisters. Sulu at once cautions everyone that the girl is a fraud. '*Baap re baap, kya ladki hai!*'

The next leading lady to come in for the attention of the con-girl is Neetu Singh. Neetu's telephone is constantly engaged with her producers, directors, co-stars wanting to know about her new secretary. It turns out that Neetu's self-appointed secretary has visited all her producers to make inquiries about her dates of shooting, her payments and so on. Here, too, the intrepid con-girl makes the *filmwallas* cough up her cab fare. They pay up quietly, for this exalted being enjoys almost as much *izzat* as the star himself. It is when the taxi bills progressed from a couple of tens to a couple of hundreds, that one producer decides to draw the line.

Neetu is perplexed, but there is nothing she can do. She has never seen her anonymous secretary though her servants tell her of a female visitor who always drops by when Neetu is shooting outdoors, and enquires about her arrivals, departures, and shooting dates. She then asks for a glass of cold water and disappears. Then one day, the whole game blows up in the con-girl's face. Shooting has been cancelled at the last minute and Neetu and her mother are at home. When the doorbell rings, Neetu answers it herself. There, on the doorstep stands the infamous 'secretary', shock and guilt written all over her face. She does not utter a single word. Nor does Neetu. Someone thinks of summoning the police, and the 'secretary' is taken to the Children's Home at Dongri.

'I cannot forget the expression on her face,' recalls Mrs. Singh. 'She was all white, and she stared at Neetu with a hungry look.

She didn't say a word in her defence. She didn't even cry. She looked very defiant.' As for Neetu, she was so petrified when she finally met the girl that she fled to her room leaving the problem to her mother. 'All I remember is that she was wearing *popatlal* trousers and she told me that she had seen *Khel Khel Mein* 50 times!'

It was evident that the vamp of this piece had progressed from being a mere fan to being a clever swindler. From time to time one hears of children who have run away from home in order to see their favourite star in person. They come to Bombay, dozens of Dick Whittingtons, and discover that all that glitters is not gold. Sooner or later they are hauled up by the authorities and most of them land up in the Children's Home.

The Children's Home is situated in a crowded street off Sandhurst Road at Dongri. As you bend your head to enter the low gate of the building, a feeling of depression, of squalor, reaches out of the dark interior. Mr. Khandelkar who looks after the place, is a man of experience. 'A quarter of the cases we get are victims of film fantasy. They either want to be film stars themselves or they want to meet their favourite stars. Some eight months ago, we had three children here, two brothers and a sister between the ages of eight and ten. They had run away from home and had come all the way from Rajasthan just to see their favourite heroine, Hema Malini. They had got her address from a film magazine and were searching the streets of Bandra inquiring about her. They were spotted and brought here.

'When Hema heard of the incident, she made her PRO call our office. He wanted to know if I could send the children to her house for a few hours. I told him it was against the rules. After a few minutes he called up again to tell me that Hema was prepared to send her car for the children. Would I send them? I told him Hema Malini could send a bus if she wanted to, but the children would not be allowed out of the Home. If she was that concerned, she could come and visit them herself. We got no more calls after that and Hema never turned up. Film stars don't realise the danger of meeting these children. They think they are being kind. They do not realise that by encouraging one child they are inspiring a hundred more to run away from home. There is this girl for instance, the one who posed as Neetu Singh's secretary. Her case-history is not unusual. She is crazy about films. In her early teens she got into bad company. They encouraged her by saying that they would make her a film star if she came to Mumbai. When she arrived here she was in a mess! She comes from a good family. Her father is wealthy. And look what she has got into!

She would not talk for months after she was brought here.

She was impossible to understand. Her interests, her ideas and her conversation centred around one topic: Film stars. She would sit in a corner and narrate stories of fantasies to the other girls. She said she had worked with Dharmendra but because one day he slapped her, she left the job. Her condition is slowly improving though,' Mr. Khandelkar goes on. 'She is on clinical treatment and psychotherapy. You can meet her if you wish to, but for not more than five minutes.' We go from room to room looking for the 'secretary sister'. Finally, in the kitchen, we see a group of ten girls, and I know instantly that my quarry is among them. There is something strange about her. She is withdrawn and tense and her face shows the hungry eyes Mrs. Singh had mentioned. I walk up to the group and say, 'hello'. There are giggles and whispered consultations. 'Do you girls see movies?' I ask. 'Yes,' they chorus. Their favourite stars, it turns out, range from Jaya Bhaduri to Jeetendra. 'What about you?' I ask the 'secretary'. 'Don't you have any favourites?'

'No' she replies, eyes downcast.

'Don't you see any movies?'

'No.'

'Don't you read any film magazines?'

'No.'

One of the other girls pipes up, 'She likes Neetu Singh.' Another bursts out: 'She l-o-v-e-s Neetu.' 'Oh, really?' I say. 'I'm a great fan of Neetu too.'

The girl sits up and stares at me. 'Do you know Neetu?' I ask her. She nods, adding that she knows Neetu's family and has been to Neetu's Bandra house often. She hadn't been able to meet Neetu personally because Neetu was in Chennai. Did she know Neetu's producers? 'Of course. I was working for her.' Had she met Chintu? 'Chee . . . no. I don't like him.'

Mr. Khandelkar interrupts us to tell me that my five minutes are up. We leave the room, with Neetu's 'secretary' staring at me all the while. On my way home, in the cab, I remember all the taxi bills that the girl had foisted on unsuspecting producers. It is tragic

NEETU SINGH

Neetu had a mysterious secretary

in a way that so many children come to Mumbai, led astray by false promises and impossible dreams. Perhaps, the answer lies in the films we make, presenting unreal worlds and glittering people. Perhaps there wouldn't be so many Dick Whittingtons, if our streets were shown the way they really are.

Super, December 1977

4

THE TREND OF 'special photosessions' where stars made exclusive time for a magazine and went through four to five costume changes was first started by *Super* magazine. The sessions lasted for hours—sometimes an entire day. The long hours spent assisting the shoots was a learning experience. Watching the star in his domestic atmosphere, going through costume and accessory trials, now losing temper, now breaking barriers, was quite different from meeting him at a formal appointment inside the studio. Social interactions are always interesting. Those involving celebrities even more so. The way they instructed the servants, the way they introduced their family, the disappearance of relatives inside the bedroom, their refrains, their comments, the door and phone bell interruptions.

Sometimes filmmakers or writers dropped by and it was easy to tell who would be working on which project. There were the 'special phone calls' when the caller's name was never mentioned. Just 'your phone' was a sufficient signal. When that happened, the star jumped and charged into the bedroom. Always, the warning echo was identical. '*Bahar se zaru* phone *rakhna.*' Fifteen minutes later the star returned, blooming. Very often the secret was let out because a foolish servant would enter a room full of people and announce, '*Ooty se* phone *hain,*' and since everybody knew everybody's schedules, there would be a moment's awkward silence. The defences invariably dropped as the hours went by and the pressures mounted. . . . The minor irritants about a missing scarf or lipstick, about how the tea was served. . . . In some homes, tea was served in ordinary glasses, in others, it arrived in mugs and a few served it in bone china crockery. Some hostesses were more thoughtful, some more pragmatic, some overfussy to the point of claustrophobia. During the elaborate hairdos and re-touching of make-up, one saw the intimacy between the star and his staff. The hairdresser knew instinctively when the heroine's hair needed brushing. In the manner in which they addressed each other, their body language, it was easy to tell the status of the relationship.

The sessions were an exhausting exercise and by the time they ended, the star was pooped and the house in a mess! Here I must give full marks to our staff photographer, Taiyeb Badshah, who had trained his assistants to never leave a star's home untidy. While they cleaned up, the exhausted star would sit on the sofa, drained and vulnerable. The last round of tea would be ordered which everyone would relish. The conversation revolved around the shoot just completed . . . which pictures would come out nice, which wouldn't. This was the most precious hour. Jokes and laughter would follow the sharing of secrets—sometimes about themselves, sometimes about their rivals and colleagues. Very often they regretted their words and phoned to withdraw it the next day. But this mostly happened at the editor's level.

There was a certain humility about the way the stars surrendered at these photosessions. An acceptance that we knew what was best for them. They threw open their wardrobes and we rummaged through the piles, picked colours and textures that we thought looked best. Observations worked overtime—how they arranged their clothes, their favourite colours, perfumes, the number of footwear in the shoe-rack, the bangle stand. Amjad Khan, for example had a cupboard full of watches, belts and aftershaves, Amrita Singh had more bangles than a shopkeeper. Zeenat Aman collected shoes that could start a store and Hema Malini possessed trunks full of sarees. Despite the invasion of their privacy, there was a *bon hommie* at those sessions that is sadly lacking today.

Star homes closed to the media sometimes in the nineties. It coincided with top photographers investing in luxurious studios. Fully air-conditioned, the studios were better equipped and more convenient for elaborate shooting sessions. This combined with the arrival of grand costumes from personal designers and make-up and hair-stylists making their own contribution. Result! the star was turned into a mannequin! If photosessions were interesting in the past, it was because the star wore his own clothes and the shooting was done in a familiar ambience. The pictures reflected his roots and lifestyle. Today, personal tastes have been substituted by designer labels. From the five-star background to the footwear, it's all someone else's, creation.

One of the popular features in the magazine was called 'Diary'. The 'Diary' required the journalist to spend a couple of days with the star and write her impressions. The aim was to get a peep into the man behind the mask. It was a terrific idea. Every day spent with the star was a revelation. I spent nine days with Shashi Kapoor, seven days with Shabana Azmi, six days with Rishi Kapoor, five days with Reena Roy and eight days with Rajesh Khanna. I discovered that I was infatuated with Shashi, cemented a friendship with Shabana and reported on Reena to a colleague who was madly in love with Shatrughan Sinha. I was confused by Rajesh Khanna, amused by Rishi Kapoor. I have sweet and sour memories because the stars blew hot and cold. My own self-image changed according to the swings in star moods but looking back, it was all worth it. I'm not saying one was always accurate in one's assessment. There were times one judged them harshly. But this was also because the stars played games and tried to live up to an image.

I did Rajesh Khanna's 'Diary' when he was at his lowest ebb, the beginning of the end. Amitabh Bachchan had overtaken him in the race but the finality hadn't yet hit Khanna. The hurt and humiliation had turned Rajesh Khanna rebellious. For a 9 a.m. shift, he would arrive at 3 p.m. and then disappear into his make-up room and not emerge on

DIMPLE

Studios were more convenient for elaborate shooting sessions

SHASHI KAPOOR

I was infatuated with Shashi Kapoor

the sets till 5 p.m. by which time the producer had been reduced to jelly. On the sets he would be accompanied by a bunch of *chamchas*. There would be endless rounds of tea and cigarettes. A few jokes, a few discussions and by the time the first shot was panned it was 6 p.m. I went through this crazy routine for the first few days, then smartened up. Before leaving home, I would phone the studios to find out if the star had arrived. After the first few phone calls, the operator got fed up. '*Kya roj roj*, Kaka *saab aaye*? Kaka *saab aaye, puchte rehte ho*? *Nau baje ki* shift *ke liya saab kabhi dopaher ke pahle aaye hain* . . .?'

Gradually, Rajesh Khanna's late arrival became a standing joke in the industry. Film-makers maintained that by the time you completed one film with Khanna, you could complete five films with Shashi Kapoor. The accusations didn't bother Kaka. The only thing he was sensitive about was when journalists praised Amitabh Bachchan's professionalism. During one such conversation when a reporter cited the example of how for a 7 a.m. shift, Amitabh reached Manmohan Desai's sets at 6.45, Khanna was vicious. 'Clerks are punctual. I'm not a clerk . . . I'm an artiste. I'm not a slave of my moods. My moods are my slaves,' he said condescendingly.

It was only when one got to know Khanna better that one saw the good side to him. There was a side to him that was difficult to dislike. Deeply bruised by the sudden betrayal of the box-office, he was hopelessly lonely and unable to contain his sorrow. Surrounded by bad company, he said and did things he regretted later but was too proud to admit his mistakes. My 'Diary' with Rajesh Khanna was more about waiting for him, than spending time with him. Even though it was more than a year now, my family's deadline of 7 p.m. for me continued. As a result, I filed my copy from whatever information I gathered from hanging around his sets—a combination of moments spent with the star, his staff and film-makers.

On the last day of my assignment, I was so saturated with the actor that I presented Khanna with a footruler inscribed with, 'For the naughty boy who needs a good spanking.' He took it in good spirit. He preserved the footruler in his make-up tray for a long time and whenever I bumped into him at a studio, summoned his make-up man, Rajaram to show me the footruler. 'I like it . . .' he would say, narrowing his eyes the way he did on screen and after that always cooperated whenever I approached him for an interview.

Neetu Singh had once told me that Rishi Kapoor was mortally frightened of flying. He would hold even a stranger's hand when the flight took off. Not surprising that pretty girls wanted to book themselves on the same flight as

Chintu's. What Neetu didn't tell me, and what I discovered on my own, was that Rishi Kapoor was a big hypochondriac. This was clearly evident during my one week 'Diary'. Every day I met him, there was some problem or the other. The first day, he had a headache, the second day, a stomach ache, the third day, he was feeling nauseous, on the fourth day he suffered from acidity, on the fifth, high fever and on the sixth day, it was low blood pressure! On the last day, when I asked him what was ailing him that day, he smirked, 'Nothing. . . . Today, I have no problems because today, she (Neetu Singh) is coming back.'

This was the first time Rishi Kapoor had openly declared his love for Neetu. All this while it was only Neetu who had been screaming her adoration from the roof-tops. Chintu neither said 'yes' nor 'no'. Till the very end, Rishi never confessed his feelings for his co-star. Not even when the press called him chauvinistic and Neetu a doormat. Neetu didn't care about the opinion of magazines. In the privacy of their meetings, she knew he cared for her and whether he said it to the world or not, it did not alter her feelings. She invested in the relationship wholeheartedly. She believed that sooner or later, he would reciprocate. He did. Rishi Kapoor's statement created a furore. Film producers were scared that she would ditch them half-way and get married. And yet the speculations were never, 'Will they? Won't they?' But always, 'Will he? Won't he?'

Time and again differences in their backgrounds were pointed out. What made things difficult for Neetu were some explosive pictures done as screen-test by the actress in her early days. Ignorant about the ways of the film world, the mother and daughter had given in to a cameraman's request, who misused their trust. They were pictures the Singhs lived to regret. Possessive to the point of paranoia, it was a sensitive subject with Rishi Kapoor. The pictures made it into print at the most vulnerable moments. Everytime this happened, the Neetu-Chintu affair went for a six. Sparks flew and Chintu went into hibernation for days, while Neetu suffered silently. I happened to visit Neetu on one such occasion when she discussed her future—'I know that I love him deeply. . . . Perhaps, I love him more than I love myself or anyone else in the world. I cannot live without him but I cannot forever die in insecurity. This constant feeling of fear and the threat that if I do this, he may not marry me is silly and unnecessary. I will never do anything to annoy him consciously. Never sign a film or wear a costume that he disapproves of. But marriage is much more serious. It's destiny. If it has to happen, it will. . . . If not, I can die but never have him. . . .'

Weighed down with pain and anxiety, she had spoken words beyond her age. We had been talking in the Shailaja Apartments balcony at Pali Hill for hours. Then staring down at the lonely street, she pointed to the laundry shop opposite and said, 'In the night, sometimes when I cannot sleep, I stare at that solitary light on the road. Do you see that name plate—Baba Laundry? (*Baba* was Neetu's endearment for Chintu). When he is not in town and I miss him badly, I stand and stare at this board. . . . Mad, am I not?' She laughed heartily even though one could see she was feeling low. Then, after a long pause added, 'This is the first time we are in town and have not spoken for so many days. . . . He's really upset. I'm suffering too. . . . What has to happen, will happen.'

Completely absorbed in each other's lives and routines, Neetu and Chintu spoke to each other at least 15 times a day. Even when shooting outdoors, they talked at regular intervals. Neetu's producers and co-stars were used to her frequent disappearance from the sets to report the progress of the day to her boyfriend on the phone. She had strict instructions from Chintu to phone him as soon as she reached the studio. Then in between shots, during lunch break, before leaving the studio and finally from home. Sometimes, she would begin her make-up without phoning because the office hadn't opened yet. When it did, Rishi's would be the first phone call. He would fire her for being negligent towards him. Their appetite for each other's interests and routine was insatiable. Neetu, in those days, spent half her time shooting and the other half locating telephones.

Mama Singh said that when Chintu went out of town, her daughter turned into a wilted flower. She said that things would work in her favour if she could restrain herself. Too much of togetherness was unhealthy and harmful. Every relationship needed breathing space. But Neetu and Chintu were beyond caring. They just didn't seem to have enough of each other. She wore, behaved, spoke, ate what he liked. Associated herself only with those he approved of. He was disapproving of her growing friendship with Rekha. 'No two people from the same profession can be friends,' he told her. There was an occasion when Rekha was forced to hide in the elevator because Neetu heard Chintu's car drive into the foyer of her building. That was the last straw on Rekha's proud back. The Rekha-Neetu friendship formed during their early careers and survived through success, split for a while. Rekha stopped her surprise visits to Neetu and Neetu stopped confiding in her about Chintu. The old friends kept their distance even at premieres and parties. Neetu missed her but nothing and nobody won when it came to Rishi Kapoor.

Ranjeeta Kaur (Robby), was in many ways like Neetu Singh. Besotted with Akbar Khan, she couldn't stop talking about him and brought him into her conversation even when unnecessary. Playing Laila in H.S. Rawail's costume drama *Laila Majnu*, Robby was known for her fiery temper. There were ugly rumours that Robby had come close to walking out of the film because of personal problems with the director. Better sense prevailed and the controversy was hushed up. It was a sensible decision on her part to swallow the humiliation and at the same time make her point. Erratic and impulsive, Robby was known to be high-strung. Her friends at FTII were used to her swinging moods. It was said that she was heavily into drugs and that was one of the reasons for her unpredictable behaviour.

Akbar Khan was the only calming influence in Robby's

life at that time. He was the only one she listened to and truly cared for. To be fair to Akbar, he never misused his power and was never judgemental about situations and people he was not directly concerned with. On many occasions when I was with the two, Robby expressed her career conflict, sought his advice on whether to sign a particular film or not. He never gave opinions, and asked her to make decisions on her own. He indulged her, felt responsible for her, enjoyed her company but I'm not sure if Akbar loved Robby the way she loved him. Whenever she was not shooting, Robby would be at Akbar's. Their regular haunt on Sundays and other holidays was the Sun'n'Sand poolside. Akbar would order beef steaks and grumble about the complacent service of five-star hotels.

I spent many such afternoons with the couple but never understood what they had in common. Akbar was suave, flirtatious and an aristocrat. Robby was earthy, serious and sensitive. And yet there was a bond. 'As long as Akbar is in Mumbai, I will never miss home,' Robby always said. I don't think Robby ever believed that she could settle down with anyone except Akbar. She hated journalists asking her again and again about marriage. 'How do I explain to them that he isn't evading me, he is evading commitment. If Akbar Khan ever marries, he will marry only me.' That was in 1978. Today, Ranjeeta has grown up kids, and Akbar tied the knot a few years ago. Some time in the early eighties Robby enjoyed a heady success paired opposite Mithun Chakraborty. All the films they did together were box-office hits. Then came Rajshri Productions' *Ankhiyon Ke Jharonkhon Se* with Sachin, followed by Raj Sippy's *Satte Pe Satta* opposite Amitabh Bachchan. The cracks in the Akbar-Ranjeeta relationship came gradually to the fore and somewhere along the line, they began to show.

The rot set into the media and Amitabh Bachchan relationship, too. Unanimously described as a proud, stand-offish actor, my colleague Pammi Bakshi, who did a week long 'Diary' with the actor, had a different story to tell. Pammi did Bachchan's 'Diary' at the time I was doing Shashi

Kapoor's 'Diary'. Every evening, we'd exchange notes on the two men in our lives. Full of praise for the tall actor, she was bowled over by him. I was bowled over by Shashi Kapoor. Only I didn't know it. My other colleague, Resham Shyam was madly in love with Shatrughan Sinha and spent a major part of her day trying to get her lover on the phone. Resham's phones would never be given to the actor by Shatrughan's innumerable *chamchas*.

It was my fortune that my editor sent me to do a 'Diary' with Shabana Azmi. If he hadn't, I would have never gained a friend so dear. It was instant chemistry between Shabana and me. I had interviewed the actress many times but it was during those seven days that we got to know each other. She was going through a vulnerable phase at that time and even though on some days she seemed in the depths of despair, like always, she rose out of the crisis! Since then our friendship has survived many storms and controversies, both in her life and mine. Shabana was the strongest source of influence in my growing years as a journalist. Citing the late K.N. Subramaniam's (*Filmfare*), she said that not a single article written by the writer was ever sensational, yet not a single article written by him could ever be called uninteresting. She encouraged me to base my relationships with stars on a foundation of trust. 'The article should be believed in because of the byline. That's the hallmark of credibility.'

It was Shabana who broke my defences about not eating on a star set. Until then, even if I was famished and close to fainting, I would restrain from accepting anything but tea. Ever since certain stars had made offending statements about journalists visiting their sets and eating their food, scribes had become self-conscious about eating with stars. It was not easy considering that most of the time I travelled directly from college to the studios. There were times I was very hungry and suffered acute acidity. I always carried biscuits in my purse but felt silly opening my packet and munching in a roomful of people. It was simpler to say, 'Thanks, I'm not hungry.'

Looking back, I feel all that control was unnecessary. What

difference does it make, when, in a roomful of people every-one is eating and you are clinging to your principles. . . . Nobody even notices your resistance. Not worth it when your intestines are coiling within and you have to do this day after day for a whole week. Fasting and bladder control were my two major lessons as a struggling journalist. After all, one cannot walk into a star make-up room and say, 'Can I use your toilet please?'

There were other disadvantages to being a staffer, too. As at trainee, I was often sent to obtain quotes from stars for a story compiled by the copy editor. Often, the story was projected in a totally different light. One such highly negative desk story involved Zeenat Aman and Shabana Azmi got me into a tight spot. Shabana Azmi met me at a suburban studio and said, 'I cannot believe that you're the same person who wrote the story.' I couldn't sleep that night. I wasn't courageous enough to defend myself and too loyal to the magazine to tell the truth. After this, I made sure that I never crossed Shabana's path again. I consciously kept away from studios and dubbing theatres that she was visit-ing. In the office, I turned extra cautious of my copy and checked it to the point of paranoia. I had burnt my fingers once and I wasn't willing to go through the experience again.

Devotion to a job to the point where it comes in conflict with your ideology isn't the right answer. Loyalty should not be more important than truth. I would have perhaps gone to the grave without clearing the misunderstanding had Shabana not made the first overtures. Shabana had often said that on different occasions, she could be a different person for she didn't predetermine her reactions. After months of silence, we finally broke the ice when she sent a message through a colleague asking me to meet her. I did. She was warm and gregarious. She hugged me and didn't mention the topic ever again. I learnt a very important lesson that day. Stars endure more than journalists. They are far more benevolent and can rise above injustice with more grace than the media is capable of. It has been proved time and again that everytime the press is betrayed, they turn vicious. Everytime the star is scorned, the outcome is isolation.

Overall, Rauf made a good editor. He nurtured those who worked under him. Unlike many journalists I know, I wasn't allowed to burn out. He treated me more like a spare tyre. I was protected and shielded from the ugly side of the film industry. He knew intuitively which assignment was right for which reporter. At that time, of course, it was difficult to understand this. Different temperaments are suitable for different subjects. And an editor knows this instinctively. With time I also realised that even though my colleague and I were diametrically opposite, there was a meeting ground of sorts. Our thought processes and attitudes were forever reflecting each other. Our perceptions to the same experiences were very different. Gradually one accepted that it wasn't necessary to be like-minded to be friends.

If Pammi was flamboyant, fearless and secure in her self-esteem, I was the opposite. She had the confidence to barge into the make-up rooms of stars, to speak her mind and making herself popular. Comparisons were obvious. Every day Pammi got back from the sets she had interesting anecdotes to recount about Rishi Kapoor's driver, Jeetendra's spot boy, Amitabh's tiffin box. . . . How many *chappatis* he ate, how many vitamins he swallowed, and how many cars he possessed. Pammi told her anecdotes, particularly those relating to Amitabh Bachchan, dramatically. We sat around her, glued to our chairs, hanging on to her every word. Part of the attraction was, of course, that Bachchan was forbidden fruit and not many had access to the man. 'Don't you have similar stories?' they often ask me at the office. The complexes set in early. . . .

5

H E WAS SITTING with his back to the camera, dark glasses covering his face. The venue, a busy street of south Mumbai, the film untitled. I stood a few steps away, rummaging in my handbag for a card to introduce myself. That's when the ace-villain, Pran Sikand, smiled. 'And I thought you were an actress.' I drew a blank. 'Only an artiste,' he explained 'can stare into four reflectors without blinking.' It needed an actor to make such an observation. Years later, on a scorching hot afternoon driving down town with Shabana Azmi, I was surprised to discover that she wasn't wearing her shades. 'Shyam Benegal has forbidden me to,' she explained. 'He feels I blink too often during shooting. My eyes need to get accustomed to sunlight.' A lot of actors face this problem. Always hiding behind their masks in public, their eyes don't get adequate sunlight. 'These are occupational hazards,' smiled Pran as he lit his third cigarette in the 20 minutes I spent with him. 'Sometimes we adopt bad habits because it helps our screen image. Ever since I was told that I looked effective with a cigarette in my mouth, I made it my trademark. I smoked in every shot of every film. Result, infected lungs.'

I interviewed Pran travelling in his car to his next shooting. The film was *Dharma* and they were picturising a *qawwali* song between Pran and Premnath. Dressed in a *sherwani* and a *topi*, Pran looked a different man. 'There is a very sweet line in this song,' he said while on the sets. 'And it's Premnathsaab's contribution. At the end of the *antra*, we've added, *'Tu hain mera Pran, mein hoon tera Prem* . . . It's lines like these which are bound to get *taalis*. . . .' After this encounter, I didn't meet Pran for a long time. The next time I met him was a decade later at the Tata Memorial Hospital. My mother and his young niece were in adjoining rooms. Pran came to visit his niece regularly. Sometimes on his way to shootings, sometimes on his return journey. In the long spell that she was in the hospital, he didn't miss a single day, except when he was shooting outdoors. Everyday, fresh flowers were sent to the patient and as long as my mother was there, he sent an identical basket for her as well. There was no mistaking his feelings for the ailing patient.

It's a cliche but all the villains I have encountered, in the film industry are fabulous human beings. After the premiere of Rajkumar Santoshi's *Barsaat*, I was waiting for my car and asked Danny Denzongpa how a courteous man like him managed to look so ruthless on screen. Where do you draw your inspiration from? 'Maybe I am evil,' he laughed. 'All the evil repressed within me just comes out for these awful roles. . . .' Then after a moment's pause added, 'Seriously, rape or violence isn't a problem unless the artiste involved begins to feel degraded. It's when the artiste's conscience reaches a crisis, that's the danger point.' I understood what he meant. I had been witness to one such incident. The film was Akbar Khan's *Haadsaa*.

Rape is repulsive

In a corner, huddled with my bag and files, desultorily, I watch Akbar Khan shoot a rape scene. The villain closes in on the girl. She retreats. He pounces on her hungrily. Tears her dress along the marked-out stitches, caresses her arm and smiles lecherously. She screams wildly . . . and 'cut!' One, two, three, four, five takes. There is humiliation on the face of the actress. 'Today, it's only the rape scene,' she had said an hour ago, while applying make-up. Now, she curls her lower lip and says, 'He pulls me so hard . . . it hurts!'

She is trying to be brave. For the next shot, the director wants the villain to tear the neck of her dress. 'No, no . . . I will not allow it,' she protests and walks away. He follows her and talks to her gently, strokes her hair tenderly—Akbar, the director, and Ranjeeta (Robby) Kaur, the heroine, have been romantically linked for seven years. 'I can't do it . . .' Ranjeeta repeats, tears welling up in her eyes. He walks to the other side, and one by one, requests every guest, spot boy, light boy to leave. They start the camera. Ranjeeta is trembling, choking with hysteria, tears roll down her cheeks and when the shot is over, she runs out of the set, races to the make-up room, enters the bathroom and bangs the door.

I come away without my interview. Seeing the rape scene distress her, has disturbed me. All this talk about the villain and the actress actually being friends, their giving each other a peck on the cheek before shooting begins, this need for establishing a friendship before the 'rape'—the facade crumbles. . . . Maybe, I'm surprised by her agitation. In an air-conditioned theatre, I've so often watched the same scene and felt nothing. But today, seeing how vulnerable the performer is to the situation, leaves me with a hollow feeling in the pit of my stomach. . . .

Rape is repulsive and all women react to it the same way. So what if they are actresses? I feel restless the whole day, until I speak about it to Shabana Azmi in the evening. She listens patiently and then says, 'In my second film *Nishant*, when the director asked me to lie on the ground, my saree hiked high and feet apart, I felt thoroughly insulted. Seething with anger, I had returned sobbing to my, room. Today, you are disturbed because you've seen rape as enacted in an unreal set-up. Probably if you had witnessed a REAL rape you wouldn't be as upset.' I am not sure if I fully understand what she says. But her words provide momentary comfort. . . .

Years later, while I'm interviewing a hero, he jumps up from his chair and locks his make-up room door. No, he isn't going to rape me, but constantly insinuated of homosexuality by the media, it's his way of proving his heterosexuality. His desperation is so pathetic that I'm disgusted rather than shocked!

Super, March 1978

Can a place like this nurture anyone? I asked myself. I wondered what kind of a jungle I had landed up in—one person had gone off her rocker, someone had lost his stability, drug addictions, secret hospitalisations, dangerous living. . . . All kinds of doctors, all kinds of therapies. The stars seemed more in need of psychiatrists and priests than medicine. I felt ill at ease in my new surrounding but crazy as it sounds, went through phases of great attachment as well. Comprised of readymade jars of intensity, these creative people accepted my eccentricities as normal. I was aware that this world had no links with my background. I would shun it if I could but having got into it, it was difficult giving up the euphoria.

Every day was a different experience, made up of different faces and different stories. Jaya Bhaduri, nee Bachchan, was shooting after a long break after marriage and kids. The film was Mehmood's *Nauker* starring her and Sanjeev Kumar. Jaya was friendly with my editor so he had sought special permission to cover the shooting even though Jaya's husband, Amitabh, was not talking to the press. I had met Jaya earlier when I was interviewing veteran comedienne Shammi, after her fifteen-year-old marriage split with filmmaker Sultan Ahmed. A broken woman, she had wept all through the interview, confessed that had it not been for Jaya's support she would have gone to pieces! While we were talking Jaya had dropped by with a *handi* of chicken curry, because it was exactly one year that day since Shammi had given up non-vegetarian food. It was a thoughtful gesture. A few months later, when I visited the *Nauker* set, Shammi was amongst the hen-group present in Jaya's room.

'Lambuji doesn't sound nice now. He's a father of two.'

It's lunchtime and in Satish Bhalla's bungalow, peace reigns. The lounge resembles a railway station waiting room. Some of the junior artistes are napping on the carpet. A few are thumbing through film magazines. One of them is fiddling with the knobs of his transistor, trying to catch a radio station. A few make-up men and unit members are still eating their lunch and a couple of kids are running around the bungalow trying to play a silent version of hide 'n' seek.

Sanjeev Kumar better known as Haribhai is having a nap, says a unit man. I don't believe him, but he points to a fat figure in a distant corner. And sure enough, it is Haribhai. Clad in a *lungi-kurta,* the actor looks enormous on the narrow sofa. When the lunch break ends, life returns on the sets. The junior artistes go off to splash some water and return looking fresh. Everyone is ready. Everyone except Sanjeev Kumar who is still asleep.

In her room, Jaya sits in a maroon cotton saree, eyes sparkling. She wears no jewellery and hardly any make-up. Her make-up man Shankar *dada* tells me of having pulled many a fast one on Jaya fans in the past. 'Jayaji didn't like visitors even those days. So I would lock her up inside the make-up room and tell everybody that she'd gone home for lunch.' Outside, a little boy sides up to the sleeping Sanjeev Kumar, thrusts a quick hand into his *kurta* and tries to tickle him. Sanjeev lazily opens one eye and shuts it again, but still refuses to get up.

Nauker, as the title suggests, is a film about servants—good and bad. About employers—good and bad. It's a story about Lalita Pawar who treats her niece Jaya as a servant. And Sanjeev Kumar who treats his servant, Mehmood, like a friend. But there is romance in the film too. For some reason or the other, Sanjeev decides to masquerade as a servant, meets Jaya and falls in love with her.

Today, they are shooting the climactic scene where Manmohan Krishna discovers that his wife has been a wicked woman and beats her up. Jaya has to intervene. She cries, 'Hit me. Break me into pieces but don't touch her.' Manmohan says, 'This is what I should have done 25 years ago,' and continues to beat Lalita Pawar. It's a simple shot and no one goofs up, but for reasons unknown Mehmood keeps calling 'cut'.

In between shots, Jaya sits in the privacy of her room. She has to go up on the tips of her toes to latch the door. Only after she has done this, does she relax. A typical Arien, the slightest thing can irritate Jaya. What annoys her most, she says, is over familiarity. As she puts it, 'If people are good, I am good. If people are bad, I am very bad.' It is a day for visitors. And there are many of them. There is a hazel-eyed lady, a friend of Jaya's who is spending the day with her. There is Shammi, who Jaya refers to respectfully as 'Shammiji.' There is director Raj Tilak and Jaya congratulates him on his new film. There is a surprise visitor—Farida, Jaya's ex-hairdresser, who is now working for Shabana Azmi. There's affection between the two women. They are meeting after ages, but they have no trouble picking up the threads. Jaya reminds Farida of the time when, while doing double-shifts, she would doze off in her car and wake up only when Farida nudged her and said, 'Jaya studio aagaya.'

'Today,' says Jaya 'I have proper sleep . . . aaraam. Those days I was busy physically with my make-up, shooting, dubbing and outdoor work. Today, I am busy mentally—with things like Shweta's school, Abhishek's meals and Amit's shooting.' I ask her when she stopped calling Amitabh 'Lambuji' and switched to Amit. 'Only recently,' she says, tossing her head in the old Jaya style. 'He is the father of two, Lambuji doesn't sound nice.'

When Jaya talks of Amitabh, there is a glow on her face. Five years of marriage have not killed the girlfriend in her. She is still the old Guddi—very much in love with her man. Only now, when she recalls the days of her courtship, she is wistful. 'I used to adore Amit's eyes. They were bright and sparkling. He always gave the impression that he had just stepped out of a shower. Today, 'she sighs, 'his eyes are sunken and hollow. Like this . . .' she says, imitating his expression. The take-off is perfect. When we ask her to put on a show for us—do imitations of other stars, she shakes her head. 'I shall imitate no one but Mr. Amitabh Bachchan!' Mid-sentence, Jaya removes a nail-cutter from her bag and without looking up says, 'Excuse me, but this is an emergency.'

Super, June 1978

Many years later as I sit in Amitabh Bachchan's van, Bachchan, mid-sentence, removes a nail-cutter from his pouch and with an, 'Excuse me, but this is an emergency,' begins to clip his nails even as he continues to answer your next question. There's a feeling of *deja vu*. So many memories—and they are all overflowing. . . .

. . . That morning when Hema Malini came red-eyed for the *mahurat* of B.R. Chopra's *Burning Train* at Bombay Central Station. When mama Jaya Chakravarthy did not leave Hema's side for a minute. And Hema didn't even once look in Dharmendra's direction. When, during the shot, she did, her eyes filled with tears which she quickly wiped with a lace handkerchief.

. . . The crazy evening when the dance rehearsals for Manmohan Desai's *Parvarish* went on and on at Bhaidas Hall and for every extra take Shabana took, choreographer P.L. Raj screamed louder, until a weeping Shabana stomped out of the theatre barefoot on the street, calling for her car in her *qawwali* costume. . . .

. . . When Vinod Mehra and Bindiya Goswami eloped and got married even though Vinod had got married, a few weeks ago, to Meena Broca. . . . The desperate days when Sulakshana Pandit was hell-bent on exposing younger sister Vijeyata Pandit's boyfriend Kumar Gaurav, his family and friends. When Parikshit Sahni kept his favourite photo the map of India in the silver frame beside his bed.

Every encounter was a journey into the stars' past, present and future, their tastes and temperaments. . . . The time when Nutan and her son Mohnish Behl were uncomfortable shooting a photosession together. . . . And everytime their hands touched, they stiffened. The time when writer-director Karan Razdan and wife Priya Tendulkar were self-conscious holding each other close. Zarina Wahab's acute competition vis-a-vis cushions and cars with Rekha. Rekha's acute problem of bedroom and round beds with Zeenat Aman. . . . The break-up and make-up of Rekha and Neetu Singh. . . .

. . . The time I mixed up comedian Asit Sen's number with director Asit Sen's and travelled all the way to Filmcity to meet the wrong man. . . . The time I dropped by to meet Johnny Walker and he did not smile even once during the long interview. . . . The time spent on filmmaker Shakti Samanta's set of *Anand Ashram*, where Sharmila Tagore, playing a Bengali belle, was draped in a chiffon saree— the Calcutta cotton border stiched over it for the 'Tangail' effect. . . . The time distributors got upset with filmmaker Hrishikesh Mukherjee for putting their favourite vamp Bindu in a saree. . . . The time Bindu's huge poster of Aruna Vikas'

Shaque, holding a black bra at Eros theatre caused a traffic jam and the poster had to be removed overnight. . . . The time when Shyam Benegal's office kept phoning, during our photosession with Smita Patil, calling her for a meeting at the now demolished Jyoti Studio. This was after *Nishant* and *Manthan*, but before *Bhumika*. Based on the life of Marathi actress Hansa Wadkar, it was the role of a lifetime. And Smita knew it.

There wasn't the slightest hesitation, fear or awkwardness about stepping into strangers' homes and asking them the most ridiculous questions. Witnessing their heartbreaks and traumas and writing about them was part of my profession.

Sometimes there was guilt, sometimes pain, sometimes relief, and sometimes pity. When Vinod Mehra got married to Meena, the woman his mother had chosen, I went to interview the newly-weds. A certain natural fragrance attached to a happy occasion was missing. Tension loomed large on that day. Vinod was awkward and Meena nervous. Their answers seemed rehearsed and it was obvious even to a stranger like me that they were not comfortable in each other's presence. Vinod suffered his first heart attack soon after the wedding and three months later, one fine afternoon, Vinod eloped with co-star Bindiya Goswami, while still being married to Meena.

It was a major scandal which took an ugly turn when Meena's brothers threatened Vinod with dire consequences. Torn between his love for Bindiya and his mother, Vinod was overriden with guilt. Bindiya's parents were upset with her for ruining a promising career to settle down with a married man. For a while the two stayed in hotel rooms. About Meena, Vinod said, 'I don't want to explain, but my marriage with her is not a marriage.' What he perhaps meant was that their marriage hadn't been consummated.

It was a sad break-up. The blushing bride, who had come with a lot of dreams, was packed away a few weeks later. For quite some time there were wild stories that Meena's *sardar* brothers were gunning for Vinod. The Goswamis were certain that the marriage wouldn't last. They knew that their daughter was reckless. Mrs. Mehra, Vinod's mother also maintained, '*Ek bar jis ladki ko* madam *bulvane ki aadat pad jaye vo bahu ya bhabhi nahin ban sakti. Vo* madam *hi rahti hai.*'

Call it destiny, but a few years later history repeated itself when one casual afternoon Bindiya Goswami left her home to get married to film-maker J.P. Dutta, whilst still being married to Vinod. It is said that Vinod went pleading to bring Bindiya back, but Bindiya had made up her mind. A few years later, Vinod made up his mind as well. He got married to Kiran. It was his fourth marriage and her second. Still, Vinod was excited. 'This is the right one,' he told me when I went for the wedding. 'You wait and watch, this will last forever.' It did, only Vinod died too young.

Vinod's death was as dramatic as his marriage. Shrouded in mystery till the very end, nobody was able to resolve why his body turned black during the last hours. Everything happened so quickly. He complained of chest pain. His wife rubbed balm on him. 'Call the doctor,' he said, 'I think I'm dying. . . .' A hysterical Kiran rushed to summon the doctor. He'd begun to turn pale by then. 'I don't want to die,' he said, again and again. 'I want to see our baby.' That was not to be.

Through the numerous marriages he went through, Rekha was Vinod's regular confidante. The fact that they had once been married but continued to remain friends was remarkable. Rekha was the first to meet Meena, to give her the customary saree and jewellery and many years later, also to meet Kiran. Even today, Kiran wears the locket Rekha gifted to her at the wedding. So does Sunita Kapoor. It's believed that presents given by Rekha are extremely lucky.

Bindu's career was soaring high, but luck was running out in her personal life. The vamp had suffered her fourth miscarriage, this time in a late stage and Bindu was in acute depression. She had consciously cut down on her assignments and had now to start all over again. Her youngest sister, Harsha, was my classmate in Government Law College and I would often accompany her home to Worli for a meal. My appointment for a, 'Diary', with Bindu was confirmed by Harsha. The actress was going through a vulnerable phase and the family was sensitive to her moods. Harsha worried that Bindu was withdrawing into a shell. '*Didi* is such an introvert that she suppresses her pain. She has never, in all these years, ever yelled at us.' To distract her pain, husband Champaklal summoned Bindu's three-year-old niece Mini to come and stay with them for a while. The couple was contemplating adopting the child legally. A few months later, when Bindu realised that Mini had got deeply attached to her and began to address her as, '*badi* Mummy,' she had second thoughts. She felt that it wasn't fair to Mini's parents and that's when she changed her mind. 'I finally found consolation in the fact that *Bhagwan ne nahin diya, to na sahi. . . .*' Her husband was extremely supportive. Not many men can be as generous or as proud of their wife's success as he is. When he married Bindu, she was responsible for her large family. He accepted this and ever since has treated his wife's family as his own.

Parveen Babi had stopped showing up for shootings for quite some time but nobody knew the real reasons. One day I was with Jeetendra, who was shooting at Natraj Studio, when Jeetendra's secretary phoned to say that Parveen's secretary had cancelled the dates once again. That was the first time I saw Jeetendra flare up! He dialled Ved Sharma (Parveen's secretary) directly and blew him up. 'You first said it's fever, then flu and now jaundice. Is she really unwell or is the problem something else?' he thundered. Parveen was committed to Jeetendra for his new production and he couldn't take the uncertainty any longer. By the next few days, rumours of Parveen absconding were all over town.

Some said she'd had a nervous breakdown and had flown to America. Some said she had gone mad and her mother had taken her to their native home in Junagadh. There were so many versions to her illness that no one quite knew what was going on. Some blamed Mahesh Bhatt, some Amitabh Bachchan and some Kabir Bedi. It was said that she followed Kabir all the way to Hollywood for the shooting of *Sandokan*, where he ill-treated her. Hurt and humiliated, Parveen returned home, a shattered soul, diffident and demoralised. That was the beginning of her self-destructive phase.

Rekha too was going through an unsteady phase. Signed for Gulzar's *Namkeen* with Sanjeev Kumar, Shabana Azmi, Kiran Vairale and Waheeda Rehman, a huge set was put up at 'Filmcity'. This was the time Rekha was not talking to journalists. One day some people from the press turned up to meet Gulzar. Rekha insisted that the director throw them out. When Gulzar disagreed, Rekha refused to come onto the sets. The two argued for a while and before Gulzar knew it, Rekha had driven away. Angry with her childish behaviour, Gulzar dropped Rekha from the film. In her place, he summoned old favourite Sharmila Tagore and continued with the schedule uninterrupted. The new starcast, however, sparked off fresh complications. Waheeda Rehman felt cheated at having to play mother to Sharmila who was almost her contemporary. Shabana felt cheated at not being considered for Rekha's role. Many years later, similar complications arose when Divya Bharti died and Juhi Chawla had to replace the actress in Raj Kanwar's *Kartavya*. Dimple Kapadia felt cheated at having to play mother to Juhi. Moushumi Chatterjee at not being considered for Dimple's role and playing second fiddle to Aruna Irani. Back to *Namkeen*. Waheeda Rehman, Sharmila Tagore, Shabana Azmi, Kiran Vairale, actresses from different generations discussed men, money and moods with honesty and abandon. Waheeda talked about the pressures of modern education—'I didn't realise I was teaching my daughter all the wrong tables until her teacher called me to complain of her tutor. My daughter, not wanting to expose my ignorance, had lied to the teacher that a tution Miss came to teach her everyday.' Sharmila Tagore talked about domestic adjustments. 'There's no need to get emotionally carried away when dealing with servants. I used to do that, but now I've become wiser. I've realised that it does not matter whether the best crockery comes out when you are entertaining guests. It's more important that you are a cheerful and relaxed hostess.'

As more months went by, I gathered more intimate details about their lifestyles. Parveen Babi loved spaghetti. Jaya Prada was controlled by staff and family. Moushumi Chatterjee suffered from eosinophilia and insomnia. Zarina Wahab suffered from a weak stomach and Sulakshana Pandit from depression. There was an eerie feeling about Kishore Kumar's home when Leena Chandavarkar, exasperated with son Sumeet's tantrums said, 'The only one person Sumeet obeys is brother Amit.' Leena looked visibly frightened of Amit herself. 'He has agreed to Sumeet's demand of not wanting to continue school. How can he? What happens to Sumeet's future?'

Reena Roy liked canopy beds, Neetu Singh liked stuffed toys, Shashi Kapoor liked eating peanuts, Amitabh Bachchan, Bisleri bottles. The sareewala who catered to filmfolks said that the three women in filmdom who bought only whites were Krishna Kapoor, Jaya Bachchan and Lata Mangeshkar. Friends of Javed Akhtar said, he only wrote at night, Amitabh, only dubbed in the mornings. Shashi Kapoor preferred to drive his own car, Rishi Kapoor was paranoid of flying, Dimple Kapadia was obsessed with playing cards. Vijay Arora obsessed with playing chess. Vidya Sinha felt cut off from the industry, living in a far away place like Matunga. Zeenat Aman said it would be a culture-shock living away from Napean Sea Road. Romesh Sharma was too earnest to give a spicy copy. Raj Kiran was far too energetic. He ate, drank and dreamt films. Ranjeeta Kaur dreamt of the day she would prove herself an actress. Shekhar Kapur, of the day when he would direct his own films. He was forever narrating story ideas to anyone willing to listen. 'I'm meant for Hollywood,' he told me, sitting on the bonnet of producer Prem Sawhney's jeep at the night shooting of *Toote Khilone*. That was a crazy evening. On the sets, Shekhar would time and again give suggestions to cousin cum-director Ketan Anand, who shrugged him off with, 'Shekhar, why don't you concentrate on your lines instead?'

A day with Toote Khilone

Juhu. It's 6 p.m. and the location looks deserted. There are two Ambassador cars, one big bus, one PRO, a few *chamchas*—and Sawhney. Sawhney seems uneasy and assures me that the shooting will soon begin. 'It's the sun that has let us down,' he says, 'Unless and until the sun goes down, we cannot shoot. But even if the sun does go down, what is the use? Where are the stars? Nobody has reported!' 'How is Shekhar in the film?' I enquire. 'You mean as an actor? Well . . . I think he's better as a friend.' 'And Shabana?' 'Thanks to Shekhar, she has been very co-operative.' 'What about the director, Ketan Anand?' 'He's Chetan Anand's son. Dev and Vijay Anand's nephew. If after all this he does not click, then Heaven help us!'

After half an hour Ketan, Shekhar and Shabana turn up. Shabana sits tight in her car in her *videsi* jeans and *desi* mood. She says it is very stuffy in the car but adds that she cannot get out because she has rollers in her hair. 'Unless and until my hair is set I cannot take off these rollers,' she announces firmly. 'And unless and until I take them off, I cannot get out of the car!' Shekhar leans over the window and says, 'Relax. You are not needed just yet. Do you want coffee, tea or a cold drink?' Shabana says, 'Nothing. I only want you.'

At this, Shekhar smiles, then Shabana smiles and then Shekhar smiles some more. And I think it is time for me to look out of the window. Shekhar says, 'I have seen some rushes of *Toote Khilone.* Shabana looks nice in the film.' Shabana says, 'Honestly! I do not trust Shekhar. When I'm looking ugly he says I look nice and vice versa.' Just then director Ketan Anand walks towards the car. He looks hassled, his bushy hair stands on end. 'The crane . . . the crane is missing!' he says. 'Without the crane, how are we going to shoot?' There is a long silence. Then Shabana lets out a low moan. And Shekhar says, 'Oh shit!' Shabana calls her driver and says, 'Mithun Chakraborty lives somewhere in that building. Go and call him. Tell him Shabana Azmi wants to meet you.' The driver says, 'But who is Mithun?' Shabana says, 'He is an actor.' The driver asks, 'what if he is not at home?' 'In that case he will be at Sarika's house in the same building.' 'What if he is not at Sarika's home?,' the driver persists. 'I do not know,' Shabana says, 'Buck up now and no more questions.'

The driver returns followed by a surprised looking Mithun. Shabana peeks out of the window and says, '*Ji hame* Shabana Azmi *kahte hai.*' Mithun introduces himself too and when he hears that the shooting has been held up, invites Shabana to come up and wait in his apartment. Shabana quickly removes the rollers from her hair, gathers up a few odds and ends, calls to her hairdresser, Farida, and the two leave for Mithun's home. In her absence, Sawhney and Ketan run up and down organising the crane. Shekhar tells me about the scene they are to shoot now. 'In this particular scene, Shabana likes a saree she sees in the shop. I cannot afford it, so I steal it. Just as we are escaping, a large crowd chases us . . . how do you like it?' he asks.

I honestly cannot say. For by now my head is spinning, with everybody complaining about something or the other. Shabana has returned and wants to know where her clothes are. 'Has my saree been ironed?' she asks. 'Unless and until my clothes are ready how can I change?' Sawhney says, 'Christ! Where is my car? Unless and until I have my car, how can I reach in time for my appointment?' Shekhar says, 'Where is my costume?' And Ketan Anand says, 'Hey look! There's the owner of this land. He says he hasn't given us permission to shoot. He wants us to get off his property immediately!'

I come home well before night. I am sure everybody else did too. As for *Toote Khilone,* the only thing I get to see from the shooting is it's *toota* organisation.

Super, October 1978

At *Super* the Gokhales were facing serious labour problems. This and other complicat-ions couldn't sustain the euphoria. They tried their very best till the end, but had to eventually close down the magazine. The tragedy of *Super* having to shut down, lay not just in the death of a quality product but in the disintegration of a brilliant editorial team.

6

I T WAS SOMETIME in 1981 that Rauf Ahmed left *Super* to join India Book House's new journal *Movie*. The new magazine was going to be daddy G.L. Mirchandani's gift to sonny boy Deepak Mirchandani. Coincidentally, Susie, Deepak's wife was expecting their first baby around this time. Ever since *Movie* has been seen more as a sibling for Rishi, Deepak's son, than as a magazine. That is why I was surprised when *Movie* had been bought over by Business India Television Video. *Movie*, like *Super* had an interesting editorial team. There was Pammi Bakshi, popular for her contacts with the stars, Neena Arora from the *Filmworld* and easily amongst the best writers in film journalism, Madhulika Sharma, equally talented from *Filmfare*, and B.R. Sharan (currently copywriting at Lintas) who had been discovered from his letters to the editor.

We were keen on featuring Rajesh Khanna in our early issues, but the superstar had been evading us. Then, one fine day, I bumped into him at Natraj studio and he promised me an exclusive interview. Khanna invariably bumped into me when he was going through a turbulent time. Mohan Kumar was shooting *Avtaar* with Rajesh Khanna and Shabana Azmi at Vaishnodevi and I accompanied them on the outdoor. This was a particularly low phase for Rajesh Khanna. He was frequently depressed concerning his personal life and rumours were rife about his rift with Dimple Kapadia. Their recurring problems in marriage had become a standing joke in the film industry. Every alternate month Dimple would walk out of Aashirwad, Khanna's plush bungalow at Carter

Road and come to her parents' home. The press would write about their divorce and about Khanna's ill-treatment of his wife.

Every time Dimple came to her parents' home, she swore that she would never return to Aashirwad yet, a few hours later, when Khanna stood before her, she meekly got into his car. This time, however, it was different. Dimple had sworn that she would leave Khanna forever. She had also decided on a date for her departure. She had warned Khanna that this time there would be no emotional drama. She was going for good. It is said that she had consulted an astrologer who had predicted that only if she quit her husband's house on that date, would she be able to live independently. Otherwise it would be difficult for her to break her ties with the past. Unaware of all this, Khanna pleaded with his wife to stay for one more month. 'Complete this year, let us part on our tenth wedding anniversary.' But Dimple was adamant. Preoccupied with all these problems, Khanna would obsessively discuss his marriage at the oddest moments. We were on the flight, eating curry rice, when without warning, Khanna began talking about Dimple. It was awkward. Perhaps, he realised it too but was weighed down with his grief that he could not be concerned with formalities. There was an intense desire in him to talk. To be heard. And somewhere along the way, came the soulful interview.

The Rajesh—Dimple break-up

It's the fourth day of shooting and it's a night shift. They are shooting inside the temple and by the time the unit packs up, it's 2 a.m. Rajesh Khanna comes out of the narrow tunnel of the Vaishnodevi temple, completely drenched. Immediately, his spotboy Raju runs to cover him up with a blanket, but Khanna brushes him away. 'Leave me alone,' he says and sits quietly by himself on the steps. Watching the snowflakes in the dark night while waiting for the rest of the unit to return from their *darshan*, Khanna appears disoriented. After a long silence, without provocation, he starts talking . . . 'Vaishnodevi is a very powerful Goddess. This is my third trip to this temple. And each time I have returned with greater faith.'

'What did you ask for this time?' I question him. He lowers his eyes. Then, after a while, surprises me with a counter question. 'Tell me, what are the rumours you have heard?' I tell him all that I know about his split with his wife. He lets out a deep sigh, 'I don't know what my life is coming to. . . . Whatever has to happen will happen. . . . It's all destiny.' By now the rest of the unit has arrived and everyone gets ready to leave. It's a long journey back to the hotel at Katra. The following interview is the result of an impromptu conversation conducted on our drive back home.

Your marriage is the biggest joke in town. Aren't you embarrassed when people call your fights with Dimple a publicity stunt?
When everyone casts stones, the temptation to come out with the truth in all its gory detail is great. But ultimately, it serves no purpose because your greatest pain becomes a source of ridicule. So I would rather be crucified than speak.

What do you mean when you say that you would rather be crucified? Aren't you being dramatic?
No. I'm a reincarnation of Jesus Christ. I'm being crucified again and again and again.

Sources close to both the families have it that you have signed the divorce papers. Is it true?
No comments.

Insiders say that this time the break-up is final, and yet you look deceptively calm. . . .
I'm tired. I'm exhausted. My cup is already full to the brim.

Who will keep the kids?
I want to keep them but ultimately it should be whatever is best for them. Let us see what happens.

Do you hate Dimple?
No. Even on the day she left, I told her, 'Rishta toda hai dosti na todna.' She is the mother of my two kids and we have shared so many beautiful moments. If, despite this, she desires a career, something must be missing somewhere. It means I have failed. The fault is mine.

Do you think you are unlucky in love?
Yes. There have been too many heartbreaks.

Would you come in the way of her career?
Never. I wish her all the best.

If it is such an obsession with her, why did not you let her work earlier?
I cannot. Period.

Do you blame her parents?
No.

If a good project comes your way, would you do a film with her? Can you imagine both of you as co-stars?
Isn't that too much to expect from me? After all I'm human.

Do you agree that you and Dimple are a mismatched couple?
When we got married, she was very young and looking for a father figure. I was very successful and seeking a mother figure. Probably, it was bad timing.

On my flight to Bombay, I think about Rajesh Khanna, Dimple Kapadia and their marriage. Nine years ago, a 16-year-old dropped out of 10 films because she wanted to marry a superstar. Nine years ago, she could not contain her joy. Today, the same woman is ready to drop her nine-year-old marriage to make a career in films.

Movie, April 1982

Overlooking the sea, next to Mahalaxmi temple, we began and summed up our day to the clanging of bells and the chanting of *aarti*. My cabin overlooked a terrace where young children gathered at 5 p.m. for dance rehearsal. Shekhar Karlekar, our paste-up artiste, made it a point to stand by the balcony every evening. 'Mili has started her dancing lessons,' he would joke, referring to a similar sequence in a Hrishikesh Mukherjee film where Jaya Bhaduri dances to '*Maine kaha phoolon se . . .*' with a group of children on Amitabh Bachchan's terrace. The endless debate of whether art imitates life or vice versa continues.

5 February 1983, was one such morning. *Movie* magazine

had completed a year and was hosting a big bash at the newly launched Hotel Centaur, Juhu. The previous evening I had gone through a dress rehearsal seeking my father's approval of my costume. In the morning I discovered that he had passed away in his sleep. One reads about such things in books, sees them in films, but never expects to have them happen to one in real life. A month later, when I hadn't yet recovered from the trauma, my editor decided that it would be a good break for me to be sent on an outdoor stint. Ramesh Behl was shooting *Pukaar* with Amitabh Bachchan and Zeenat Aman. It was Bachchan's first outdoor shooting after his brutal accident and the producer was keen that he got adequate press coverage.

Travelling with me on the same flight were both the Bachchan and the Behl families. Jaya, Shweta, Abhishek and Ramesh's wife Bubbles with her four kids—daughters Nano, Tanya, Booboo and son Goldie. The six kids together were a riot! The encounter was published as our cover story that month. It was a cheerful story brimming over with domestic chatter.

The Bachchans after the crisis

While waiting for the security-check call, Jaya Bachchan signs a fan's autograph book indifferently. Her seven-year old, pragmatic son, Abhishek, irritatedly pulls at her *dupatta*, 'Ma, look, this buckle does not close.' Jaya glances over her shoulder, hurriedly returning the pen to the eager fan, who lingers on with a compliment. She smiles politely, but her concentration is focussed on Abhishek's satchel, with which he's fumbling exasperatedly. 'Ma, this stupid buckle does not shut,' he yells angrily this time. Jaya rushes to him, takes away the satchel and fastens the buckle effortlessly. The child stops frowning and stares at his mother, his eyes full of admiration. The mother and son exchange meaningful smiles. As if enjoying some private joke, Jaya now plays with the clasp—opens it, shuts it, opens it, shuts it. Abhishek, watches on, wonderstruck at the miracles an adult touch can produce, then impishly grabs the satchel from her hands and scuttles over to another corner, where he is immediately surrounded by his young friends.

With deep concentration, nine-year old Shweta examines the buckle, then in a tone of superiority, asks, 'Ma fixed it, right?' The brother nods. From where I'm standing, I witness this scene with amusement. Children have their own world where adults cannot trespass. Not even if you are the child's mother. Dressed in a blue silk *churidar-kameez* with a printed *dupatta*, her bag (which matches her footwear) tightly clutched under her arm and her freshly shampooed hair left loose, Jaya looks more glamorous than she ever did in her star-days. Huge sun-glasses cover her small face and when she removes them, I notice that her face looks rested. 'I'm feeling calm and at peace with myself,' she says softly, tossing her hair. 'Only the last few days I have been a bit worried about his health because, after all, this is his first outdoor after the accident and already he's been away for two weeks. . . .

'Initially, we had decided to give him a surprise by landing in Goa. But, as usual, the kids got excited and told him about out our visit on the phone. Once you are married your conversation on the phone is different. You don't coo on a long-distance line. My primary concern in calling him is to inquire after his health and, of course, to give him news about the children—about what happened at school, what they did at home. Yesterday, when I called him, the line was awful—full of disturbances. All I could hear was the repeated 'Jaya, I cannot hear a damn word.' Amit gets very frustrated with a bad telephone connection. To not aggravate his impatience, we hung up.

'He does not know by which flight we are arriving today, but of course, Abhishek expects his father to receive him at the airport.' So does daughter Shweta. Dumping her large straw hat in her mother's lap (because the ribbon has come off), she flops on the chair next to her mother's and asks anxiously, 'Will Pa come to the airport, Ma?' 'I don't know, *bete*, but I think Pa will be at his shooting,' Jaya replies, automatically tying the ribbon on her daughter's hat. Shweta surveys the hat and promptly returns it to her mother, saying politely that the 'bow' is not yet perfect. Jaya re-ties the bow, this time carefully. 'And now?' she asks her daughter. Shweta smiles, clings to her mother, tells her in whispers about something that had happened in school and mother and daughter giggle.

Fans continue to stand in a corner and stare at the children. But the Bachchan kids are unaffected by this. They run helter-skelter, screaming 'statue' to one another (a game they play all through the weekend) and laugh heartily at the oddest jokes. Time and again they sit on the squeaky chairs, get up feeling restless, sometimes dropping their hankies, sometimes their hats. The whole airport seems to come alive with their chatter—they talk in broken sentences, their conversation is erratic. One moment, they are singing a song from *Masoom* and the next, comparing their socks. 'Mine reach upto my knees,' says one. 'Mine has a border,' says another. 'Are these your school socks?' asks the third. They talk about school, about homework, about teachers.

When the call for the security-check comes through, Abhishek is confused about whether he should go through the ladies' section (with his mother) or the gents' section. 'Ma, where should I go?' he asks petulantly. Jaya observes the long queue of men and says, 'Children can go anywhere. You can come with me.' So all of them follow Jaya. Getting cleared at the security-check turns into a competition for the kids.

'First . . .' 'Second . . .' 'Third . . .' they scream as they emerge from behind the curtain. All of them insist on carrying their own boarding cards. The security officer shows sign of disapproval. 'Why do you people leave boarding cards in the hands of children?' he asks Jaya. 'Don't you realise it's risky?' 'Our children are responsible enough, they are used to travelling,' Jaya replies. For a minute, I'm stunned by her answer.

She seems an overprotective mother, constantly covering up for the children and I wonder if I'm disappointed in her. But the next instant, frowning deeply behind her sunglasses, she looks at her children and says firmly, 'Did you hear what uncle said? Next time, don't insist on carrying your boarding cards. It is risky.' Immediately, the kids walk up to their mother and return the boarding cards. I'm touched by their blind obedience. They are well-behaved kids. Considering that they are the children of a superstar, I'd expected them to be spoilt brats, but both Abhishek and Shweta are disappointingly normal. One wouldn't blame them if they were not. Not every child has his father's face staring down at him from hoardings on the streets. In the evenings, huge crowds collect outside their gates and in the mornings, when they leave for school, everyone points excitedly and screams, 'See, that is Amitabh Bachchan's son. . . . That is Amitabh Bachchan's daughter.'

On the flight, they fight for window seats. 'Auntie, please, may I sit in your place?' Ramesh Behl's son asks me. 'No . . . do not sit behind the grown-ups, you will get bored,' Abhishek warns him. 'But I want the window seat too,' he complains. 'Okay, we'll take turns,' Abhishek promises reluctantly. At last, when the flight takes off, they fasten their seat-belts and settle down . . . Jaya reclines on the seat next to mine, lazily looks out of the window, then excitedly taps Abhishek in the front seat, 'Look, *Bhaiyyu*, that is our house . . . did you see it? And that tall building behind is Sea Rock.' She continues to look out of the window. Then, suddenly remembering something, she leans over to Shweta's seat and asks her to pass the Walkman. Bubbles, looks at the Walkman and sighs deeply, 'You, your husband, your kids . . . all of you are paralysed without the Walkman.' Jaya smiles, 'In our house you will find batteries of the oddest shapes and sizes.'

'Her house is a different world altogether,' interrupts Bubbles. 'Everything is so organised, so functional. Every ash-tray, every table is spick and span. Just now, when I went to fetch her, I was taken aback by the goodbye scene. A row of servants waited for umpteen instructions, while Jaya filled them on with the minutest details. For the next few days that she will be away, she has planned the menu, decided on the table mats and even advised as to how much *masala* should be added to the curry that will be cooked for dinner. Jaya is a perfect housewife and a perfect hostess.' I look at Jaya for confirmation but she looks away, too embarrassed to discuss herself. But about her husband and her children she can go on and on . . . and lovingly, too. 'Everybody tells me that Abhishek looks like me and Shweta resembles her father. But I'm certain that Abhishek will be a tall boy. Sometimes, I feel the strong resemblance myself. When he makes a certain gesture, or when he frowns, I watch him and tell myself, he is so much like me. Every time Amit returns after a long outdoor, he is very demonstrative with the kids. But Abhishek keeps his cool. When Amit gets hurt and says, 'I have come back after so many days why aren't you greeting me warmly?' he merely pouts and says, 'But I said hello . . . and I shook hands.'

Then after 15 to 20 minutes, he warms up on his own and

becomes as affectionate as his father. He is like me. I can't be overt even when I feel very strongly. I guess I'm shy of showing my feelings. This shows in my performances. So does my stubbornness. *Bhaiyyu* is very stubborn too. Very often, during a serious argument with him, I give in out of sheer exhaustion.

'My daughter, on the contrary, is very composed. Just the right kind of girl to have around the house. I find it absolutely amazing that a child of her age should have so much poise Temperamentally, she is very much like Amit—not shy, but distant and reserved.' Long pause. 'I wouldn't mind having one more child,' she says hesitantly, 'If it is a girl, I have a very beautiful name for her. I picked it from one of my father-in-law's poems—Naveli. Isn't it beautiful? It's a beautiful experience watching your children grow. When Shweta was small, every time Amit went out of town, she would fall ill. It used to be a harrowing experience. Now that she's grown up, she understands. . . .

'It's quite a challenge, bringing up children. Too many books and too much introspection on how to rear children can make things complicated. When *Bhaiyyu* used to suck his finger in infancy, I'd worry endlessly because the books said it was due to insecurity. Later, I realised it was foolish of me to worry. Why must we invite so much guilt on ourselves? After all, are we not doing our best for them? Giving our best both emotionally and financially? So why must the child feel insecure? Instead, why can't we accept his sucking of the finger as a bad habit? Our parents brought us up by sheer instinct and we grew up to be normal beings. I think that's how we should bring up our kids. Shweta is at a phase where she wants to imitate her mother. She does it all the time, specially when she thinks she isn't being watched. Abhishek is boisterous and brazen in his relationship with his father. The other day Reena Roy was at home when Abhishek called Amit 'Tiger' on the telephone. She was so shocked. '*Yeh apne baap se baat kar raha hai?*' she asked disbelievingly.

'My son has his moods. One day during lunch, he decided he'd get married to Shweta. So off-handedly he proposed to her, but Shweta refused. So now he has decided to get married to me! Every fourth day he tells me, "Ma, you and I are getting married, okay?"' Shweta has decided that she never wants to get married. 'All the time Pa says, "Jaya this . . . Jaya that . . ." Pa does not leave you alone for a minute. Don't you feel tired, Ma?' she'd often ask. Just as we are talking about Shweta, she joins us and complains about her cassette-player. 'Ma, Pa didn't buy me new batteries for my cassette-player. He bought only for Abhishek.' Jaya sighs deeply and says, 'Okay . . . okay . . . tell him when you meet him. We will reach the hotel in a little while now.'

Jaya looks out from the aircraft window and in a voice full of nostalgia says, 'The airport has changed so much. It has been a long time since I last came to Goa. It seems like ages. Do you think it will be cold in Goa? Amit is sure to find fault with my wardrobe. I have taken a shawl just in case the evenings are cool. My this habit of "just in case" always upsets Amit. He will sigh deeply and speak thus . . . (She imitates him). You-have-travelled-all-around-the-world-yet-you-always-bring-the-wrong-clothes-to-the-wrong-place. Why-are-you-so-thick-Jaya?' It seems to be a family trait to imitate one another, and enjoy it. Just as it is the family trait to rag one another and not mind it.

Whenever it is time for Amit to return from his outdoors, Abhishek puts on a solemn expression and says, 'Ma, watch out, the old man is coming back.' Not that the father lets him get away. He has his own private joke to rag his little boy. When recently the parents discovered that their son had a massive crush on Amit's leading lady, Zeenat Aman, they lost no opportunity to tease him. The father now referred to him as Zeenat Aman. 'My husband would say, Zeenat Aman will you eat an apple? Or Zeenat Aman, would you like a Thums-up?'

With the daughter, the parents' attitude is more serious. A few weeks ago, when Jaya took Shweta for a hair-cut to the beauty parlour, Amit was very upset. Jaya recollects, 'Girls look nice with long hair and you have gone and chopped it off. . . . He kept grumbling about it for several days. To this day, everytime I comb her hair he says, "Kitne achche bal the, kaat diye?"'

At the Goa airport, Ramesh Behl has come to fetch us. His children rush into their father's arms and hug him tightly while Abhishek and Shweta look on awkwardly. With covert glances they convey their disapproval to their mother because their father has not come to receive them. 'Pitwana hai kya?' Ramesh Behl asks, when he hears of Abhishek and Shweta's disappointment. 'As it was, his popularity was incredible, but after the accident he's turned into some kind of a cult. We need two security cars—one ahead and one behind him before he can travel to the location. If your husband comes to the airport there will be riots!'

Her husband's accident is still a sensitive topic with Jaya.

Though she tries to be brave, it is her Achilles heel, because suddenly there is a lump in her throat and her eyes seem distant. For a long while, she sits quiescent, and then introduces the topic on her own. 'Today, I cannot believe I survived the whole experience. When there is a crisis, God gives you the strength. You survive. Still, when I ponder over what must have been Amit's frame of mind, I shudder. . . . Millions of people prayed for him, the reactions of people were touching. They were all very individual, very sincere reactions and I feel he feels overwhelmed with gratitude. He wonders how he will repay so much warmth. The memory of the day we left the hospital will stay with me forever. I saw a sea of faces, all the way to Juhu. Amit was in a tizzy himself. When the TV interviewer thrust the microphone at him, he was too choked to speak. . . .'

Were you frightened when you saw all that overwhelming affection and adulation? 'Crowds always frighten me because I get claustrophobic. Because I get scared that my children might get lost.' Are you emotionally frightened that you are the wife of this popular man? 'No,' she says softly. There is no pride on her face, just surprise. At the hotel, Amitabh has been informed about our arrival. When we enter the Taj Village he is pacing up and down with impatience in the garden. It seems he has been doing so for the past one hour. When he hears the cars, he marches forward to meet the family. In a white *churidar-kurta*, with a huge shawl thrown across his shoulder, his face softens with unconcealed joy. The kids run into his arms. Amitabh embraces them. Shweta and he walk together hand in hand, while Abhishek lurches behind to latch on to his father by his trailing shawl. Amitabh turns around and offers his other hand to his son. Jaya watches on. Only through her eyes does she communicate with her husband. She follows the three of them a few steps behind. I can hear echoes of their conversation. Shweta says, 'You didn't buy me batteries. You only bought them for Abhishek.' Abhishek says, 'Pa, we will go swimming tomorrow. You don't go for shooting. . . .'

I watch them from a distance, feel an outsider in the family scene, collect my keys from the reception desk and go to my room.

Movie, April 1983

7

THE NEXT DAY, outside an old church, a fight sequence was in progress. After the accident, everytime Amitabh Bachchan was involved in an action scene, there was tension on the sets. And the paranoia wasn't without foundation. On this day Kareena (Bebo) Kapoor, the younger daughter of Randhir Kapoor, aged three, was perfectly happy as long as Amitabh punched the villain. It's when the villain began punching Amitabh, that Kareena began to howl loudly. She pulled her mother's scarf and asked them to stop or else 'Uncle would get hurt'. The shot had to be cut and the shooting stalled for a while because Bebo wouldn't stop howling. It was only when Amitabh carried the young girl in his arms and assured her that he was fine, that she was pacified. Babita and Bebo returned to the hotel and the shooting resumed. There was no denying that Bachchan's accident had left a lasting impression on the girl. Perhaps, the hysteria was a reflection of an entire generation deeply affected by the tragedy.

Fight masters admitted to over-caution. They confessed to checking and re-checking the most mundane action scenes involving the superstar. The actor, who had in the last twenty years never come home without a cut or bruise, was suddenly having to do with molly-coddling. For years, Bachchan had believed that, 'Whenever in doubt, avoid it. For if you are uncertain, you are sure to muck up the shot.'

I wonder if the superstar had any doubts before doing the action scene for *Coolie* with Puneet Issar that day. Years later I often saw him cut jokes with unit hands before enacting dare-devil scenes. He would coax junior artistes on sets to cheer him up when he was about to jump from a height. It never occurred to me then, though it does now, if in his horsing around, he was in fact mustering courage. Showbiz is full of contradictory signals.

Dimple who had defiantly walked out on her husband was frightened about staging a comeback after a long gap. She was lucky to find a godfather in Ramesh Sippy who was launching her in *Saagar*. Elaborate photosessions to put the lead pair, Rishi Kapoor and her at ease had been organised by the director at hotel Holiday Inn. Dimple was nervous as hell every time the lensman said, 'Smile'. 'If I'm so nervous for this session, how will I face the camera?' she asked Ramesh Sippy. Ramesh Sippy and Rishi Kapoor went out of their way to make her feel comfortable. During the shoot, there were constant interruptions from Dimple's home. Dimple's daughters, Tina and Chinky would call from time to time to inquire if mummy was fine and needed help. It was truly a reversal of roles.

Return of Dimple Kapadia

28 February 1983. Dimple's first day of shooting for *Saagar*. A hundred thoughts, a hundred fears cloud her mind when she wakes up restless in the morning. Will everything run smoothly? Will she achieve the goal she is set for herself? In the drawing room, four huge baskets of flowers await her attention. The message on the cards are brief: 'Best of luck—and may you be happy', says one. 'We are with you', says another. 'I have just a few friends, but with their genuine support I'm certain I'll survive,' Dimple tells me when I meet her in the evening on the sets at Dariya Mahal, Juhu. Her make-up man, Ram Tipnis, is giving the final touches to her face, while sister Simple, playing her hairdresser for the day, is busy brushing her hair, pinning her saree, hunting for her sandals, and serving her carrot juice.

The first shot requires Dimple to race down the staircase and bump into Rishi Kapoor who is coming from the opposite end. A long shot of the two . . . a tight close-up . . . and 'cut!'.

'Are you nervous facing the camera after so long?' I ask Dimple when she returns to the chair in between shots. She sighs deeply. 'All morning I had been worrying about today's shooting. The last time I faced the camera was ten years ago. Yet, half an hour ago when I actually stood before the camera and performed, acting seemed the easiest thing in the world. Those few moments before we actually began were a frenzy. But finally, when I heard Rameshji shout c-u-t, I knew I was back.'

The prodigal has returned. At last. 'This is what I have always wanted!' Dimple says, drawing deeply on her cigarette. She gazes at herself in a full-length mirror, her beauty complementing the ambience. Apart from the regal trappings, the make-up room is filled with the paraphernalia of any regular star—a huge ice-box stuffed with salad and fruit juice, Dimple's vanity case overflowing with cosmetics and jewellery. Finally, her innumerable books, cassettes, music equipment, a shawl and other accessories carried over from home. Her escorts include her mother and her sister.

The atmosphere in the room reeks of old routine. In fact, just now, watching her sitting cross-legged on the bed and playing chess between shots, it's difficult to believe that it is her first day at work. It's difficult to believe that she could have spent the last ten years of her life anywhere but in the studios. Dimple laughs, 'Javed Akhtar said the same thing when he came on the sets two hours ago. He said he'd expected to find me sitting in a corner, chewing my nails. Instead, by not being nervous I had disappointed him!' She laughs constantly, but it is a defence mechanism. The actress in her is preparing. One can see she's been out of touch. She admits that it will take some time before she can be called a professional.

'I have yet to get used to my own body movements before the camera. To learn to concentrate on continuity. Everytime I touch up my make-up I'm conscious that the size of my *bindi* is changing. During the fourth shot I suddenly realised that I wanted to wear a nose-ring. But since I had not worn one in the previous shot, I could not. So sad!' There is a knock on the door and she is summoned for her next shot. On the sets, a unit boy waits with two buckets full of water and two fresh towels. The scene requires Dimple and Rishi to be soaked to the skin. They are shooting a romantic duet. In different corners of the garden, assisted by their individual make-up men, Dimple and Rishi pour dozens of tumblers over their bodies. Ramesh Sippy stands next to them supervising. 'More . . . More water on the arms', he tells Rishi. Then looking at Dimple, he says 'Wet your hair . . . more . . . still more.' Dimple splashes water onto her hair.

There are several rehearsals and retakes. From behind the camera, Ramesh Sippy frowns deeply. It's apparent that he is bursting with energy. From one end to the other he parades, sometimes to pull at Rishi's coat and sometimes to straighten his collar, but most of the time to correct Dimple's posture, her angles. Time and again he requests Simple to brush Dimple's hair, adjust her saree. He is a perfectionist. And it shows. For every 'take' he personally fills tumblers from the bucket and pours water on his artistes. Every time he does that, Dimple shivers. 'It's cold. I'll die. Can I have hot water, please?' Rishi watches on amusedly, 'I'm fortunate to be wearing a suit. It must be awful for her in a chiffon saree,' he says.

He talks about Dimple casually. Their past does not matter today. Both have outgrown their *Bobby* infatuation. There is no hesitation, no self-consciousness. His behaviour is normal and relaxed. 'Thanks to you folks, we are comfortable with each other today. It was your photo session which helped to break the ice. The first day's shooting would have been difficult under normal circumstances. Dimple and I would have been extremely self-conscious and tense. It sounds funny to say this, but in a strange way it's like old times. Only, during *Bobby*, I was friendly with Dimple and Simple and now, during the making of *Saagar*, I'm friendly with Dimple's daughters!' The daughters, Tina and Chinky, sit in a distant corner sipping Thums-up. They sit quietly, without communicating. Temperamentally, they are perfect star children—they understand the discipline of shooting. It's intuitive probably, but everytime a 'take' is on, they sit in pin-drop silence, watching their mother with utmost concentration, deeply engrossed in her every movement. But no sooner does the director shout 'cut', than the girls rush to the mother with, 'Mummy are you feeling cold? Do you want a towel? Some tea?' When they are not around, Dimple says, 'I don't think I could have made it without them. You should see the letters they have written to me. So sensitive. They tell me they want me to make it. That I mustn't be frightened and mustn't give up.' Her eyes glisten. Tears threaten but she fights them. Older daughter Tina is more like her father. Watching her expression just now, it's difficult to gather what she is thinking. Arrogant like her father, she is stingy with her reactions. Chinky, on the other hand, is dreamy and self-absorbed. Everytime the clapper boy rubs off the number on the slate, she watches delightedly. During the 'take', when the mother sings, '*Chchuo na chchuo na . . .*' Chinky silently sings with her. When the mother moves her shoulder, she moves her shoulder too. And finally, when the director pours water on Dimple, Chinky crosses her arms and shudders. Simple observes this and is immediately concerned. 'Tina, Chinky, let us go home. It is bed-time for both of you.' They shrug their shoulders: 'No, we will go home with mummy.'

It is 8.30 p.m., when the electricity goes off. 'Fantastic,' says Dimple. 'All evening we have been waiting because the director wanted a gorgeous sunset, and now when they finally settled for this artifical sun, the lights go off!' I decide to make a move, and just as I do so, the lights come back. 'Action!' screams the director. Immediately there is a frenzy of activity. The artistes take their positions and as I walk through the gate, I notice Ramesh Sippy pouring some more tumblers of water over Dimple.

Movie, April 1983

One day a young, bespectacled *sardar*, cigarette in hand, casually strolled into Shabana Azmi's residence. The actress was relaxing at home in the company of old friend Farooque Shaikh. The door-bell rang and Shabana got up to answer it. She found herself face-to-face with a young boy who refused to explain the purpose of his visit. Instead, he blew a neat cloud of smoke on Shabana's face. 'What do you want?' she asked. In answer, the *sardar* blew another jet of smoke. That is when Farooque decided to intervene, but Shabana stopped him. A split second before Farooque's punishing hand could descend on the *sardar*, the jigsaw puzzle suddenly fell into place. Shabana shrieked, 'Wait. It's Sarika!' Playing a *sardar* in a film, Sarika decided that she might as well have some fun before removing the disguise. Forever pulling jokes on friends and family, once Sarika got back from America with a laugh-machine she played on my phone waking me up late at night. It's difficult to understand her sense of humour unless you know her closely. But then, that is Sarika. I met her in the late seventies and became friends with her in the early eighties and ever since she has remained my confidante.

The film world was forever springing surprises. Nobody believed that Reena Roy would eventually settle down. Madly in love with Shatrughan Sinha, she was on a constant see-saw, a now-on and a now-off relationship. Shatrughan Sinha was unable to make up his mind between Poonam Sinha, his childhood sweetheart and Reena, his current leading lady. He met one at home, the other on the sets. Shatru's indecisiveness drove Reena to Rajneesh. A chronic manic-depressive in those days, Reena was forever driving to Osho's *ashram* in Pune. Vinod Khanna was responsible for getting her out of this phase and Jaya Bachchan apparently, for encouraging her to say 'yes' to Mohsin Khan's marriage proposal. Once she made up her mind, Reena left no stone unturned in her effort, to play the perfect *bahu begum* of Pakistan. Every time there was an India-Pakistan match and the Indian team fared better, the common refrain in the film fraternity would be, '*Jal gayi* Reena Roy.'

Reena had made a place for herself in the industry and when she quit, her absence was noticed. But all this didn't matter to Reena once she went through her *nikaah*. Or so she said in her good-bye interview.

Goodbye Reena Roy

'I don't know why, but I'm suddenly beginning to resent work these days. I think I am tired. Half my time goes in travelling to the studios and the other half in waiting endlessly for my shot. I'm fed up of costumes, wigs, make-up. I think I need to settle down. I wish some Prince Charming would come galloping my way. The day he does, I will get married and go away like Mumtaz. Never to return to the arclights again.' This was in May 1980.

Three years later, Reena Roy is attending the Amitabh Bachchan show in London. Every evening Mohsin Khan calls her up at her hotel. Sometimes they go for long drives, chatting all the time. Mohsin talks to her about his game, his ambitions, his future. Reena listens. Then tells him about her flagging interest in her profession, her dilemma, her growing insecurities. They discuss their parents, their friends. Slowly but surely, a relationship is cemented. A strong and secure relationship, which promises a future.

Back home, in India, Reena thinks often of Mohsin, misses him, confesses to herself and to her friend Jaya Bachchan that she is in love with the man, but cannot make up her mind. Jaya gets to work. She makes Reena conscious of her own identity and the need to find some happiness for herself. She brushes aside Reena's doubts about her family, her career, about Shatrughan Sinha and prods her into making a decision. After all, Reena has known Mohsin for more than six years. He is talented, successful, famous, rich. Reena has had long innings in the film industry herself. Has enjoyed stardom for ten years. Seen good times. Earned enough money, name and fame. If she didn't get married now, she would probably never get another chance.

An uncertain, undecided Reena broods. At home. At work. Maybe Jaya is right, after all. It is true that she is tired of acting. She is tired of futile relationships. There is a definite vacuum in her life, and she isn't getting any younger.

And one day Reena makes up her mind. Yes, she'll call it a day. She'll marry Mohsin Khan. She does. Reena leaves for Pakistan. As a little girl, Reena had fantasized of a royal wedding for herself. Lots of people. Flowers. Music. Illumination. Reena liked being pampered, liked being spoilt. Hadn't she always romanticized about being the reincarnation of a princess? 'I'm blue blood,' she would tell friends. 'That is why I wear gold *payals* on my feet. Don't you know only princesses wear gold *payals*?' It was a fantasy she believed in and it showed in the manner in which she decorated her bungalow in Pali Hill. Her bedroom was like a dream sequence in a Hindi film—a large oval-shaped bed with a heavy furry quilt and velvet cushions of all shapes and sizes. On window-sills and on tables there are dolls, toys, mirrors. On the ceiling, a canopy from which hang silver threaded braids with tiny bells. The bells chimed everytime Reena changed her position on the bed. 'Isn't this music sensuous? It's a warning to my servant that I have woken up.'

Reena enjoyed luxury, her larger-than-life existence. She loved playing princess in her films, loved wearing flowing costumes, the trail carried by slave girls. 'When I get married I will do so with *shaan*,' she had once told me. 'I will explode crackers, blow bugles, pound drums. Everyone must know that Reena Roy is getting married!'

On 1 April, it was a quiet wedding. Without bugles, without crackers, without illumination, without noise. The over-indulgent, little girl, who lived in a world of fantasy, had grown up. At last. A fairy tale had ended. Many years ago, a garish, uncouth girl had come thumping her way into films. She desperately wanted to make it as an actress. The directors snubbed her. The actors made fun of her. The heroines laughed at her. Yet, she made it! Today, she is on the threshold of a new dream. She has taken on wings and flown to her kingdom in Karachi. All she wants is to be happy.

Movie, September 1984

There were changes in the office atmosphere. Rauf Ahmed was wooed with a job offer again. *The Times of India* group wanted Rauf to launch two magazines—*People* and *Entertainment*. Art director Amrut Kondekar, Madhulika Verma and I were to join Rauf a month later. My mother was against my submitting my resignation until I had secured an official appointment letter from my new employer but of course, I thought I knew better. Publisher Deepak Mirchandani talked me against leaving, saying that I was making a mistake and I ought to rethink my decision. I didn't. After having worked with Rauf in *Cinema Journal*, *Super*, *Movie*, I was reluctant to believe that anything could go wrong. But it did.

I joined the *Times of India* in the month of August. The year was 1985 and I travelled by the harbour train every morning from Wadala to V.T., swallowed sandwiches during lunch break and returned home before dusk. After 20 days of this routine, I realised that I was still not signing the muster and at the end of the month was not paid my salary. A family crisis took me to Ahmedabad for a while and when

I returned, I decided to stop attending office. Since those senior to me were not able to come to a decision, I took a decision on my own. Rage and regret alternated with doubt and fear in the days that followed. Plunged into uncertainty, I realised for the first time the value of a secure job. Ever since, I've made it a policy to never trust anyone until they put the proposal in writing.

In my low phase, the only one to support me with sufficient freelance assignments was Vir Sanghvi, editor of *Imprint*. I knew Vir because he did a lot of re-writing for *Movie*. Coming from mainstream journalism, Vir brought a distinctive flavour to film writing which was more perceptive and less familiar. The trend of referring to a star by his surname was first adopted by Vir. Prior to that, film magazines addressed stars by their first names, if not pet names. *Imprint* paid freelancers well but in return Vir was a very demanding editor and would extract the very best out of you. I enjoyed writing for him because his work-briefs were precise and when he disagreed with what you wrote, he cared to analyse it. At the same time, he was open to suggestions. When he asked me to do a story on the new breed, I wrote instead on stress and how film stars cope with it. He gave you a free hand as long as you delivered the goods. Photographer Gautam Patole, his discovery, described him as the most democratic editor. My opinion being that he wasn't as generous with his praise as with his remuneration. He seldom complimented, so when he said 'good', his staff believed him.

Those were the days when almost every married actor was involved with another woman. When Dharmendra announced from the roof-tops his marriage to Hema Malini, lovers, all over the film industry stopped suffering! The seventies were a volatile decade. Illegitimate relationships, love-children, eloping, suicide, sex scandals were the order of the day. Old

SALAAM BOLLYWOOD • 101

partnerships like that of Salim-Javed broke up. Old rivals like Sridevi-Jaya Prada patched up. Naseerudin Shah declared war on art cinema, Shabana Azmi got married. Neetu Singh delivered the first grandson of Raj Kapoor. Shyam Benegal made a film on prostitutes and Sanjay Dutt admitted that he was on drugs.

'I'm pregnant,' Sarika said looking out of the window. 'And I've decided to have the baby.' We were travelling to a friend's wedding in Colaba and it was a full moon night. Whether her man stood by her or not, whether society condemned her, Sarika was determined to have the baby. Earlier, she had had afterthoughts and suffered immense guilt. This time she wasn't going to make the same mistake again. 'If I do so it means my love wasn't true. Why must society put so much pressure on me when all I ask is a little space?' The wind lashing on our faces (air-conditioned cars didn't exist those days) and her eyes filling up from time to time, Sarika talked and talked and talked. About her childhood, her past and present. It was a poignant evening. The beautiful moon followed us like a loyal friend. It peeped from behind the clouds from time to time. This was the time when Sarika had moved out of her mother's house and was roughing it out in PG accommodations. Except for the rickety Fiat car and driver Narayan, Sarika had taken nothing from her mother's home, even though everything in the flat was bought from her earnings.

What she missed most in the constant shifting of homes was a telephone. Most of the accommodation she rented out had no phones. Those that did, had restrictions. As a result she was always on the run, thinking of the right time and the right place when she could talk to her man, Kamal Haasan. Whenever he wanted to trace her, he would get in touch with one of her friends. She drove from Juhu to my home in King Circle only because he was going to call her at a particular time and she needed privacy. It was heartbreaking to see their suffering. The chemistry between the two was

SARIKA

'I'm pregnant and I've decided to have the baby'

electrifying. The romance blossomed before either of them knew it and then followed the heartaches.

Morality, I read somewhere, depends on circumstances. I may not follow someone else's lifestyle but that doesn't mean I have a right to judge another person's choices. And to have the baby was Sarika's choice. We discussed the unborn baby, her fears, her future, the pressures on an unwed mother, but no matter which way I argued she had a solution. Predictably, there was a lot of backlash. All kinds of insinuations were made and a lot of them were painful, but there was an unnatural calm about Sarika. I would often visit her on her sets those days. She was shooting for *Sindoor* with Shekhar Suman and had the sense of humour to see the irony of life.

For hours at a stretch, she would talk about the growing changes within her. 'I have decided,' she said pushing away a film magazine from the table, 'I'm not going to let any negative aspect influence my life. This is a beautiful phase and I'm going to relish it.' A collector of memories, Sarika was forever jotting her thoughts and feelings, recording them on paper and in pictures in an unusually imaginative way. Her writing has always fascinated me because though grammatically incorrect, she is an original. Self-taught, Sarika is in the true sense a survivor! That Kamal Haasan was ready to stand by his lady-love, face the wrath of society, stake a decade-old marriage was indicative of their relationship. The press should have credited Kamal with more sincerity and attached more importance to the love story. But all the couple got was accusation and condemnation. Perhaps that's the tragedy of love stories. They are realized only when the trauma is over. Damned as a home-breaker in the eighties, Sarika was celebrated as the feminist in the nineties.

8

A N EARLY EIGHTIES, SCANDAL to rock the film industry was the liaison involving Dilip Kumar with a Pakistani woman, Asma. When he was caught red-handed, it was the beginning of a nightmare for the actor and his wife Saira Banu. To settle the dust once and for all, the thespian took the Koran on his head and swore that he had nothing to do with the other woman. A month later, his *nikahnama* with Asma was released in the press. What followed was a vicious cycle of denials and defences. The husband and wife gave separate interviews explaining, explaining, explaining. . . . Skeletons tumbled out of their creaky cupboards and love turned into martyrdom. Saira Banu blamed the press and Dilip Kumar blamed the world for not understanding him. 'There was a lot of breeze and the door got locked,' he told a reporter. Truth turned stranger than fiction. According to grapevine, Saira Banu hid a journalist under her bed to record Dilip Kumar's confession. With every passing month more gory details emerged and their marriage became a laughing stock. It baffled me how a fifty-plus man could not see reason and make a mess of his life? It would have been so much simpler if Dilip Kumar had accepted he was in love. He owed explanations to none, except his wife. Besides, his religion even permitted a second wife. Instead, the thespian let down a million fans and more important, two women he loved and who loved him.

Years later, in a similar situation, the Hyderabad chief minister N.T. Rama Rao in a public gathering in Andhra Pradesh, declared his love for his biographer, Laxmi Parvathi and sought their permission to make her his wife. It was a moving moment. There was pin drop silence. Confused in their new role of a jury, the Andhraites became emotional. Mesmerised by the superstar's charisma, sycophancy took over principles and they cheered him in unison. Idols have a way of overruling logic. Twelve years ago, when Kamal Haasan first became a father, his fans gathered in huge crowds outside the Willingdon hospital in Chennai. All they wanted was a brief glimpse of the baby. They wanted to bless the child. It didn't matter to them that their idol wasn't married, that the baby wasn't legitimate. What mattered was that their hero was happy. Had Dilip Kumar mustered enough courage, had he been completely truthful, I'm absolutely certain that his love story, too, would have been accepted.

Sanjeev Kumar could never sustain a relationship because he was paranoid about his money. Every woman who fell in love with him, Sanjeev suspected was after his wealth. Result: Sanjeev lived and died a lonely man! Heavily into drinking at one stage, the only time Sanjeev, better known as Haribhai, gave up drinking was when he signed a film with his favourite director, Gulzar. The actor and the film-maker shared a special bond and when the former died, Gulzar felt his absence. Our magazine published a nostalgic feature on him where the star travelled to his roots. I remember travelling with Sanjeev Kumar to his old home in Bhuleshwar. He showed us the shanty room's they lived in, introduced us to his old neighbours and humbly pointed to the stinking toilet at the end of the chawl, where he waited every morning in a queue. It is said that Sanjeev was standing with the *dabba* in his hand one morning when a producer dropped by to sign him. His two favourite people in the industry, till the very end, remained Sachin and Sarika. The former emulated him, the latter worshipped him.

The only other person Sarika has equally fond memories of is Meena Kumari. Strangely, everyone who came into contact with the legendary actress spoke about her warmth and generosity. Sarika did a number of films with her as a child star. The senior actress would often take her home after the shooting of *Majhli Didi*. Sometimes, Sachin and she travelled together in her car. Meena Kumari enjoyed being in the company of children. At one point, Meena Kumari had become so attached to Sarika that she wanted to adopt her. Whenever she was not shooting, she would send her driver to fetch the little girl home and spoil her silly. *'Bahut achcha khana khilati thi aur bahut pyar se khilati thi . . .'* Sarika says today. Meena Kumari would insist on the young girl calling her mummy. 'Her house had velvet beds and satin pillows. The bedroom was a collection of dolls and all of them were dressed as brides.' Hours later, when it was time for Sarika to go, the senior actress would cling to her and plead with Sarika's mother to let her stay one more day. Kamala Thakur was not easy to persuade. Reflecting on those days now, Sarika says, 'She was a fountain of love— ethereal and attractive. It's only when dusk fell that things got a little scary.'

I have been fascinated with Meena Kumari as long as I can remember. She was my favourite heroine as a child. I have never seen such tender eyes. Her sheer presence was so warm, like a lush banyan tree which protects you from sunlight and rain. Every time I saw her in roles relating to children, I wanted Meena Kumari to tuck me in bed and sing me a lullaby. Nutan was feminine, Waheeda Rehman was fragile, but Meena Kumari was an addiction. When she died, she left her diaries for Gulzar. It is said that Nargis maintained an infrequent diary, which she left for her sister Zaheeda. After Nargis' demise, Sanjay Dutt went astray. His producers complained of his late arrival on the sets and directors of his unprofessionalism. Only his heroines seemed to be besotted with him. Invariably, all his co-stars were romantically linked with him. He had a lost look about him that made women around him over-protective. That was a part of Sanjay's personality.

I once had an appointment with Sanjay Dutt for 9 a.m. at his house. When I reached the bungalow, Dutt junior was still asleep. An hour later, when he woke up, he called the photographer and me for tea in his bedroom. The first thing he did was to put on the video. 'Yesterday, I left the film at an important scene,' he said, switching channels. Still sleepy-eyed, he smoked three cigarettes with one cup of tea. Another hour passed while Sanjay had a leisurely bath and changed four shirts. The long wait was making everyone impatient and we also needed to visit the toilet. That's when one noticed that none of the toilets in the bungalow had a latch. It was only later, my colleague Gia D'Cruz, who once worked as Mrs Dutt's personal secretary, let out the secret of the missing latches. Nargis Dutt, after failing on every attempt to control her son from taking drugs, had removed all the bathroom latches to ensure that Sanjay did not smoke inside the toilet. We spent a whole day with Sanjay, met various people, but none of us suspected that he was on drugs. In fact, it was a fun-filled afternoon. There was Waheeda Rehman who embraced him and said, 'Bachchon pe maa se zyada khala ka haque hota hain.' He flirted with Tina Munim outrageously and even kissed her on the mouth in our presence. This peeved Tina's current boyfriend Rajesh Khanna no end and he made his spies ring up our office to find out when exactly the interview had been conducted.

Rekha was still sulking with the press and not wanting to make up. 'I will never talk to them,' she told a friend. 'Instead, I will put my energies into looking better and giving better performances so that when they go to the theatre and see my film, they will not be able to hate me even if they want to.' She had the killer-instinct and used it mercilessly. Around this time, once I happened to be on her sets. It was a song sequence and I thought nobody would notice me from where I stood. But she did. And minutes later, the assistant clapped his hands and asked everyone on the sets to clear out. Even in her worst moments, you cannot accuse Rekha of being rude. That's why I was surprised when she went through the absolute mad phase of treating her white bungalow as a Taj Mahal. No one was allowed to trespass into Pushpavalli and producers wanting to sign her had to wait outside the bungalow while contract letters went inside for madam's signature. Naturally, film-makers felt humiliated and condemned Rekha's obsession with privacy. It seemed unbelievable that even the most private person could go to such extremes. Maybe Rekha had her reasons, but she never spoke about them.

Nor did Hema Malini. I invariably caught Hema at her worst moment or perhaps I brought out the worst in her. I had been waiting for her for over two hours chatting with her director and Dina Pathak on the sets of Mushiar Riaz's *Meera*. When she arrived, she disappeared into her room to get ready. After that, she was memorising her lines and then she sat before the mirror doing her make-up. Finally, on the sets, she was putting glycerine in her eyes when I asked her for an interview. Today, I would be more tactful. There is something like creative space but you do not realise all this when you are young and new on the job. In retrospect, I feel it is not fair to expect a new scribe to understand such fine points. There are no ground rules. How does a budding journalist strike a balance between pressure from the office and the film firmament? Always and forever, the star has either just arrived, or is preoccupied, is either having his first cup of tea, or is giving an important shot, is meeting important visitors, or important things are on his mind. After what seems ages, the star finally takes a break. He's all by himself and appears relaxed. You catch him smiling, even cracking a joke with his colleagues. This is the time, the scribe thinks to himself, and hesitantly approach him. The dialogue writer interrupts just then. After that the director, then the cameraman, then the make-up man, then the hair-dresser and finally the costume-designer. When you are older and wiser, it's easier accepting these as professional hazards, but as a fresher, a studio round-up is sheer hell.

HEMA MALINI

I caught Hema at her worst moments

That's why I've always maintained that it is far more difficult pursuing film journalism, than mainstream journalism. Other journalists report on events. We are traders of emotions.

I remember Moushumi Chatterjee as a high-strung actress and the only young mother amongst her contemporaries. She was forever discussing domestic crises. During one emotionally-charged interview she confessed that she was insanely jealous of her daughter's maid because the maid got to spend more time with the kids than her. 'The shooting keeps me away for weeks. There was a time when everytime I went outdoors, my daughter fell ill. When I got back, even if I was at home, my daughter wouldn't come to me. Payal had got so attached to her *ayah* that she wanted the *ayah* to do everything for her. I was insanely jealous of the *ayah* and wanted to chuck her out, even though I knew I was being unreasonable.' Beneath the giddy-headed, scatter-brained actress was a serious girl, prone to introspection. 'It isn't easy being married and remaining a star. The pressures of home are too many and too complex. Either I should have a representative, a mother, or a mother- in-law who can impart the same values to my kids in my absence, or I quit my job. I had become an insomniac and was heading for a nervous breakdown, unable to cope with the dual roles. I would come home exhausted and even before I could remove my make-up, I would be drawn into servants' squabbles. Depressed about doing a scene badly, I would sit in my room in darkness. It disturbed my daughter to see me withdrawn. To reassure her, I had forcibly turn on bright lights and peppy music to liven the atmosphere. Children are sensitive and need reassurances which adults don't always understand.'

Unlike other stars who give emotional interviews and later recant, Moushumi Chatterjee forgot the interview once it was over. I preferred that. Journalists need that much time and space to assess and reassess their encounters. A constant flow of interaction can be suffocating and restricting. I've been on the receiving end, when stars perpetually phone to add and subtract from their quotes, fill in more details to interviews given weeks ago. They change their answers and opinions. All this is very unprofessional. On moral grounds, all individuals are entitled to second and third thoughts. But there are ground rules to every game. Interview must have them too. The stars must know what to speak and when. After so many years in the profession, excuses of, 'I didn't mean it that way,' don't work.

Sometimes, circumstances land one in awkward situations. I was in Sridevi's hotel room one early morning. Sri was getting ready with the greasepaint for our cover shoot. Suddenly, the doorbell rang. Thinking it was the room service, she said, 'Come in.' Everyone was surprised when Asha Bhonsle strolled in accompanied by her son, Hemant Bhonsle. If Sri was offended, she didn't show it. Asha Bhonsle realised she had taken the actress offguard, '*Humne kal* mummy *se baat ki thi . . .*' the singer started defensively. She got down to explaining the purpose of her visit. She wanted Sridevi to be part of her show abroad. Sridevi heard her in silence, self-conscious about not being appropriately dressed. 'I will talk to mummy and get back,' she said politely. When they left, she got back to doing her make-up, visibly distracted. Decorum demanded that Asha Bhonsle should have phoned the actress from the lobby before coming directly to the room. This is common courtesy, even when one has a confirmed appointment. Considering it was only 8 a.m. and she was visiting a female star's room, Asha Bhonsle should have forewarned the actress. Weighed down with something personal, Sridevi wasn't in the best of moods that morning. She mumbled non-stop instructions to her make-up man in Telugu. In the bedroom, her mother was talking to her father on the trunkline. Something terrible seemed to have happened the previous evening because the tension in the room was unmistakable.

Sridevi was unable to concentrate on the photo-session. After a few futile attempts, Sri pleaded with us to postpone the shoot for another day. The photographer agreed instantly. It wasn't a day for arguments. Something was amiss and we knew it. The next time we met was on the sets of Shekhar Kapur's *Mr. India*. Rekha was shooting in the same studio for Manoj Kumar's *Clerk* and Sri had dropped by to meet the senior actress. Director Shekhar Kapur was preparing to picturise the song, '*Kaate nahin kat ti* . . .' Shekhar commented that Sri grasped what was told to her quickly. 'Projecting a kiss to an invisible man on screen is not simple. When you explain the scene to her, she appears blank. But start the camera and she's a live-wire.' Another interesting insight Shekhar gave me into the actress was that everytime he explained a scene to her, she in turn, would explain the scene in Telugu to sister, Srilata. 'I don't know why she does this,' he added.

In Michael Jackson's biography, it is revealed that Jackson could never directly communicate with his interviewer. He never made eye-contact with any journalists. It was always a family member—sister, brother, uncle to whom Michael replied to and who in turn repeated the answer to the journalist. In a mysterious way there is a striking resemblance between Michael Jackson and Sridevi. It is something about their expressions while dancing and the energy they exude. There is conviction in whatever Sridevi does. Without conviction, an illogical film like *Nagina* would never have worked. She has an instinctive feel about the character she plays. In Feroz Khan's *Jaanbaz*, her body language during the climax, after she is injected drugs by the villains, was so mesmerising that the censors had to cut it out for they felt that it glorified drugs. In *Roop Ki Rani Choron Ka Raja*, where she walks down a flight of stairs without looking down impressed Amitabh Bachchan immensely. An observation like this could have come only from an actor.

With Raakhee, somehow, each encounter was a vale of tears. The first time I saw her she was shooting an emotional scene at Natraj Studio. This was immediately after her comeback with *Tapasyaa* and she was still vulnerable to questions regarding her break-up with Gulzar. An hour later, lunching with director Shakti Samanta, she seemed particularly low. The two spoke in Bengali. Months later, I was talking to her on the phone and out of sheer lack of topics, mentioned a song picturisation in *Thodisi Bewafai*, director Esmayeel Shroff showed it to me the other day. 'Has *he* (Gulzar) written the songs in the film?' she asked, her voice cracking. 'Yes,' I said. She asked me to recite the lyrics. I told her the few lines I could recall: '*Hazar rahen mud ke dekhi/ Kahin se koi sadaa na aayee/Badi wafase nibhaee tumne/Hamari thodisi bewafayee.*' There was silence. Unintentionally, I had touched upon a raw nerve. Our next meeting was on the sets of Ramesh Sippy's, *Shakti*. Preoccupied with Bosky's school problems, she seemed more stable but ill-at-ease playing a mother to her one time hero, Amitabh Bachchan.

There was discomfiture, mixed emotions and undisguised pain. I don't think Raakhee had bargained for playing character roles so early in her career. Beginning with the role of a *bhabhi* in Ramesh Sippy's *Shaan*, she had now graduated to the role of mother in *Shakti*. Raakhee knew that she was saying goodbye to sex appeal forever. But films are full of surprises. Anil Ganguly's *Aanchal* was an interesting film, of a complex relationship between Raakhee and her brother-in-law Rajesh Khanna. This was clearly a happy phase for Raakhee and it was evident in her bouncy and cheerful mood on the sets. Once I was on her sets when the producer of Rose Movies, Ramesh Behl dropped by to discuss dates for the shooting of *Basera*. She ragged him endlessly while he blushed like a school boy. Raakhee wore beautiful sarees in *Aanchal*. That was the first time I discovered how innovative our actresses can be in areas that interest them. Rejecting the colour combinations brought by the shopkeeper, Raakhee motivated her dress-designer Meeta, to mix 'n' match different borders with different *pallus*. Theirs was an old association. When Meeta died, Raakhee was inconsolable. 'My wardrobe will never be the same without her,' Raakhee said. And she meant it.

I have myself designed Shabana Azmi's costumes in a couple of films. It happened like this. Shabana was leaving for Delhi for the outdoor shooting of Sai Paranjpye's *Sparsh*. Her hair-dresser Farida and she were trying out a couple of hair-styles that would be appropriate for a young widow in love with a blind professor. 'I'm wondering if the character would wear a plait or a french bun.' Shabana asked me casually, I asked her why Hindi film heroines always dressed in such a stereotype fashion. The wife on screen would wear gold chains and diamond rings, but her arms would be adorned with cheap plastic or glass bangles. From Nirupa Roy to Neetu Singh, the bangles have never changed. The only time the *sone ke kade* came out was when the mother-in-law had to gift them to her prospective daughter-in-law with a patent dialogue, '*Yeh mujhe meri saas ne diye the.*' No middle-class houswife, I told Shabana, wore half-a-dozen glass bangles in the house. Not when she had to attend to so much housework. Most housewives wear two gold bangles intermingled with red or green glass bangles. And this for traditional, not aesthetic reasons. She heard my sermon in silence and at the end of it asked if I'd do her costumes in films.

I did Dasari Narayan Rao's *Aaj Ka MLA*, D. Rama Naidu's *Kamyaab*, Pravin Bhatt's, *Bhavna* and Tinu Anand's, *Main Azaad Hoon* and they were all learning experiences. Shabana was knowledgeable about textures and weaves, had prefer-ences in colours and fabrics but, most important, had an instinctive way of working on her characters. She said it was simpler to model the look on somebody she was familiar with. The columnist of *Main Azaad Hoon* was modelled on Shobha De. The village woman in *Aaj Ka MLA* was mod-elled on me. In the second half, when her husband became the chief minister, modelled on Shalinitai Patil. We gave her *chanderi* and *garhwal* sarees with huge, *kumkum bindis*. The director was particularly impressed because I had packed two separate *mangalsutras*—a simple one for when she plays the barber's wife and another diamond one after her rise in status. Javed Akhtar found our dedication amusing. During *Bhavna*, it was my suggestion that she wear Bhopali *salwar-kurtas* during the honeymoon phase. Normally in Hindi films, the minute the heroine is married, she is wrapped in tissue sarees and *suhaag ka choodas*. Of course, these days things are changing. I discovered that if Shabana's performances are effective, it's because they reflect both the heart as well as the mind. She taught me the significance of colour in cinema. Colours play an important role in cinema that cannot be underestimated.

The lessons came in handy when doing costumes for Deepa Sahi for her teleserial *Tamas*. I met her during my Film Appreciation Course in Pune. When Deepa Sahi arrived in Mumbai for the screen-test of *Party*, director Govind Nihalani went to fetch her at the airport. The first question Govind asked his prospective heroine was, 'Do you smoke? You have a smoker's mouth.' Deepa lived as a paying guest in Juhu, then in Bandra, until she got married to Ketan Mehta after he was divorced. In the interim, she often dropped by at my home.

Stories of the Shabana-Javed romance had been in the air for quite some time. And even though they neither confirmed nor denied then, the rumours persisted. Friends of Honey Irani talked about Javed leaving the house freshly showered with a trail of aftershave behind him. His neighbours at Sea Spring, Bandstand whispered about his late and sometimes early morning arrivals. And then came 10 December 1984. It was a magical afternoon and the mood carried on till evening. Both had innumerable appointments, but neither was willing to budge. As the clock ticked, they wangled out of the day's commitments. Javed had an appointment with his producer. Shabana had a recording with music-director Khayyam for *Anjuman*. We were all sitting in the garden, Shabana, her friends, her mother's friends. As dusk fell, some more friends dropped by. Cousin Rajjo came with her daugher Farha. And some more regulars. The sequence of events is not very clear but the two decided on the spur of the moment that they wanted to get married that very night. Anu Kapur, a regular at Janki Kutir those days, and Farha went hunting for a *maulvi*, while Shabana as always was unable to locate her cupboard keys at the opportune moment, sat motionless in her room. She grabbed the saree lying outside, tied a rubberband around her hair and the bride was ready.

Much later, she regretted not wearing a *gharara*, not having a photographer on her important day. 'How sad that I have absolutely no memory of the moment. It was over

SHABANA-JAVED
They owed no explanations

before I knew it.' For a long time after, everytime Shabana attended a wedding she missed the celebration she could never have. 'We had no lights, no *shehnai*. It didn't even feel like a wedding. . . .' It was all said in humour. Deep down, she cherished what destiny granted her. Also, it isn't as if she was deprived of the customary rites completely. Her room was decorated in the traditional *mogras* and *agarbattis*. The backlash came soon after. The press condemned her marriage. They called Javed a cad and Shabana a hypocrite. From someone championing women's issues, they expected something better. Some of them even landed up at Shaukat Kaifi's *Umrao Jaan* set at Mehboob studio to extract a statement from Shabana's mother. Somebody took a press cutting to Shabana's father, Kaifi Azmi in Mijwan, UP. That was the time when MTNL was on a strike and the news of the marriage couldn't reach him. When finally it did, Shaukat broke down—not because she wasn't sure of her daughter's choice, but because she had taken a major decision in her husband's absence. Kaifi Azmi was relieved that the problem had found a solution and envious that there would now be one more writer in his daughter's life. The media, however wasn't going to let Shabana get away so easily. She defended herself with dignity. Till the very end Shabana and Javed maintained silence. They owed no one any explanations and did not offer any.

9

WHEN NEETU SINGH and Rishi (Chintu) Kapoor finally got married, it was truly a Cinderella story. He had given Neetu one month's notice to complete all her assignments. 'Once you are a Kapoor, you will not step into the studios.' The month prior to the wedding, every studio in Mumbai held a Neetu Singh set. And this included projects shelved for five and ten years. Neetu made sure that she honoured all her commitments. She didn't want to repeat what happened to Dimple Kapadia after she became a Khanna. The last schedule of *Bobby* was shot after her marriage. Dimple reported for work in a BMW, wearing solitaires. She sat by herself in between shots and refused to mingle with the unit. It was the beginning of her alienation with the Raj Kapoor camp and as years went by, the barriers between RK and Dimple got higher. Neetu had heard this painful story many times from Chintu and didn't want to repeat it with her producers, some of whom she had worked with since childhood.

Shooting round the clock, Neetu was doing triple-shifts and dubbing after that. By the time she came home it was often midnight and she would be pooped. One morning, when she was particularly tired and had difficulty waking up, she snuggled next to her mother and said, '*Hum bahut thak gaye, aaj kahin nahin jana.*' Her mother humoured her with, '*Humne nahin kaha tha shaadi karne ko.*' Contrary to her image, Mama Singh was a vulnerable, easy-to-tears woman. Forthright and practical, her philosophy was, to get something in life, you ought to be prepared to give up something. 'If my daughter wants marriage, she should be ready to give up her career.' All alone in the savage world of films, Rajee Singh singlehandedly pushed her daughter's career. When success came and luxuries multiplied, she mellowed. Her restraint was unmistakeable when Chintu came into her daughter's life.

Initially, the two couldn't see eye to eye. During their courtship, Chintu would come home every day to meet his girlfriend but would disappear straight into her room without greeting the mother. The rejection hurt, but Rajee Singh swallowed it for the sake of her daughter. On her part, Neetu suffered, trying hard to balance the two relationships that mattered most to her. The strain persisted and if Rajee Singh worried about Chintu's motives towards her daughter, she did not voice her fears. Time went by but Chintu never officially proposed to his girlfriend. Like all men, Rishi Kapoor was unable to make up his mind till the very end. Not because he didn't love her, but because he was frightened of commitment.

How the engagement came about is an interesting story by itself. There was a wedding in the family of Ritu Nanda, Rishi's elder sister in Delhi which the entire family was attending. Neetu was invited too. Once there, everyone decided that there would not be a more opportune moment for Chintu to announce his engagement. He kept dillydallying, making silly excuses. That's when elder brother Randhir Kapoor pulled him aside and made him see reason. He asked his brother pointed questions for which he wanted direct answers. 'Do you want to get married and have children?' Chintu: 'Yes.' Do you love Neetu? Chintu: 'Yes.' Would you rather marry someone else? Chintu: 'No.' So what the hell is your problem? Chintu: 'Nothing.'

Randhir went out of the room and made the announcement. Rajee Singh was summoned to Delhi by the evening flight. A week later, a radiant Neetu said, 'I don't know who ordered my saree and who decided upon my jewellery. Somebody was putting on my make-up. Somebody was putting on my nail polish. Everybody did what they felt like.

I was being overdressed but I was too overwhelmed to protest, so I let people do what they wanted to. I felt it wouldn't look nice for a young fiancee to give so many instructions. I wore a peach chiffon, a colour that doesn't suit me and was as nervous as hell! Chintu caught me trembling, pulled me into the next room and forced a glass of champagne on me. "Calm down," he ordered, "I don't want you to make a fool of yourself." After this, I was flying high. Nothing mattered anymore.'

Three engagements were announced around the same time. Two star daughters—Raj Kapoor's second girl Reema Kapoor was to marry Kumar Gaurav. Rajendra Kumar's daughter—Dimple Tuli was to marry Ritu Nanda's brother-in-law. And one actress—Neetu Singh to Rishi Kapoor. Call it destiny, but while the first two broke off in the following months, only Neetu Singh took the *pheras* round the fire. It proved that bloodline does not control destiny! The wedding invitation had just Neetu's mother's name on the card which had the film industry buzzing with gossip, but I think it calls for a lot of courage and Rajee Singh proved that. It was the wedding of the decade. The ceremonies began days in advance—*Sangeet, dandiya raas, akhand path, mehndi*, etc. Stars got special wardrobes made for the event. The entire industry was present.

Prior to the wedding, Raj Kapoor threw a lavish party at the Deonar bungalow. That was the first time I witnessed the much-talked about Krishna Kapoor's *mehman nawazi*. The lady in white was charm personified. Attentive and smiling, she looked after every guest personally. Her test came when around midnight, Nargis, escorted by Sunil and Sanjay Dutt stepped into the R.K. lawns. Raj Kapoor, in a black suit and a red muffler, noticed them but took a while to get his act together. Krishna Kapoor had in the meanwhile taken charge. A perfect blend of warmth and restraint, she escorted her guests to her husband and after a few lingering moments left them alone.

There was a stiffness in the atmosphere. Everyone was

conscious of the fifties sensational pair amidst them. It was indeed a historic moment! Nargis was stepping inside the cottage for the first time, meeting her hero after two decades. Even the telephone operator who had connected Ajanta Arts, Sunil Dutt's bungalow for Raj Kapoor to invite the couple personally, was emotional about RK's old heroine. 'After 20 years . . .' he said mushily. Much later, when a dear friend asked Nargis how it felt to come face to face with the man she had loved after all these years, she said, 'It was like the climax of a film. We are both old, tired and with our children grown up. How could I feel otherwise when I have two handsome men on either side, my husband and my son?'

A year later, when she was pregnant, Neetu said, 'Everyone tells me that I'll have a son. Actually it doesn't matter whether it is a son or a daughter. Even Chintu is not particular. I've put on so much weight that my mother-in-law joked that in all probability I will deliver twins. I would want my child to be educated and become a good human being. I'm glad we are still in the Chembur home. I would have been lost being all by myself with a new-born baby. It's nice to be with the family. I feel more secure. By the time I shift to my new home the baby will be manageable.'

From the strong headed girl who could do everything, from driving to swimming, Neetu vegetated into a meek girlfriend when she met Rishi Kapoor. For a while it seemed as if Chintu would subdue her natural exuberance, but as the relationship grew, the two complimented each other. If, during the courtship, Chintu's influence on Neetu was stronger, after the engagement Neetu had a stronger hold on her fiance. After marriage, everyone said that Chintu had mellowed considerably. And after fatherhood, he was completely besotted with his wife.

One would have expected her to miss the arclights. She didn't. 'This is the first time in my life that I'm enjoying a super holiday. Why shouldn't I live it up thoroughly? In fact, some mornings when I see Chintu leave for work, I feel sorry for him. I feel fortunate that I can laze in the house without bothering about shooting. People ask me how I spend my time. I don't know what I do, but I'm busy the whole day, maybe busy doing nothing, but all the same I'm occupied.' Domesticity suited Neetu. With her mother-in-law's guidance, Neetu was becoming an expert hostess and a responsible daughter-in-law. Gone were the days when she played pranks at her mother's home, teasing her cousin, singing loudly, ragging the maid, hitting her hairdresser or dancing a John Travolta on her bed.

Without her, Shailaja Apartment became a lonely house and it was a lonely life for Rajee Singh. 'I do worry a lot about mummy, but she had to accept this some day. My mother is a strong woman and she has many friends. We are lucky that we are in the same city and can speak on the telephone daily. That's life.' Neetu was changing. Her old insecurities had vanished. Marriage had provided her with an anchor. Earlier, she was too absorbed in her singleminded relationship to appreciate other relationships—be it Rekha, co-star Randhir Kapoor or any other close friend. Now, Neetu was more receptive and invested more time in friend-ships that mattered to her.

When, once in a while, she visited her husband's set, she felt ill-at-ease when photographers clicked her. On outdoors, she didn't like hanging around on location. 'It was all right when one was acting. Now that I'm out of it, I find it all very inconvenient. The children need more comfortable surroundings. I prefer to stay in the hotel or go shopping instead. Now, when I think of it, I don't know how I could sing and dance in the rain and sun for so many years. They were tough days, but I survived.'

No other profession requires you to make as many physical adjustments as stardom. Babu Mukherjee, Moushumi Chatterjee's husband, once said that the stars deserved every penny of the price they commanded for the sheer discomfort they underwent. They are pushed into rain or fog, made to roll on mud, wear furs in mid-summer and shorts for a song-sequence in the snow in Kashmir. I've known actors refusing roles because they could not go through the torture of wearing a beard for so many hours—'The glue bites into the skin and there are no words to describe the discomfort,' said Anil Kapoor during the shooting of *Eeshwar*. Amrish Puri said that elaborate wigs gave him a headache and there were times he wanted to throw it all up but couldn't. Forever stuffed with a pillow inside her petticoat because she was playing a pregnant woman in many films, Shabana Azmi would throw away the cushion immediately after pack-up. 'What a relief and thank God, it's not a real pregnancy. Imagine what pregnant women go through for nine months.'

Whether it was Madhuri Dixit, whose feet were blistered because of dancing 9 to 5. Rekha who endured chipped nails because of regular rape scenes, no generation has been spared the ordeal. It is said, Madhubala fell ill because of the heavy chains she dragged during the shooting of *Mughal-e-Azam*. The late Geeta Bali died of small-pox during the shooting of *Ek Chaddar Maili Si*. Rajesh Khanna was allergic to synthetic fabrics, Waheeda Rehman to stick-on *bindis*, Sharmila Tagore got a headache because of the hair pins and costume jewellery did not suit Jaya Bhaduri. Once, during an elaborate dance shooting involving 50 dancers, Dimple felt embarrassed because a fly had got into her blouse. On another occasion, Jaya Prada refused to drink water, because there was no facility for a toilet at the outdoor location. While film-makers erected the most opulent sets, they invariably left out basic amenities. For *Mr. India*, Sridevi would drive all the way to her hotel to change her costumes. Overworked and constantly in the public eye, film stars deal with more stress than ordinary people. The glamour world is full of complexities, passion and magic. There is triumph, euphoria, loneliness and innumerable memories. . . .

I remember the time when Amitabh Bachchan was in the hospital and blackmarketeers sold tickets of *Khuddar* at Rs. 200 each. When he returned home after five months at the Breach Candy Hospital, the roads were blocked with

cars and people all the way to Juhu. When he was shooting
Pukar in Goa an old woman slipped her address into his
hand and said, 'It's my dream that you come home. And I
don't have many years left to dream.' She didn't have to
wait long. That same evening Amitabh drove into her
compound after pack-up. I remember the time Padmini
Kolhapure's directors discussed her acne problem in public.
'Why can't she do something? It disturbs my close-ups.'
Rishi Kapoor ragged Padmini mercilessly on the sets of Raj
Kapoor's *Prem Rog* and a horrified Neetu Singh proclaimed,
'She's too confident. When he used to do that to me, I used
to be in tears.' I remember the time when a doctor had to be
summoned to the sets because both Neetu and Chintu were
suffering from low blood pressure. I remember the time
when Hema and Dharmendra couldn't talk about each other
without blushing. The time when Chimpu Kapoor was
linked with Padmini, then Divya Rana, then Nagma, in fact,
every heroine he worked with. I remember the time
Rameshwari promised a job to her canteen boy at FTII and
the day *Dulhan Wohi Jo Piya Man Bhaye* was released,
summoned Shivaji to become her personal cook. The time
she fell off the horse's back during *Sunaina* and lost *Amardeep*
to Shabana. The time Rati Agnihotri and Anita Raj produced
hits and flops alternately and got married to have babies and
quit films. I remember the time Poonam Dhillon denied
romantic involvement with producer Ashok Thakeria and a
few months later got married to him. The time Kumar
Gaurav confessed infatuation with Vijeta Pandit and later
changed his mind. I remember an emotional Sunny Deol
weeping at his sister's wedding. The time Zarina Wahab
signed a film opposite Asrani and regretted it for life. I
remember the time Mithun Chakraborty would park his car
below Yogeeta Bali's building in Pali Hill and talk to her for
hours. The time Aruna Irani described an extra-marital
relationship as a curse. She said, 'In the end the wife always
wins. The man always returns to her.' The time Amol Palekar
made a serial on fading stars called *Naqaab* starring Bengal

superstar Anil Chatterji. 'The future belongs to the small screen,' he predicted. The time Dev Anand invited me for lunch and served me biscuits and fruits. I remember the time Boney Kapoor was a struggling producer, but behaved like he owned Mumbai. He wasn't linked with any top heroines yet dominated all the girls in his college. He didn't have a penny in his pocket but ordered the most expensive dish on the menu, had a zero bank balance, but travelled by air and had never been abroad, but wore only imported shoes and shirts. I remember the time Mandakini was making it big. The time Shashi Kapoor couldn't shed weight after Jennifer's demise and *Utsav*. The time Raj Khosla began appearing drunk on the sets. The time Waheeda Rehman felt diffident doing an old woman's role. The time Dilip Kumar watched Amitabh Bachchan's *Akayla* stone-faced. The time Raaj Kumar watched Dilip Kumar give a shot for *Saudagar* and then disappeared into his room. I remember the time Javed Akhtar explained the significance of rape on screen. 'The more traditional the heroine, the greater the humiliation of the audience.' The time Mahesh Bhatt analysed why in a scene depicting an attempt to rape, the heroine cannot be draped in trousers, 'Because it's important for the heroine to look feminine to arouse the villain.' The time Raj Kapoor said that, 'The more covered a woman, the better she looks.' I remember the time Dimple Kapadia complained that she hated going anywhere because all people said was, 'Look at her hair and look at her eyes.'

As time passed my perception of the film firmament began to change. I cannot say when exactly the balance tilted, but slowly my inverted snobbery made way for a new modesty. Initially, when I was still new to the line, I believed firmly that film stars were a bunch of illiterates without style or substance. A lot of this had to do with pre-conceived notions and peer pressure. It's not fair to pre-judge people. A lot of them were uneducated, but rich in experience. They taught me some valuable lessons in life. These have come in handy in my stressful moments. The film industry has a lot to offer. It depends on how you absorb these influences.

It taught me tolerance and caution. One morning *Movie* publisher Deepak Mirchandani invited Pammi Bakshi and me for lunch at the Willingdon Club, Mahalaxmi and offered me the joint editorship of the magazine. It was decided that I'd take care of the day-to-day office while Pammi would take care of the stars. Only, this time I wasn't willing to take any chances. I insisted on an official letter confirming my appointment and received it the same evening. It was only later that I learnt that Bharati and the publisher had parted in bad blood.

The responsibility of the job was enormous and I was unsure of living upto expectations. Again, it was my mother who gave me strength. 'Only those who join the race can lose it,' she said. I didn't mind losing. My fear was not knowing the game. My attitude was simple. By the time they discovered that I was no good and threw me out, I would at least have some bank balance. I had been without a job for two months and was feeling the pinch.

8 October 1985. Within seconds of my stepping into the office, I knew I wasn't welcome in my new surroundings. There was acknowledgement of my authority but no support. Looked upon as a traitor who had done injustice to their earlier editor, my colleagues resented me. The tension was evident though no one had the courage to confront me directly. They wouldn't submit their manuscripts and after a few attempts, I stopped asking them. The only person to support me whole-heartedly during this period was our newly promoted production manager, Govind Sawant. On a new post himself, Govind didn't want the internal politics to ruin his career prospects. He did all within his capacity to put the magazine on the stands.

If we managed to hit the stands on the 22nd of the same month, the credit goes to Govind's enterprising nature. In the weeks to follow Govind taught me many pertinent

JACKIE SHROFF

The debut issue was a disaster

production lessons—how to make up a page, push colour formes so as to not delay printing schedules—all boring but essential details of an editor's job. People have often ask me how male colleagues react to a woman in power. Strangely, I have never sensed resentment from any of my male colleagues. The men I have worked with have never felt threatened or subjugated by me. If Govind taught me one side of production, my art-director Amrut Kondekar (now art-director of *Filmfare*), made me aware of the technicalities of art jobs. A swift worker himself, he was forever hurrying me with pictures, titles, captions. He could decorate a page within moments. Without the unflinching support of freelance friends, achieving the first deadline would not have been possible.

The debut issue was a disaster. When I went home, I wept at my helplessness. It was going to be a tough battle but the show had just begun.

10

KAMAL HAASAN had gone on record to say that Sarika was not the cause of his split with his wife, Vani Ganpathy. 'No marriage breaks because of an outsider, it breaks because there is something lacking in it.' The sad thing about a marriage breaking up is that everyone involved with the couple has to take sides. From the people who dropped by to see the baby at the hospital it became very clear who was their friend and who wasn't. When I visited Sarika at the hospital she was still under sedation and kept dozing off in between the conversation. I utilised the time to go shopping for sarees at Nallis on Mount Road in Chennai. This was the first time I could afford to buy eight sarees at one go—one of the perks of being an editor. For somebody perpetually thrown in the company of glamorous people, I wasn't particularly fashion conscious. I wore the same kind of sarees I did during my college, except that now they were of a better quality. My needs were not extravagant and my home was simple but aesthetic.

At office, administration took up a lot of my time. I began to understand, for instance, why editors wrote so little. Every day was a learning experience. I learnt that it is better to be inaccessible than to be rude to people. I also began to understand why most editors were short-tempered. The only good natured editor I have known so far, is Rauf Ahmed. Scoops were slipping from under my nose more out of a genuine lack of curiosity than out of incompetence. I wasn't interested in getting more information than necessary. My co-editor, Pammi Bakshi and I had our share of ideology conflicts. But we didn't let the undercurrents affect our attitudes. Despite serious differences in vision, the first two years were euphoric.

I was in London visiting our international office, when I went to see Jeena Agha, mother of the *Nikaah* fame singer-actress Salma Agha. In her sprawling apartment, full of persian carpets and chandeliers, servants bent low and did *adaab*. With familiar music playing in the background, the green-eyed lady, over lemon tea and cookies spoke incessantly. Her limpid eyes told me the sad story of her daughter's destiny. 'With so much beauty and so much talent, my baby is still marked for sorrow!' Quite like the *begum* she played in B.R. Chopra's *Nikaah*, who was forever looking into the sea and singing, '*Dil ke armaan ansooon mein beh gaye . . .*'.

1985 coincidentally was the year of tragedies. We were driving down the Juhu-Versova road after an evening show at Prithvi Theatre, when the car bumped heavily. '*Gaadi dhire chalao . . .*' Deepti Naval snapped at the driver. Then, turning to me, in a very matter-of-fact tone said, 'Have to be careful. I'm pregnant.' She said that she first felt giddy whilst sitting beside husband Prakash Jha at the National Awards function at Raj Bhavan in Delhi. Four months later, the stomach was showing even though she cleverly tried to hide it in the folds of her saree. 'It's because I'm short,' she said, blushing. Deepti often met Sarika during her early pregnancy and living in the neighbourhood. The two women exchanged notes on the progress of motherhood. 'Does your baby move?' asked Sarika. 'It kicks often,' replied Deepti. 'My doctor says it's important to oil your stomach everyday or you get stretch marks.' 'I want a son. A son who looks like Kamalji though I feel I'm going to have a daughter,' said Sarika. 'I want a daughter,' said Deepti. 'And I'd like to bring her up like a man.'

On 15 October, the last day of her shooting, Deepti was driving back from Madh Island and stopped to browse at the Holiday Inn bookshop. That's when she started to get cramps. She knew something was wrong and drove straight to Daftary's Nursing Home in Santacruz. She was admitted the same night. Prakash Jha was location hunting in Rajasthan for his new film and could not be contacted. It was a desolate night and for years to come Deepti would remember it. There were ominous sounds that didn't allow her repose. A drunkard yelled on the street outside her window. Another woman in the adjoining room whimpered during her labour pains. There was something forbidding in the atmosphere. It was when Deepti's amniotic bag burst the following night that they had no option but to induce labour and deliver a premature, still-born baby. 'They let me hold the baby for a while. It was a girl,' she said weeks after the tragedy when I went to meet her one late evening. Seated in a dimly-lit terrace, she said, 'I have lost my baby. Call it ignorance, but I didn't know that the stomach ache I had been feeling for many days, was the beginning of the end.'

Two years ago when Deepti was required to do a scene for Buddhadeo Das Gupta's *Andhi Gali*, she had wondered what would be the right expression to depict the trauma of a mother delivering a still-born baby. 'Today, I do,' she smiled, this time unable to hide the tears gathering in her eyes. The last time I had met Deepti, she was trying to sleep, tossing and turning in her bed, trying to find a comfortable position. Sighing deeply she had said, 'The only negative thing about pregnancy is that it is physically inconvenient. It should last for only five to six months. Nine months is too long.' Deepti's pregnancy lasted only six months.

Many summers ago, I remember a breakfast appointment at Smita Patil's home. It was 9 a.m. and Smita was still in her nightie. Over black tea stirred with honey, we sat on her huge bed, sunlight peeping in through the glass window in the ceiling. It was a rather controversial interview but Smita took the accusations on her chin. After this, I consciously avoided interviewing her because of my close friendship with arc rival Shabana Azmi. I was not sure if I could be objective and didn't want to be unfair. Still, whenever we met, the vibes were warm and spontaneous. We spoke about sarees, *khand* blouses and *mangalsutras*. Once, while on flight from Hyderabad to Mumbai, she spoke about receiving threats from dacoit Phoolan Devi. She said the voice on the phone had asked her to throw Rs. 50,000 in a dustbin at Goregaon on S.V. Road. She was warned against informing the police. On landing at Mumbai airport we discovered that there was a *bandh* in the city. As a worried Smita ran helter-skelter looking for her car, a passing fan in a *burqua* pulled Smita by the arm and said, 'Smita Patil *ho na tum?*' Offended by her familiarity, Smita surprised me with, '*Amma lagti ho kya meri?*'

Fans can often be selfish in their adoration. I had read about fans mobbing Shashi Kapoor when he went to visit his dying father at the Tata Memorial Hospital. Read about the crowds surrounding Sunil and Sanjay Dutt when Nargis died. In Hyderabad, during the shooting of Shyam Benegal's *Mandi*, Smita and a few others had gone shopping in Pochampalli village. They were inside a weaver's hut when suddenly Smita developed cramps in the stomach. Suffering from colitis, Smita was in agony. The village women gathered from all sides and would not let her go. They pulled her arm and hair for a closer look. It didn't matter to them that she was in a critical condition and needed medical aid. Not even her tears could disperse the crowd. Shocked and dismayed that anyone could be so insensitive to another human being in pain, a furious Ila Arun had to literally jostle Smita into the car and rush her to a doctor.

From the very beginning, there was something very fragile about Smita's constitution. She was the kind who could go to pieces easily. And yet, in her better moods, she was very adventurous and sporting. Smita understood cars and mechanics, could change tyres with an ease that was uncharacteristic and could drive down from Mumbai to Pune in a jeep all alone. Till the end, a silent wall persisted between us. When I went to see Smita on her last day at the hospital, director Arunaraje Patil, Smita's close friend wept unconsolably on my shoulder. Those were desperate moments. Months later, at a private gathering in a warm moment, Aruna said that she and I were connected for life—we could have had so much in common but we were on different sides of the fence. She came for g's fifth anniversary bash and we discussed Smita yet again.

There was an uncertainty about Smita—a certain hesitation, an insecurity which was in complete contrast to Shabana's wholesome, confident presence. The two shared an inexplicable bond that can best be described as a love-hate relationship. Insatiably curious about each other's careers, men and lifestyles, their progress and failures were interconnected and forever running parallel. A turning point in Shabana's professional life was inevitably marked with a turning point in Smita Patil's career and vice versa. A retrospective of Smita Patil films was followed by a National Award for Shabana Azmi and a controversial link-up for Smita was followed by a personal crisis for Shabana. Almost inevitably if the previous year had been beneficial for one, the subsequent year was better for the other. From attending parties to film festivals, the entry of one was timed with the exit of the other. It was as if the two had made a silent pact not to cross each other's paths. And yet, their lives, forever ran parallel.

There were sudden spurts of warmth and hostility. Of understanding and betrayal. I was at Shabana's home one sunny afternoon when a persistant caller insisted on talking to Shabana personally. Out of exasperation Shabana took the line and disguising her voice said, 'Madam *ghar pe nahin hain.*' 'If you are avoiding a call you ought to change your accent,' said the caller. Shabana knew this was no ordinary caller. It wasn't. Feeling particularly low and in a need to talk, Smita had sought Shabana on an impulse. Shabana was equally reciprocal. 'Come over right now,' she urged. They spent a whole day together and embraced when they parted.

The similarities in their temperaments were uncanny—the

transparent enthusiasm, the compassion, the generosity and the hysteria. When hurt, both could sink to the depths of despair, lose courage and feel pessimistic. In an intensely engrossing conversation that went on into the late evening, the two shared tears, traumas and triumphs. Smita confessed that whenever she felt weak and couldn't cope with the pressures of a demanding relationship, she imbibed courage from Shabana. 'When you feel weak and lose hope, do not give up. Phone me and I'll give you strength. As many times and forever,' she told Shabana. Together for a whole month during the outdoor shooting of *Mandi* in Hyderabad, on Shabana's birthday, Smita sent her a card which said, 'We are like fellow passengers.'

The rivalry between the two reached its peak during the making of *Arth*. A film about extra-marital relationship. Starring Kulbhushan Kharbanda, Shabana played his wife and Smita the other woman. Whenever the two were shooting together tension was evident on the sets. The person, more often than not, to bear the brunt, was director Mahesh Bhatt. A good friend of both, it was a tight-rope walk for Mahesh. He had predicted that it would be a nerve-wracking experience to cast the two women together, but he wanted it all the same. From the very beginning, he made it clear to both what their roles entailed. Smita and Shabana knew that it wasn't going to be easy. The film would cause a lot of heartburn but they trusted the director. And more important, they liked challenges.

It was New Year's afternoon when Mahesh narrated the script to Shabana. Pooja Bhatt was sleeping on the cane couch at his home and Kiran, Mahesh's first wife had gone to the church. 'You are at the right phase to enact this role,' Mahesh said dramatically. Shabana had just split her seven-year-old relationship with Shekhar Kapur and was at a vulnerable phase. The timing was perfect. Shabana knew intuitively that the role would be a turning point in her career. And it was.

Mahesh Bhatt of the eighties was far more attractive than

the Mahesh of the nineties. Then, he was Mahesh. Today, he is Bhatt *saab*. And Bhatt *saab*, according to me, is merely repeating what he said and did in the eighties. Mahesh has always enjoyed shocking people. He thrives on sensationalism. It was his high! This is true today as well. The famous drunken brawl in *Arth*, where the wife confronts the other woman during a party scene is proof of this. On the morning they had to shoot the scene, Shabana woke up feeling ill. While drinking her morning tea with her parents in the garden, she discussed the scene in detail. She asked her parents if they found the dialogue offensive. Her father did. He disapproved of undignified behaviour. Poet and lyricist Kaifi Azmi never saw films where his daughter played a prostitute (*Doosri Dulhan, Mandi*). Shaukat Kaifi, an actress herself, was more liberal. She reacted to the purity of the emotion and said, 'A woman who is about to lose her man has no dignity. A wife can go to any limit to save her marriage. And she should.'

The conflict wasn't resolved and as Shabana drove for the shooting, she retreated into a shell. It's an old habit with her to develop withdrawal symptoms everytime she is to shoot a difficult scene. Unusually quiet, she said she wasn't sure if she was capable of delivering the goods, wasn't sure if she was a good actress. When the car reached the slope of Satish Bhalla's bungalow in Pali Hill she turned completely pale. Preoccupied to the point of detachment, her weariness was indicative of an actress preparing. Only on that morning, somehow, she looked a little more nervous than usual.

Later in the evening when I dropped by on the sets, I was told that Shabana couldn't stop crying even after the director had called 'cut'. This can and does happen in their kind of profession. A spillover of emotions. Something deep was churning and Shabana knew what was happening and why. She wasn't the only one suffering though. Smita Patil was going through her private hell too. A bundle of nerves, she felt degraded about portraying a character so completely diffident and self-destructive. And when Mahesh Bhatt told

Smita that she had to look morally inferior to the wife in the drunken scene, she was devastated for deeper reasons!

Arth came at an important point for both the actresses. Involved with married men, Shabana with Javed and Smita with Raj Babbar, the two were discovering new equations. There is no denying that both affected each other strongly. There was a strange kind of power and an undefined pain. The sheer presence of one altered the body language of the other when in the same room. The love-hate relationship was unique in the sense that it fell and rose in a mysterious rhythm that only the two of them recognised and understood. Much later, it was the men in their lives, Javed Akhtar and Raj Babbar, who worked out a truce between their warring women. A rendezvous was organised at Smita's Bandra flat. The women were reluctant, defensive. They agreed to come together after a lot of persuasion. The conversation was initiated by the men, but eventually it worked. When they parted, Smita and Shabana shook hands and as Shabana slipped into her *mojris*, Javed commented, 'Even your footwear is similar.' Despite all the efforts, the relationship was a mad mix of happy and sad moments which continued till the very end.

There were a lot of sniggers when Shabana appeared at Jaslok Hospital where Smita was dying, hours after the great industry event Hope '86. And much later, when Shabana broke down during her TV interview on Smita's demise. Film folks described it as a publicity stunt, but I knew, watching it from close quarters that her pain wasn't false. Regret, grief and guilt combined with a sense of loss. Something died within Shabana that day. The actress lost her energy and zest. In Smita's death, Shabana lost competition, the need to outsmart herself. The tragedy was the breaking of the umbilical cord. Something broke inside Shabana, which she has not been able to recover in all these years. For a long time she was obsessed with the fantasy of adopting Smita's son, Prateik. Ironically today there's a unique bond between Shabana and Smita's family. Smita's sisters, Anita and Manya, share an independent relationship with Shabana. So does *Mai*, Smita's mother. Perhaps this wouldn't have been possible if Smita had been alive!

13 December 1986. The bleary eyed city had barely started on its mid-morning chores when a hint of the terrible tragedy that was to follow first came. Following a PTI flash, the afternoon papers screamed, 'Smita Patil critical!' The suspense continued all evening and then at 12.30 in the night, the voice over the phone said, 'It's all over!' A mere 12 hours later, the hideous suggestion had become an irrevocable fact. Smita Patil was dead! The city was shocked. After Guru Dutt's demise, some two decades ago, this was possibly another untimely tragedy to hit the film industry. At 31, she died an idol, a cult figure reaching beyond her grave. As Kaifi Azmi said in his inaugural speech at a charity function, 'Smita Patil is not dead. Her son is still amongst us.'

Smita Patil Dies

12 December. It begins like any other ordinary day. At 6 a.m., when the baby begins to cry, Smita turns in her bed, feeling slightly weak. Then softly, very softly, taking care not to wake up husband Raj, who has been up all night working for Hope '86, she moves out of the room, carrying the baby to the nursery. There, she plonks herself on the bed, and nurses the baby, thinking for the hundredth time of all the wonderful things she will share with him, when he grows up.

He is going to be a great man. Of that, Smita is absolutely certain. No other child, when he is only six days old, could lift his head and blink his eyes the way he did. She often wonders if he would be an actor like his parents or a politician like his grandfather. She likes the name Prateik and calls him by the name while playing with his tiny hands, laughing, feeling happy. Only the baby isn't in the mood. Cranky, and a little restless, he keeps turning his head away from her.

It's then that Smita realizes that it's her body temperature that is annoying the baby. She's been feverish for the last two days and hasn't touched the baby, just in case he catches the virus. But today, she decides she isn't going to deprive him. So Smita puts a damp cloth around her and feeds him. It helps and after a while, the baby falls fast asleep. Next, Smita goes to wake up Raj. He has to attend the Action Committee meeting at 10 a.m. She touches his forehead to check if his fever has subsided. It's normal. 'Thank God,' Smita sighs. It's going to be a hectic day for Raj. He's been working the entire month for the show and she hopes for his sake that everything goes all right. After all, this is the first time that Raj is actively involved in an event like this and Smita wants it to be a success.

An hour later, when Raj leaves, Smita attends to her daily chores. She washes her hair and like always worries about her falling hair. She recalls her first meeting with Raj on the sets of *Bheegi Palkein*. 'You have an old world look,' he had said to her. Smita is feeling nostalgic. Full of old memories, she remembers her sisters. Anita, whom she calls *Tai*, has played a surrogate mother to Smita in childhood. Younger sister Manya, Smita has mothered all along. She remembers the time when, as children, they played around their favourite banyan tree in the backyard of their old house in Pune, while their mother sang Marathi folk songs.

Rinsing her hair, she decides that she must copy all those songs in her note-book today. 'Why do you need them now?' her mother asks surprised by Smita's sudden passion to collect them. 'Just like that. I feel like singing them once again.' Smita spends a major part of the morning scribbling the songs dictated by the mother. Just like old times, mother and daughter sit by the window, drinking tea from large mugs. It's sometime in the evening that Smita begins to feel slightly melancholic. Somewhere in her body, a slight ache has begun.

At 10.30 the doctor comes in for his regular check-up. 'There is slight fever, but nothing to worry about,' he says, putting her on saline. Then he leaves for his next visit. Perhaps all she needs is rest. Smita lies on the bed, trying to read. She can't. Memories crowd her mind as she stares at the bottle, waiting for the drip to get over.

Maya, her hair-dresser, drops by with a copy of the video cassette of her *godbharni* function. 'The tape is only of 30-minutes,' informs Maya. 'We'll complete it during the naming ceremony when *Tai* and Manya are here. They haven't been photographed with the baby at all,' says Smita. Then, as an afterthought, adds, 'Maya, I'm not feeling too good. Pray for me, please. Pray that I get well soon.' 'Silly girl, nothing has happened to you,' Maya replies ruffling Smita's hair affectionately. Though the two women have been working together for only a couple of years, they share a deep bond.

The last two years have been exceptionally trying for Smita. Maya had often witnessed Smita's bouts of depression and had, at times, even consoled her. Protective to the point of being maternal, Maya did not hesitate to scold her if she found Smita worrying unnecessarily. Today, once again, she reprimands her with, '*Vedi ahes ka? Kai jhala ahe tula ki itki ghabharte?*' (Are you mad? What has happened to you that you are so worried?)

Smita tries not to worry or think too much. Two hours later, when the first bottle of saline is over, Smita, who has by now become impatient insists that she change the room. Cuddling up to her mother she says, 'Ma, I haven't been good to you these last two years. I have quarrelled with you all the time but now it will all be fine. Now I have sorted out my problems and everything is going to be just fine.' She feels restless and low and is hankering for contact. To Poonam Dhillon, who calls her at 3 p.m., Smita says that she is feeling low. 'All women feel like this after pregnancy,' jokes Poonam. 'Besides, now that you have all that you have always wanted, why worry?' 'That's true,' Smita muses, 'but I'm feeling very uneasy. Why don't you come home just now? We can sit and chat, I will feel better.'

Poonam, who is calling from the sets promises to drop by. Then as she says goodbye, Poonam coughs and hysterical mother that Smita is, she shrieks, 'Don't come if you have fever. I don't want my baby to catch an infection.' Then, almost laughingly, adds, 'I'll be okay in a few hours. I always go through such moments.'

In the evening, by the time Raj returns from his meeting, Smita's tubes have been removed and she's already feeling better. Humming a tune, she pulls out the clothes that Raj plans to wear for the Hope '86 function. She pleads with him to let her accompany him for the show. 'I'm feeling better. I always do when you are with me. Let me come along too. When will I ever get to see a show like this?' But Raj isn't willing. He tucks her into bed, covers her with a blanket and goes into the bathroom for a shower. He returns barely 10 minutes later to find Smita looking pale as chalk, doubled up

SMITA PATIL
'I'll be happy if I cross 30'

with convulsions, cringing in pain and vomitting blood. He panics. Moments later, quick arrangements are made to get in touch with the doctor.

'I won't go to hospital,' Smita pleads, as they put her on the stretcher. 'I don't want to be away from my baby. Don't take me to the hospital. Please don't take me away from him. I want to be at home with everybody.' Her hysteria increases as she weeps and argues with Raj and her mother. Then somewhere anger gives way to fatigue and Smita leans on Raj's shoulder and falls asleep. It's only when they reach the hospital that they realize that Smita isn't sleeping but has slipped into a coma.

News of her critical situation spreads rapidly. In a couple of hours, a lot of people from the film industry and the press have gathered at Jaslok hospital. Everyone has only one question, 'How is she?' The hospital staff have only one answer. 'She is the same!' Worried visitors do all they can to extract further information. Different people have different reasons for her illness. Some say its meningitis, some say viral encephalitis, some say its disseminated introvascular coagulapathy, some say it is DSC and others describe it as stress. The speculations continue while every half an hour a fresh health bulletin is circulated.

It's late evening. Somebody comes down and says that she has finally stopped bleeding, but now it's her blood pressure that is falling. Smita is on the respirator and twenty doctors are examining her. Some say her brain has stopped functioning but the doctors still have hope. 'Her brain gave away,' says Smita Patil's mother next morning at the funeral held at Smita's Bandra residence. In a room filled with people clad in white, Mrs. Patil, who had been unconscious for long hours, now sits in a daze staring at her daughter's photograph. 'Otherwise my daughter was a fighter. She fought all her battles. Her career. Her sorrows. She would have fought death too, if only her brain hadn't let her down.' Mrs Patil breaks down. Everytime tears fill her eyes she wipes them away angrily. Shivaji Patil, Smita's father, watches his wife from a corner, trying to be brave. There will be plenty of opportunities to break down later, he seems to have told himself. But right now, the show has to go on. Even Smita would have liked it that way. 'The loss is ours,' he says dispassionately. 'The world will continue and life will move on. What is unforgivable is that we lost her through negligence. If only we had been more careful!'

'I'll be happy if I can cross my thirties,' Smita had once said in an interview, irritated with her constant ill-health. She wasn't in the least bit surprised when a dear friend read her palm and predicted that she would die early. 'I don't mind. But as long as I live, I want to lead a healthy and a wholesome life. A life I believe in.'

And Smita did. It showed in the way she took her decisions. In just a decade, Smita graduated from being a mere TV announcer to becoming an actress to reckon with. The youngest star honoured with a Padmashri, she was the first Indian star to be honoured with a retrospective abroad. When that happened people said, 'Isn't she too young? She has a career that only spans a decade. There is still plenty of time. What's the hurry?'

There was, for somebody up there knew that there was very little time. And in that time, God wanted Smita to live life fully and passionately. The way Smita wanted to.

Movie, December 1986

11

THE HOPE '86 show organised by the Cine Artistes Association was to compensate for the technicians and the daily wage earners of the film industry. What led to the month long Maharashtra film industry strike and how it was eventually resolved is a story in itself. The echoes began in mid 1985.

The protests against the government's total apathy towards the film industry were in the air. The industry had been decrying the imposition of heavy taxes for years, but the government refused to reduce the burden of taxes. Eleven days later, a massive morcha led by stalwarts V. Shantaram and Sunil Dutt wound its way from Shivaji Park to Mantralaya. The smallest unit hand to the biggest star, participated, to garner public support and present their long-standing demands to the then chief minister, Mr. S.B. Chavan. The chief minister maintained that the government would arrive at a decision after the Godbole committee submitted its report. Nine days later came the All India film *bandh*. A mammoth public rally was held on the sands of Chowpatty. It was a Black Diwali for film folks. This time the stars participated in a prayer march from Opera House to Mahalaxmi race course. The same day witnessed the start of an indefinite hunger strike by veteran character actor, Jankidas. The month long strike affected nearly four lakhs daily wage earners.

All the studios were empty and all stars at home. A round of meetings being held at Amjad Khan's home at Pali Hill. The Film Makers Combine and the Cine Artistes Association were trying to resolve the problem, but it was not easy. Not recognised as an industry after 75 years of existence, the industry was on a war footing. When after several attempts to get aid from the government it failed, they roped in Sunil Dutt. Everyone felt that Sunil Dutt, as a Congress MP, would have some clout. He didn't. Eventually, much against their wishes, they decided to seek Amitabh Bachchan's aid. Bachchan wasn't in the country at that time so they had to wait till he got back. When he did, a committee of five representatives went to meet the actor. They met late at night and Bachchan agreed to advocate the case to High Command—Rajiv Gandhi. By the next morning, the problem had been resolved. Just one phone call had achieved what the entire committee couldn't achieve after days of sermons and strikes. It was the first time in 15 years that interim relief had been provided to the film industry. Bachchan said that he was confident that more concessions would be granted after the Godbole committee report. But the terms of agreement weren't acceptable to the industry because none of the major demands of the industry had been conceded. Something just snapped after that. The hero was made into a villain and the impression created that Bachchan had sold the film industry to the government. The feeling of betrayal was universal and it took years before the scars would heal completely.

At the General Body meeting held at Gaiety theatre in Bandra the same afternoon, there was a strong resentment against Amitabh's role in the matter. The speakers at the meeting termed the settlement as a shameful sell-out to the government at the hands of Amitabh. The workers decided to return the cheque of Rs. 2 lakhs which Amitabh had contributed to the Workers' Welfare Fund. In the following week Mr. Ramraj Nahata, president of the All India Film Producers' Council and convener of the Action Committee, resigned from both the posts to express resentment against the midnight settlement. When contacted, he said, 'The settlement is dishonourable. I was compelled to sign on the dotted line because of other members.'

Months after the strike, the film industry continued its protests by wearing black arm bands and refusing to shoot at the government owned Film City.

Rajesh Khanna and Anju Mahendroo had broken off almost 15 years ago, when Khanna, on the rebound, got married to friend Chunibhai Kapadia's beautiful daughter, Dimple. It was said that Khanna deliberately led his *baraat* on the 7th road of JVPD Scheme to embarrass Anju. One wasn't surprised. When scorned, Khanna was capable of turning venomous. The two didn't meet despite being in the same city for over a decade. And when they did, my co-editor Pammi Bakshi was instrumental in bringing the two together. A common friend of both she would often talk about one to the other. Apparently one fine day, Rajesh Khanna just picked up his phone and broke the ice. Next, Anju invited him over for a drink. He agreed, then dropped by one evening, just like that. The old bungalow on Juhu road, his parting gift to his girlfriend, was not an unfamiliar address to him. When he parked his car outside the gate, it was as if time stood still. The Mahendroos recognised the honk and the old dog rushed to greet his master. Kaka entered the room like old times, a cigarette in his hand and settled down in his favourite chair and ordered his favourite drink. Emotions have a way of adjusting to the impossible. A nervous Anju taking large puffs on the cigarette came out to greet her special guest. Contrary to expectations the evening went off very smoothly. Over the months, both of them made a special effort to rejuvenate the old ties. From ex-girlfriend to best friend, slowly Anju slipped into the role of his confidante and soon began assisting him at his office. This was the time he was launching himself as a producer with *Jai Shiv Shankar* and consequently changing as a person. He had even come to terms with wife Dimple's comeback to films. Dimple had come to terms with her separation. 'He should have married Mumtaz. They would have been perfect for each other,' she said. Dimple believed that Rajesh and she were mismatched. They had married each other for all the wrong reasons. Dimple was too young to handle Khanna's complexities. She looked upon him as a priceless gift that everyone admired but only she possessed. He looked upon her as a beautiful statue everyone desired but only he owned. Romance flew out of the window after just a few flops. The deeply disturbed man sat sulking on his terrace, drinking till the wee hours of the morning, mourning the shadows of his slipping stardom. Confused and anxious, the wife sat beside him, too frightened to trespass into his private thoughts. Young and restless, she suffered and endured until she could take it no longer. And that's when she decided to walk out.

Rekha and Raj Babbar were shooting on a long outdoor for T. Rama Rao's *Sansar* in Chennai. When they returned to Mumbai rumours about their romance were in the air. What spilled the beans was the midnight drama that unfolded on the streets of Juhu. Our office phone rang with bizarre stories that seemed stranger than fiction. It all started when a speeding car threw out a woman onto the road. The woman, in a white sari, collected herself and started walking. Spotting a passing taxi on the road, she hailed it. The voice was familiar. A few sex workers strolling by lazily recognised the actress. Even without a trace of make-up, Rekha was too dazzling to go unnoticed. 'It's her. Rekha, the film actress,' they yelled. Within moments she was surrounded by a whole group—someone pulling her hair, someone her hand. It was her good fortune that a unit hand returning home stopped by. To his disbelief, he found Rekha sobbing, begging them to let her go. He pushed his car right into the crowd, pulled her from the madness and dropped her home! To his credit, the assistant remained forever anonymous. To this day, nobody knows the man who saved the damsel in distress.

The next morning the whole of Mumbai was buzzing with the news. We phoned Rekha to find out if the story was true. She wasn't available for comments. We had anticipated it. Everytime a serious controversy crops up, the star is never available for clarifications. This is an eternal problem for a scribe chasing deadlines. It's always after the storm has subsided, that the star emerges and everytime the line of defence is the same. 'How could you do this? I would have told you the truth.'

Sarika had gone into voluntary exile, left Mumbai for good and settled in Chennai. Despite wild rumours and raging accusations, Kamal and Sarika offered no clarifications. Sworn to silence, for her fans and the Mumbai film industry Sarika remained a mystery. But the time had come to tell the complete story, unravel the mystery.

Sarika mystery solved

'I want this baby. I want it because it's his,' she had said nine months ago. And the problem, as expected, started soon after. With every passing month, the controversies multiplied, both in Chennai and Mumbai. Fortunately, around that time Sarika had moved out of her PG accommodation into her own flat, Trishul at Seven Bungalows. She was more comfortable, but not having a phone, she still had to keep going to her friends' homes all the time to receive and make calls to Kamal. One day, after having spoken to him for an hour, she called me up to say that she was leaving Mumbai and migrating to Chennai for good. 'Kamal*ji* wants me to have the baby there. I'll have to leave soon because the doctors have advised me not to travel after that.'

When I went to her flat that weekend, Kamal was there too. In a room devoid of curtains, the afternoon glow seeping in through the window, the three of us struggled to pack Sarika's umpteen trunks.

There was a serenity about the afternoon. A strong feeling of security was exuded by the sheer presence of Kamal Haasan. 'I don't want to take any risks,' he said, climbing on to the sofa to shut the ventilators. 'So I came down personally to take her back with me. She was dilly-dallying and I didn't want her to have second thoughts.' The truth is, that initially Sarika was quite hesitant about having her delivery in Chennai. She felt that since Kamal would be busy with shooting every day, she would feel lonely in an unknown city with nothing to do and no friends. She gave in for she accepted that there might be complications in the advanced stages of pregnancy and surviving all alone, without even a servant or a car, would be difficult. 'Do keep coming to see me,' she said with misty eyes while hugging me at the airport.

In the six months that followed I could not make a single trip to Chennai. Having recently taken up the joint editorship of *Movie*, I was caught up with the teething problems of a new job. However, we kept in touch, more through letters than through phone. Sarika was paranoid that the operator would overhear our conversation. She was certain her phone was being tapped. There were a few occasions when she felt she was being followed too. Whom she met and whom she talked to was being monitored by a detective agency. She even received threatening calls from the same caller at fixed hours every afternoon. Obviously, Sarika was frightened.

As expected, living in Chennai wasn't easy for her. After Kamal left for work in the morning, the day seemed long and lonely. Till he returned after pack-up, late in the night, Sarika was all alone in an empty hotel room, shifting from the bed to the chair to the window—restless and full of anxiety. Her only source of entertainment was the television and the video. During this long stay in the hotel she saw all the films available in the hotel library and tried out all the different varieties of food listed on the menu card. For recreation, the only place she could venture into was the beauty parlour. But even here she was the target of gossip! In voices loud enough to be heard, society women, dripping with diamonds, bitched openly about the actress. Sarika saw humour in their uncharitable behaviour. 'Such a pity they are wasting their effort on someone who doesn't even understand the language,' she laughed.

The bravado slipped as weeks went by. As she grew enormous, her restlessness increased. Living on the edge, she became hyper-sensitive and suspicious of strangers who tried to befriend her. She preferred being a recluse rather than trusting an imposter. When she felt very lonely, she went for long walks or drove to Kamal's office to make long-distance calls to friends. But as the date of delivery approached, even driving to his office became difficult. However, her letters came regularly and by the dozen—sometimes spirited, sometimes abstract soliloquies, immature but rich in thought, scrawled on different stationery pads from addresses which changed from time to time.

It took Sarika and Kamal months to find a house. This despite Kamal Haasan being an important name down south and despite the whole city knowing that they were house-hunting. Everywhere they went, the reply was in the negative. Doors were shut with feeble excuses. The trauma continued for months as the hotel bills soared and their privacy was trampled upon. Demoralized and exhausted, they finally knocked on Hema Malini's door. It was a rainy day in September and Sarika and Kamal were drenched when they entered the low gate of Hema's bungalow on a famous street of Chennai. Their problem was solved within five minutes. After house-hunting for months and returning dejected everytime, they had finally got the key to their love-nest, even if the nest was bare.

I had seen them living with make-do curtains, a make-do kitchen with a second-hand refrigerator, paint chipped walls, a leaking bathroom, a *kaccha* gate, an asbestos sheet over a supposed garden and second-hand furniture to fill up the drawing room. That's why every time I read stories of Kamal Haasan's wife accusing him of taking away all the money, I was confused. If Kamal had really taken all that she accused him of, why was he living like a vagabond? They went through it bravely. 'You know, delivering a child is more of a lonely than a painful journey. It was the first time I realized that I was all alone in my battle. I had to push the baby myself and nobody could help me, not even God.' It was a philo-sophical statement, but not an unusual one coming from Sarika, who made serious statements very casually.

I met Kamal's father for the first time after Sarika's delivery at the hospital. *Atti*, I discovered is a spirited, feisty old man. Accompanied by his friend Anantaswamy, also in his late seventies, the two old men would drop by every evening to give Sarika company. 'They were the only two who regularly spent time with me. It was so funny. Normally old women tell you what you should do and what you should not at times like this. In my case, it was old men guiding me. It was so odd, even embarrassing at times but I had no option. *Atti* taught me how to walk, how to take short strides when the baby kicks within. Always sit down gently, he would caution. He said he knew this because he had supervised his wife's pregnancy.' Thirty years ago, Kamal Haasan was born in the same room and even then *Atti* had amused his wife with similar wisecracks.

To the father's credit, it must be admitted that despite stiff opposition he didn't let outside influences prejudice his relationship with his grandchild or the child's mother. 'To me all my children are the same. And I will go wherever love beckons me,' he said. After Sarika came home, *Atti* continued to drop by to look up Sarika and Kamal or to play with little Shruti. So did Chandra Haasan, Kamal's older brother, who also manages Kamal's business. Their relationship remained untarnished contrary to the reports in the press.

If Kamal and Sarika were affected by the scandals raised by the fourth estate, they preferred not to show it. Kamal was able to snap out of the depression faster for he had other diversions. For Sarika it was more difficult. When the servants read out what was written in the local papers, the trauma became unbearable.

'I go through phases of immense anger and rage,' Sarika once said. 'I want to shout out the truth from the roof-tops. But it's of no use. Wisdom lies in keeping quiet and I hope I have the strength to be quiet always. What happens in the future we will face as it comes.' As always, her face was expressionless. A cool exterior hid a sea of turmoil. Very quietly, she continued serving *rasam* and *sambhar* to Kamal at the dining table while Shruti played in the background. She called out to the cook, who was in kitchen, to ask him where the pickle bottle was and the two chatted in Tamil. Then she looked out of the window to give instructions to the driver. In a cotton *khaki* skirt and blouse with an apron and a bunch of keys jingling at her waist, she was the *memsaab* of the house! For all the scandals and defamation, the harmony within the walls of their home remained untouched.

In the meanwhile, arguments over Sarika's right to happiness continued. How could Sarika expect to be happy after stealing another woman's husband? How could she demand justice when she herself had been unjust? How could Kamal expect anything but slander and defamation after the way he had behaved? Opinions.

Discussions. Judgements. Sarika and Kamal expected this and had in fact, three years ago, gone through a clinical decision to part ways. After four months of unbearable separation they had come to realise that if living together was difficult, living apart was impossible! Weeks went by without domestic help, but Sarika would cope. 'It's just a passing phase. Besides, I need to keep myself busy. I am going to give birth to a tough baby—just like the mother.'

The baby was tough, a healthy eight pound child. And when the nurse laid her in Sarika's arms, the first words Sarika cooed to her infant were, 'If only you knew what I have gone through to have you.' To which Kamal said, 'She will and her parents will tell her.'

The hospital matron was tired of the number of times Sarika buzzed to ask for her baby. 'Can't I keep her with me for a little longer? Can she sleep with me tonight? What is she thinking?' Childish queries, but understandable, for Sarika had at last found a companion she could cherish as her own. 'How does it feel?' I asked her. 'At the moment I'm delirious with joy. I'm so glad I had her. I will never regret this decision. Never. No matter what happens. I'm 100 per cent sure of that,' she replied. Sarika preserved every press clipping which she neatly pasted in a scrap book with dates and names. 'I want Shruti to know all that happened. I want her to read all the good as well as the bad things written about her parents and then decide for herself what was right and what was wrong before the world starts poisoning her innocent mind with horror stories. It's awful to grow up surrounded by mystery. Ask me, I should know. I grew up with questions that were never answered. I want my daughter to be unafraid of asking and me unashamed of telling.'

Sarika never mentioned her mother unless I specifically asked. Does she keep in touch at all? 'No,' she replied briefly. After a pause she continued, 'I'm told she's given a statement somewhere that I will know what it means to be a mother when I become one myself. Today I do. And I am even more convinced that what I'm doing is right.' She didn't elaborate further and we never discussed her mother again.

She didn't like discussing the past. For Sarika, the present was too exhilarating to talk of bygone days. She talked passionately about Kamal's forthcoming film *Vikram*, Shruti's first foreign trip, Kamal's silent experiment with cinema *Pushpak*, Shruti's teething problems, Kamal's histronic performance in Mani Ratnam's

Nayakan, Shruti's *mundan* ceremony, her photography, her occasional writing for South Indian magazines, her single-minded participation in Kamal's script sessions at home, and finally, her renovation of Kamal's office. From time to time gossip mills churned out rumours involving his leading ladies—sometimes Dimple, sometimes Radhika. Horror stories tumbled out of Sarika's past too. Sometimes, there were outbursts from Sarika's mother and once in a blue moon they even witch-hunted her father. 'Everyone is so keen on giving interviews now, flaunting relationships. Where were they when I needed them? There are too many scars. And it has taken me a long time to wipe them out. I can't go through it all again. Not now.'

In all the years that I have known her, only twice have I seen Sarika close to a breakdown. The first was when she split with Kamal and the second when she discovered a voodoo doll in the truck-load of items that appeared from Kamal's old house at Alwarpet. I was in Chennai to cover an outdoor shooting at that time and we were at the dining table, when the baggage arrived. We got up half-way through the meal to direct the crates to the room upstairs. As the men moved to and fro, a plastic packet containing a skin-coloured broken wax doll fell on the carpet. Kamal's make-up man was the first to notice it. He was about to throw it out but Kamal snatched it away. Seething with anger, he locked himself in his bedroom. When he finally emerged, he was calmer, but not Sarika. Sitting on the sofa, her face hidden in her hands, she wept as she had never done before. 'I don't say a word when they say anything against me. But why don't they leave my baby out of this?'

For a long time after this incident, I didn't get any letters from Sarika. I knew that she was miserable. After months of silence, I received a small card. It said, 'The temptation to lash out is tremendous. But I mustn't. Years later, when this mess is sorted out and the washing of dirty linen in public is over, I'll feel proud of myself for not talking. And you'll be proud of me for helping me take this decision.'

With every passing year, her domesticity spread further roots. She wrote about making a study for Kamal, a video room for the family downstairs, an extension of the porch to include a make-up room for his staff. Having mastered the local language and become familiar with the city, Sarika had overcome her fears of the new city. Involved in many activities, the most important being *Frames*, her Film Society which screened Adoor Gopalkrishnan amongst other eminent film-makers, she was also supervising the construction of her new house. Two months ago, Sarika had flown down to Mumbai to shop for Kamal's costumes for his forthcoming film *Satya* (remake of *Arjun*), but ended up mostly shopping for Shruti's birthday. She picked up a red plastic doll containing three identical smaller dolls. 'In my childhood, I played a lot with a similar doll and was surprised when I discovered it in a shop after all these years. When Shruti plays with this doll, she will be re-living a part of my own life . . . .' Stopping mid-sentence she said, 'I don't want Shruti to re-live anything I have gone through. Nothing unpleasant at least. She should have a glorious future, sound and secure. I want her to be fearless and I'm confident that my daughter is going to be a very sensible girl.'

Movie, April 1988

12

PRODUCER G. VENKATESHWARAN and director Mani Ratnam had made a film in Tamil about Varadarajan Mudaliar, the Mumbai underworld don, starring Kamal Haasan. I knew about it because I travelled with the unit all over America on a promotional trip. Entered for the 1988 Academy Award nominations in the Best Foreign Film category, producer G.V. and Kamal were the official invitees of the Tamil Sangam Association of America. In the ten-day tour, I saw the film half-a-dozen times and each time, I wept at the very same scenes. A lot had to do with my feeling extremely homesick. It was Christmas and at every airport or shop we visited, people were hugging and screaming, 'Merry Christmas'. The whole world seemed to be celebrating, while I was, in the true sense, lonely in America. After a while, the endless switch of aircraft and hotels became meaningless. So did the constant buzz around the stars by fans seeking autographs.

It was during one such gathering when, perched on a high stool, I was watching a jam-packed crowd indifferently. The city was Detroit and the occasion, one more screening of *Nayakan*. Suddenly, I noticed that a woman had plonked on a stool next to me. I was surprised that there was someone else in the room who wasn't part of the circus. 'What's your name?' the lady asked. 'I am part of the film unit, I'm a journalist,' I replied absentmindedly. 'But you must have a name?' she asked. That's when I became conscious of my low self-worth.

Constantly being in the company of a celebrity can alter one's self-image. It's the effect of the halo surrounding them. The sharp focus put everything else under an eclipse. I had begun to search for answers which didn't occur once I was back home in secure surroundings.

One evening I was shopping for vegetable in Matunga market, when suddenly the idea of meeting the underworld don Varadarajan Mudaliar whose home was somewhere nearby struck me. To find out, I stopped at the nearby *paanwala* and asked him to direct me to Vardarajan's home. A little surprised, he pointed to an inconspicuous building at the end of the road. I climbed the dark, creaky staircase and knocked on the wooden door. There was a long pause. Someone peeped from the eye-hole but didn't open the latch. I knocked again. A little later a puny man in a white *lungi* and *tilak* adorned on his forehead opened the door slightly. '*Yenna ma?*' he asked me in a tone which was polite but firm. 'Is Vardarajan Sir, there?' I asked, suddenly unsure of myself. Silence. 'I want to speak to him,' I said slowly. Hearing my voice another man appeared from behind. After a brief discussion between the two and I was finally allowed in. A small wooden partition blocked the entrance and one had to jump over it to get inside. A narrow passage led to a small room with a window overlooking the street. Dark green curtains covered the door. A strong aroma of coconut oil filled the nostrils, as I settled down with my vegetable basket on a *chattai* spread on the floor. More *lungi*-clad, dark skinned, *tilak* decorated men poured into the room and settled on similar *chattais*. I tried smiling at one, but he was disapproving. After about ten minutes, a dimunitive but power exuding man entered the room. He seemed to be the leader judging from the manner in which the rest of them got to their feet. He stood for a while staring at me, then keeping a safe distance, settled down in a corner. He cleared his throat. It was an indication for me to tell the purpose of my visit. I did. If he was surprised, he didn't show it. 'Leave your number. We will get back,' he said politely. They didn't.

After a few days, I called again. 'We will get back,' they said again and didn't get in touch. This went on for weeks. In the interim, *Sunday* asked me to compile a story on *Nayakan*. I filed my story without talking to Mudaliar. When it appeared in print, I was scared that he might try to cause me harm. Nothing so dramatic happened! When the film was released, there were bigger controversies. The *Illustrated Weekly* carried a raging story profiling the don. A photograph of Mudaliar sitting on the *chattai* was so similar to a working still of Kamal Haasan from the film that for once, it was difficult to tell the original from the imitation.

As coincidence would have it, Varadarajan Mudaliar died a few weeks later. He died the way he would have liked. With pride and honour. All the shops in Mumbai pulled down their shutters. The crowded streets of Matunga were deserted. Crowds thronged to watch the funeral procession. They threw flowers all the way to the crematorium. With tear-stained faces they bid farewell to a favourite hero.

Kamal Haasan plays Varadarajan

In the seventies when Salim-Javed wrote *Deewar*, based on the smuggler Haji Mastan and cemented Amitabh Bachchan's star-status. Now, over a decade later, South Indian star Kamal Haasan has tried to replicate that success with *Nayakan*, based on the life and crimes of Varadarajan Mudaliar alias Vardha, the Mumbai don who died on 2 January in Chennai.

Varadarajan's sudden death gave the film a massive publicity boost with even the late don's eldest son, Mohan, raving, '*Nayakan* is a powerful film with great work from director Mani and actor Kamal.' Mastan, on the other hand, has never been happy with *Deewar*, claiming that his life had more in common with the characters of *God-father II*!

What makes *Nayakan* special is that Mudaliar actually collaborated with its film-maker. Both director Ratnam and Kamal Haasan,

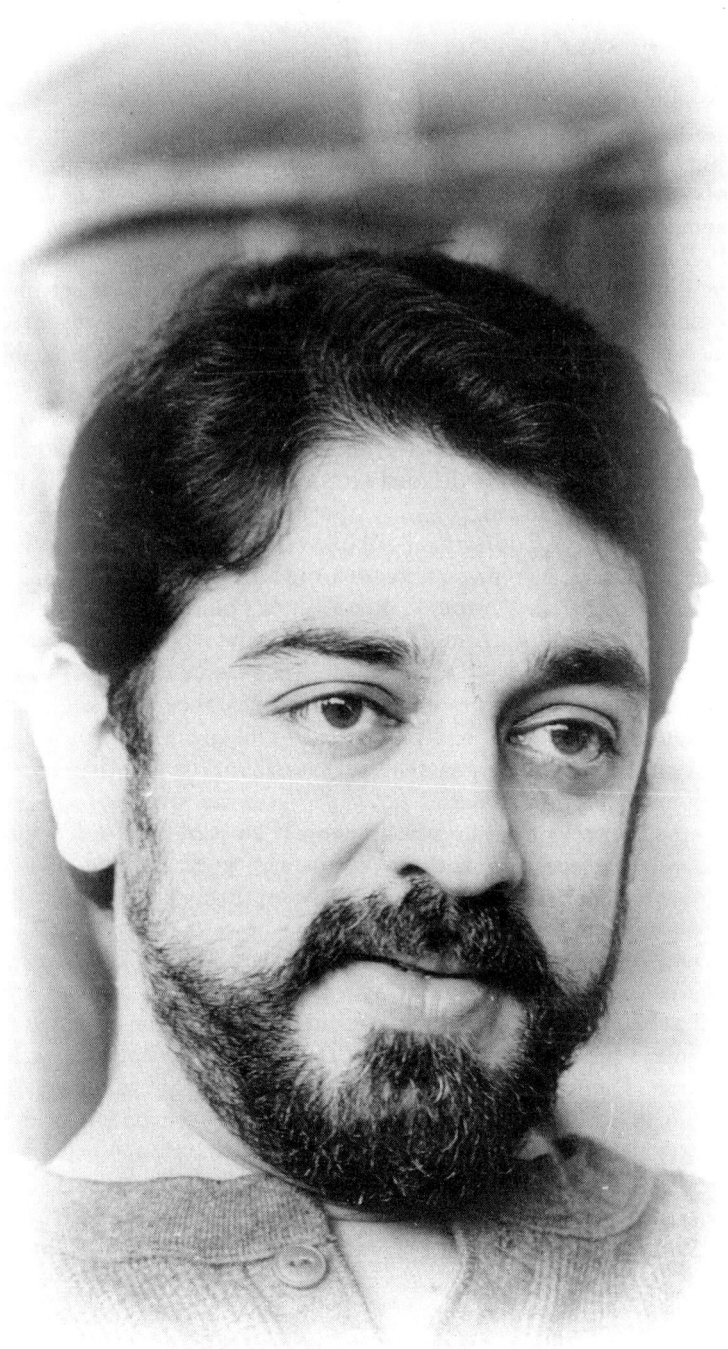

KAMAL HAASAN
Nayakan *was a role to remember*

his star, have always fought shy of admitting that *Nayakan* is a 'bio-pic.' Nevertheless, word got round in Chennai that it was based on Vardha's life. (To this day, Kamal Haasan will only say, 'My character, Velu Nayakan, is an inspiration and is not an exact imitation of Varadarajan Mudaliar)'.

Clearly, Vardha heard the talk and wanted to find out the truth for himself. Last May, the crew was shooting a sequence set in a slum colony when they noticed that several obvious *thugs* appeared out of nowhere and hung around the sets, silently watching the shooting. Some of the *thugs* were recognisably Vardha's men; others appeared to be their accomplices. Ratnam had three options: To ask the *thugs* to leave, to find out who they were, or to simply ignore them. He decided on the third option and finally his patience was rewarded.

On the fourth day, Ratnam's phone rang. The voice on the other end, delivered a cryptic message. Could he come to Mudaliar's house on Chennai's Santone Road? And could he please come alone? A terrified Ratnam decided to take the risk, to see Vardha, and to find out what he thought. He was reassured, he recalls, by the non-menacing nature of Mudaliar's appearance. The don wore a spotless white *dhoti*, had his forehead emblazoned with a white *tilak* and seemed more genuinely curious about the film than upset. 'Tell me about your hero,' he said. 'Does he wear a red scarf around his neck? Does he beat up people? Does he bark orders into a cordless telephone?' Clearly, Varadarajan knew a thing or two about the manner in which Hindi cinema portrayed its villains.

As Ratnam listened, Vardha told him how he thought the don should be portrayed. 'Whatever you do,' he lectured, 'See that the film is not biased. Nobody, not even a Mafia don, is as black and evil as he is projected. It is true,' he admitted 'that one gets used to an image bestowed upon one. But the image need not necessarily be true. The truth goes far beyond what meets the eye. Have you ever wondered?,' he asked rhetorically, 'Why the underworld is always a step ahead of the police? (In fact, at the time, Vardha was on the run from the Mumbai police.) We have no facilities and no big force, but we are intelligent. We have the knack.'

Ratnam understood that the lecture contained an implied threat. Vardha could, if he wanted, have blocked the entire shooting schedule of the film using the strong-arm tactics that he was notorious for. But as time went on, it became clear that Mudaliar did not want to block the shooting. In fact, he probably wanted the film to be made, he just wanted his character to be portrayed as accurately as possible. Kamal Haasan met Vardha twice, though initially he was hesitant to see him for fear that the real man would overshadow his performance. When, in fact, Kamal met the don, he was struck by the contradictions in Vardha's character. 'I would describe him,' he now says, 'As a vociferous talker and a very energetic man. He was not a loud-mouth. For all his vivaciousness and fire, he could be extraordinarily paternal while talking to people who asked him for help. I'd call him a disturbing man. He had a way of sitting at the edge of the seat, whether in the car or at home and he spoke with furious gesticulations.'

Ratnam decided to use the opportunity to obtain as many authentic details as possible. He went to Mumbai to meet Mohan, Vardha's son and heir. 'I had a lot of questions to ask Mohan,' he recalls, and many of them were inane and boring but he answered them all patiently. His contribution to the film has been immense. A lot of the scenes set in the hero's residence were inspired by my conversations with Mohan.'

Vardha himself decided to contribute his mite to the creative process. Movie tradition has it that a gangster hero must die in the last reel if the film is to glide past the censors. But how was Kamal's character to die? What would make sense in the context of Vardha's turbulent life? Foxed, Ratnam decided to approach the don himself with this problem. Vardha thought it over and then announced, 'I would like to die quietly and in peace. But I feel that this is not how it will happen. I feel I will die amidst tension and panic all created by the people who love me deeply. In wishing me well, these people will destroy my peace for me. Sad, isn't it?' Keeping Vardha's philosophical meanderings in mind, Ratnam arranged a violent death for the character. Only to find that, shortly after, Mudaliar himself died as he had predicted—on the run from the Mumbai police and beset by doubt, worry and tension.

Early one October evening in 1987, Mani Ratnam held a preview of Nayakan at Chennai's T. Nagar Preview Theatre. Ratnam had held other previews before but this one was special. There, in the front row, was a beaming Varadarajan Mudaliar, accompanied by his family and friends. Most of the audience seemed to enjoy the film right from the early scenes in which a rationale was built up for the hero turning to crime to the gory denouement: The don is acquitted by the courts when the case against him is thrown out for lack of evidence and is about to savour his triumph when his favourite protege (played by Tinnu Anand) shoots him at point-blank range. The don crumbles to the floor in an inert heap. Early the next morning, Ratnam's phone rang. It was Vardha. 'I loved your film,' he said. 'It wasn't at all what I had expected.' And then, with unexpected humility said, 'I was a powerful man but your film has made me realise that I could have been a better human being. I could have done much more. Do me a favour. Don't tell anyone that the character is based on me. I feel embarrassed.'

Ratnam respected Vardha's last wish, but less than three months later, Mudaliar died of cardiac arrest. His death set off scenes of mourning that topped anything a film director could have imagined.

Vardha's one-time boss, Haji Mastan, chartered an aircraft and flew to Chennai from Mumbai to collect his body. In Matunga, shopkeepers downed their shutters (cynics said that Varadarajan's gangsters forced them to) and tearful mourners thronged the streets for a last glimpse of the don's body.

Sunday, 21-7 February 1988

Three months later, Raj Kapoor, the irrepressible showman, maker of dreams and the last emperor of the movies, passed away. He was only 64.

Raj Kapoor Dies

'I want you to be the hero of my next film,' Dr S.S. Sahni, professor of anasthesia at the AIIMS, wasn't sure that he had heard right. Was Raj Kapoor, India's greatest movie director, really offering him a role? He would never find out. It was three weeks since Kapoor had been admitted to the AIIMS in a serious condition and all his body systems seemed to be failing one after the other. He had all but lost the ability to speak. Nine days after he entered the hospital, a tracheotomy was conducted and his neck slit just below his chin so that a tube could be inserted into his lungs. This had the effect of restricting his speech and so the doctors planted a small electronic gadget, no bigger then a microchip, into his throat. This device was called a Ventrivoice and it had the effect of registering his lip movements into sound. It was through the Ventrivoice that Kapoor would communicate with his doctors and his family, though most of the time he was too weak to say much more than 'Good morning'. So when he apparently offered Sahni a role, nobody was sure if he meant it. Sadly, those were the last words Kapoor ever spoke.

It had been a tense, worrisome month. On 2 May, television-viewers who tuned to Doordarshan's national news broadcast were distressed to see an obviously unwell Kapoor struggling for breath as he accepted the Dadasaheb Phalke award for outstanding cinematic achievement from President R. Venkataraman at the National Film Awards. Later, the same evening, it was announced that he had been rushed to the AIIMS for medical treatment. Within the Kapoor family there was gloom. The decision to attend the awards function had been taken after much deliberation. Nobody had forgotten how Prithviraj Kapoor had also won the same award and had then died before he could collect it. Raj had ended up accepting the award for him. To the superstitious Kapoors, the Phalke award symbolised bad luck and attempts were made to dissuade Raj—already in poor health—from flying to Delhi to receive it. But he overruled the objections, insisting that to refuse to turn up would be to insult the President of India and went off to Delhi along with his family.

When he had his asthma attack at the auditorium, the family's fears seemed confirmed. And yet, ironically, he would probably have died instantly, had he not been at the awards function. Doctors attending on Kapoor contended that if he had had the same kind of attack at his residence in the Mumbai suburb of Chembur, he would not have survived the drive to the nearest well-equipped hospital. At the National Awards, however, the President of India's ambulance (which always forms part of Venkataraman's entourage) was available. Kapoor was rushed into it and para-medics began to give him oxygen on the drive to the AIIMS itself. Within half an hour of the attack he had been intubated and put on an artificial respirator as a life-saving measure.

The swift action saved his life that night and after that Kapoor's own body took up the battle. Says Dr J.N. Pandey, assistant professor of medicine at the AIIMS who headed the team treating Kapoor, 'Anyone else in his place would not have survived for 24 hours. He was a tough fighter.'

The problem was that Kapoor had too many medical complications. On 2 May, when he was admitted to the AIIMS, he was already close to death: his lung passages were severely obstructed and he had acute bilateral pneumonia. Doctors attacked the pneumonia with antibiotics and on 6 May, Kapoor began to respond to treatment. This caused some optimism but efforts to take him off the respirator failed.

For a while, it seemed that he would cheat death. But at 3.30 p.m. on Thursday, 2 June, Raj Kapoor's heart stopped beating. Word got out quickly. The Press Trust of India (PTI) announced his death and so did the Mumbai station of Doodarshan. Ever since the moghul had taken ill a month earlier, his condition had been critical, and the news was not a surprise. Nevertheless, doctors at the All Indian Institute of Medical Sciences (AIIMS) in New Delhi, following standard procedure, tried to revive him. An external pacemaker was connected to his body and a long transvenous electrode was inserted from his thigh to the right trium in his heart. As the machine thumped life into him at the rate of 120 beats per minute, the incredible happened. Kapoor's heart started beating again.

Then it stopped. The doctors revived it once more. It stopped again. The heartbeat was brought back. This went on for an anxious ten-minutes during which his heart stopped beating five times. Each time, Kapoor's body, assisted by the pacemaker, fought back. Finally at 5.30 p.m., after two hours of treatment, the doctor felt able to turn off the machine. Kapoor's heart continued to beat without assistance. He was alive. As the message went out to the news agencies the obituaries were withdrawn. Doordarshan was told to correct itself. The director of the AIIMS read a prepared statement into the television cameras. Raj Kapoor's condition, he said, was critical. But no, he was not dead. The master showman had come back from death's door and his body was fighting the severe illnesses.

Alas, it was too good to be true. Finally, harsh reality intruded into the movie-like magic of the dream-maker cheating the reaper. At 8 p.m., Kapoor's blood pressure began to drop. It was a sure sign that he was losing the battle. As all his vital indicators dropped dangerously low over the next hour, doctors told the family that it was all over. After a month-long grapple with illness, Raj Kapoor's body was giving up. By now, the whole country was concerned about the moghul's health and the corridor outside his AIIMS room was full of well-wishers, politicians and virtually the entire Mumbai film industry. As messages of support came pouring in, so did unsolicited packages of alleged 'miracle' drugs, Ayurvedic medicines, good luck charms, vials of *vibhuti* and *taaviz*. The Kapoor family, God-fearing as always, bedecked the patriarch's bed with all the *taaviz* and charms and hoped for the best.

Alas, things got worse from that point on. His muscles develop a marked weakness and doctors became reconciled to keeping him on the respirator. Next, a state of polyneuritis set in. Then, all of Kapoor's old health complaints (gout and heart disease among them) began giving cause for concern. As is inevitable with prolonged artificial respiration, his kidneys began to fail till finally there was complete renal failure.

For the family, the final days were torture. Kapoor's three actor sons, Randhir, Rishi and Rajiv had flown in from Mumbai as had his two brothers, Shammi and Shashi. All of them kept vigil at his bedside, rarely leaving the hospital and using the empty room next to Raj's (kept for the family by the AIIMS authorities) to rest. His two daughters, Ritu (married to Escorts managing director Rajen Nanda) and Rima, his favourite (he would call her 'my production controller') refused to move out of the hospital and his wife, Krishna, began to visit temples, *sadhus* and *dargahs*, hoping to find the miracle that was eluding her husband's doctors. She was told by astrologers that Raj would live out the month of May, but not last much longer after that. Nevertheless, she feared that he would die on 25 May, Prithiviraj Kapoor's death anniversary and steeled herself for that day.

Kapoor lived through the 25th of May, but the grim messages from the doctors were compounded by the bad taste displayed by the media. Sensation-hungry editors printed obituaries of Kapoor, even as he battled for his life, figuring that he would probably die by the time their issues hit the stands. The family was disheartened by this foolish behaviour and Krishna now began to get paranoid about Thursdays, which she said had always been bad days for her husband. The entire family fasted on every Thursday and waited for the worst, given her resolve that he would die on a Thursday.

As Kapoor's body began to give way, the kidney failure was combined with a liver failure and he developed severe jaundice. Septicaemia spread to his lungs and his heart seemed to be giving way. Around 26 May, doctors came to the conclusion that multiple organ failure was imminent. In effect, this meant that all hope had vanished. Finally, on 2 June, after he had been put on dialysis Kapoor suffered the five cardiac arrests that led to his death that night. It was exactly one month since he had been rushed to the AIIMS from the National Awards ceremony.

And yes, it was a Thursday.

After the first false alarm about Kapoor's demise, the film industry refused to believe any rumours till Doordarshan confirmed the news half-way through it's 9.30 p.m. news broadcast. After that, everything stopped for Raj Kapoor. A party to celebrate the release of Mahesh Bhatt's *Kabzaa* at a suburban hotel was just getting into high gear when news of Kapoor's death arrived; most guests simply went home. Elsewhere in the industry, stars and moghuls parked themselves by their phones and jammed the trunklines trying to find out details of the funeral from Delhi. Some of Rishi Kapoor's closest friends, among them Jeetendra, drove straight to the airport and took the last flight to the capital. Rajesh Khanna, who was already in Delhi, rushed to the AIIMS and helped with the arrangements.

At 5.45 a.m. the next morning, a specially chartered plane carrying Kapoor's body arrived at Mumbai's Santa Cruz airport. To receive the body were collected hundreds of the late showman's fans, close friends and assorted film personalities. The family was escorted to a waiting bus in hushed silence and left for home immediately.

From 11 a.m. onwards, the house was packed with visitors. Politicians such as H.K.L. Bhagat and Saroj Khaparde (who had accompanied the body from Delhi) and many Maharashtra leaders, including chief minister Shankar Rao Chavan and Bombay Congress chief Murli Deora all came. Virtually the entire film industry showed up. Amitabh Bachchan and Manmohan Desai were in Kashmir, shooting for *Ganga Jamuna Saraswati* when they heard the news. They chartered a plane and flew to Mumbai for a day. Bachchan, solemn in dark glasses, sat quietly near the body. Dharmendra, who had also flown down from a shooting schedule in Kashmir, wept uncontrollably remembering the director who had given him one of his best roles in *Mera Naam Joker*.

At 3 p.m. the body was taken to RK Studios for *darshan*. The short distance from the family residence to the studio was jam-packed with fans and mourners and over 1,000 policemen, personally supervised by deputy police commissioner P.S. Pasricha (police commissioner V.K. Saraf was there as a mourner, so was former director-general Soman), were unable to keep the crowds from completely dislocating all traffic. After the cortege entered RK Studios the gates of the studio were shut and hundreds of enterprising fans pleaded with the guards to let them in. At 5.30 p.m. the procession left the studio for the Chembur crematorium. Thousands of fans joined Kapoor's friends and colleagues and by the time the procession reached the massive, 30-foot stage on which the body was to be placed, its size had swelled immeasurably. Randhir, Raj's eldest son, lit the funeral pyre while Vedic *mantras* were chanted and as the flames enveloped the body, the crowd shouted, 'Raj Kapoor *amar rahe*.'

In the background, the sun was setting and when they lit the pyre, the flames just spread in all directions. It was an eerie moment, quite like his own film *Aag*. How appropriate that a showman like him should have such a dramatic exit. Kapoor would have approved of the imagery. As he himself once said, 'If you can't go in style, don't go at all.' It seemed a fitting end to a man who had lived life in 70 mm and technicolour.

Sunday, 12-18 June 1988

Funerals are reflective of human behaviours. In the film industry, even more so. A predictable pattern of expression and attitudes follow. Tear-stained mourners arrive with cliched words of consolation. It would be unfair to undermine their pain. As artistes, they are an emotional lot but all moments, happy or sad, can be sustained only upto a point. A stubborn domesticity takes over after a while. As hours went by and the men folk carried the body to the crematorium, it was time to attend to hungry servants, cranky children and exhausted relatives. It was dusk and we were all upstairs, in Rima Kapoor's room—Neetu putting little Riddhima to sleep and Babita feeding *dahi chawal* to Bebo. Exhaustion has a way of bringing down defences. We spoke on disconnected topics. Rima recalled her hospital days with papa and how he had regressed completely and fought with the nurses because he wanted cheese on his toast. 'Whenever I was in conflict, I always went to papa. Somehow he always had a solution,' said daughter-in-law Neetu. 'That's right,' confirmed Babita. 'Whenever I was low, he somehow knew it. He always phoned at the right time. I wanted Dabboo to be like his father.'

Krishna Kapoor was in the room as well. Surrounded by well-wishers and cushioned by attendants but still devastated! This is the other mystery on occasions like these. The bereaved more often than not chooses a complete stranger for a cathartic outburst. On that evening too, something similar happened. I happened to stop by Krishna Kapoor to say goodbye, when she held my hand and broke down. It didn't matter that we weren't exactly friends, that we would never meet again, that she was reacting more to her memories. What mattered was the moment, her grief. 'The older he grew,' she said tears streaming down her face, 'the more stubborn he became. In his later years he was worse than a child. When he got upset with me, he wouldn't talk to me for days. At the same time, he wanted me to be around him all the time. So despite sulking with me he would make some excuse or the other to summon me to the dining table when he was eating his food. He could never eat his food alone. If he had his way, he would invite the entire neighbourhood everyday. He was a man of *mehfil* and enjoyed a full house. As the children got older and moved on their separate ways, we became more and more dependent on each other's company. His childishness amused me sometimes. And sometimes I got angry. This huge, burlish man had begun to behave like a teenager. He would make blank calls to me from outdoors. His ego wouldn't permit him to talk when he was fighting with me so he'd make silly excuses, phone and ask me to send more clothes or papers left on the table. At home, he was forever cooking up excuses to summon me from my room, 'Nal mein pani nahin hain . . . memsaab ko bulao,' or 'Mali nahin aaya hai . . . garden ki haalat dekho.' He could go for shootings or sit at the R.K. office, but he wanted me in the house when he was home. 'It will never be the same again,' Krishna Kapoor said sadly, 'Every part of this house has a story. We have sat at this dining table drinking tea, reading our separate papers, without words because even silence was so comforting.' She was right. The house was never the same after Raj Kapoor's demise. The white cottage in Deonar that lent glamour to all of Chembur wasn't a distinguished address anymore.

Sadly, stories of the studio being mortgaged began to circulate soon after. The brothers vehemently denied the rumours which as time went by, died down gradually. Krishna Kapoor, though not completely recovered, learnt to lead a normal life and her sons helped her. Contrary to what I had expected, I bumped into the lady-in-white from time to time. At Amjad Khan's condolence meeting, Shammi Kapoor's jagrata or producer Bubbles Behl's trial show of Aisi Bhi Kya Jaldi Hai, based on the story of Steve Martin's Father of the Bride, Krishna Kapoor and I sat next to each other, sharing a bottle of Bisleri and a box of tissues.

It was a ladies show and all of us cried non-stop through the screening. During the interval, everyone turned nostalgic and discussed their daughters' weddings. Krishna Kapoor had a story too. Raj Kapoor apparently had behaved the same way when they confirmed their first-born, Ritu's engagement. 'When we got home, he was so upset that he started yelling at the servants for no rhyme or reason. In the following weeks, everytime we had to visit my daughter's in-laws, or they were coming over, he was looking for excuses to get out of the meeting. It was so embarrassing. He just could not adjust to the idea of becoming a father-in-law. And more important, of giving away his favourite girl to another man. '*Kya ghar chod ke chali jayegi hamari bachchi?*' he would ask me again and again. And as she said this, Krishna Kapoor wept again.

13

F OR FOUR YEARS I'd been driving down Worli Seaface, staring at the sunset at 6 p.m., wondering how many more years I could go through with the same routine. There was an anxiety within me and a strange restlessness was creeping in. I don't know when exactly the rot set in, but my relationship with *Movie* had reached a stalemate. My joint-editor and I, with our contrasting outlooks, should have churned out a sensational product. Instead, the magazine was a compromise between her perspective and mine. The smallest decision needed a consultation and patience has never been one of my virtues. It was during a casual meeting with Maulik Kotak and Bharat Kapadia, publishers of *Chitralekha* at the coffee shop of Palm Grove Hotel that the idea of a new magazine cropped up. We were talking about the power of positive journalism. I emphasised the importance of a visual magazine. Kotak pulled out a copy of a foreign magazine, *Hero*. 'You mean something like this?' he asked. 'Like this!' I echoed, flaunting my own copy of the same magazine.

My association with the group went back more than a decade. When I started writing for them in the seventies, I was paid Rs. 50 per article, then Rs. 75, then 100 and so on. If I continued writing for the group even after I took over the editorship of *Movie*, its because its difficult to say 'no' to Madhuri Kotak, the dignified owner of *Chitralekha*.

The job offer followed a few months later. Initially, I didn't take the proposal seriously. The publishers and I met a couple of times, brainstormed, but that was about all. They got back to me again in August 1989 and asked me if I was ready for the challenge. I wasn't sure. But I was sure that I had outgrown *Movie* and the time had come for me to move on. I remembered a memorable column by veteran journalist, M.V. Kamath. He had written that whenever he had to make a crucial decision he weighed the pros and cons on paper. A mental calculation, he analysed, could misfire but when you put things on paper, you're clairvoyant. I never forgot that.

I jotted down my points and by the end of it, I had made up my mind. I phoned Pammi to inform her of my decision. She said she was quitting the job as well. She was getting married next month. If my problem was joint-editorship, *Movie* could now be exclusively my baby. I didn't want to re-consider. My next problem was how to break the news to my publisher. I phoned Deepak Mirchandani for an appointment to tender in my resignation. *Chitralekha* wanted me to sign a contract immediately and I thought it unethical to do so before I had resigned from my present job. Mirchandani was leaving for London that evening. He suggested I postpone the decision for a while. He emphasised that this would be my second mistake. The first was, when I left to join Rauf Ahmed at the *Times of India*. 'Let me get back from my trip and we'll talk.' I didn't want to wait. There were no second thoughts.

I don't remember much about my last day at *Movie*. I had started packing days in advance and there was nothing dramatic about the goodbyes. Years of working had turned me pragmatic and I believed that no emotion could be sustained for too long. As weeks went by, I settled in my new routine. At the new office, I went through my gamut of anxieties as I adjusted to new people and a new environment. There were highs and lows, moments of excitement and moments of agony. Those were desperate weeks of preparations and promises, of commitment and confusion. I had imagined that I would miss my old office. I had been travelling to the same address for almost eight-and-a-half years, but I surprised myself.

Before starting on my new job, I took a short vacation to

visit my native place in Ahmedabad. I have always turned to the city at all critical moments in my life. Ten days of complete relaxation at my sister's home and I was rejuvenated for action. I joined the *g* office on 10 October 1988. It was Dassehra and there was a small *puja* at the Press. Its been an old custom with the group to celebrate all major festivals with their workers. The other annual traditions the group religiously observes are, a Satyanarayan and Ganpati *puja*, and Dhanteras, which falls on the day before Diwali. For a month, until the present Andheri office was ready, my art-director, P.G. Ghawali and I functioned from the head office at Vaju Kotak Marg, near the G.P.O. at V.T. The teething problems were many, but we survived with each other's support.

Call it ignorance, but I hadn't bargained for the problems involved in launching a new journal. Today, I'm not sure if I would take such a chance. Without a suitable team, I had dared to dream. A dream my art-director P.G. Ghawali and photographer Jayesh Sheth helped to realise. Eventually, the 'look' of any magazine depends on three people, the art-director, the photographer and the editor. The set-backs were many. The first came on the title. I wasn't excited about naming the magazine *Jee*. Forty years ago, the title had some social relevance. Founder-editor Vaju Kotak saw humour in this reverential form of address. For regional readers it still does but for an English audience, the title posed an identity crisis.

I had yet to resolve the conflict when one day, hunting for some number in my old telephone diary which had been compiled by my ex-secretary, Lucy Lewis, I noticed that she had registered *Jee* numbers under the alphabet g. That's how the title *g* came about. To prevent people from asking g for what, we came up with the three words commonly identified with the film industry—glamour, glory and grandeur. Using the logo on every alternate page was the art-director's idea. He felt we needed to familiarise our readers with the logo.

I don't think anyone expected the magazine to succeed. A

lot had to do with *Chitralekha* not being mainstream. That was the last of my fears. The publication was as old as the hills. A copy had been coming home ever since I was a child. Not just my parents, grandparents, aunts and uncles but my entire neighbourhood read the weekly. If I was unsure, it was of my own potential. What if I failed in the experiment? Eventually, I adopted the same attitude as my mother's. I'd give the magazine my best shot. If it didn't succeed, I'd opt out and do something else. My publishers tell me now, that in those days I would speak in hypotheticals. It was a defence mechanism. Deep down I know I am a survivor and can sustain relationships both personal and professional. On one of my birthday bashes I had invited photographer Rakesh Shrestha. He saw a group of people laughing heartily in a corner and remarked, 'The crowd there doesn't seem familiar.' When I told Rakesh they were my college friends, he was surprised. 'You mean to say you are still in touch with them?' He had his reasons. The film industry has a way of destroying your contacts. It takes over your life and routine like a jealous lover. That's its power. Also it's magic. And there is no escape.

A new breed was taking over the film firmament and re-establishing contact with yet another generation of stars was not going to be easy. My friends felt concerned about me because I was not social or gregarious enough to enjoy star company. Amidst all this chaos, the first issue was somehow ready. *g* was the first film magazine to introduce an editorial column and the first to launch a fashion feature at Rekha's suggestion. Now of course, every magazine has a few pages devoted to styling but we initiated it. During my EST training, many years ago, I had learnt that unless there is commitment, there is hesitancy and the desire to withdraw. We made a commitment too. No matter what the pressures, we promised not to succumb to yellow journalism.

The first year was a big high! Stars went out of their way to cooperate for photo-sessions. Photographer Jayesh Sheth, the man from Mulund, was suddenly the hot-shot guy of the glamour world. Our critics found fault in this too. They missed no opportunity to throw barbs at us. Their definition of aggressive journalism was bedroom stories. Discussing careers or analysing star performances wasn't significant. Well-wishers like Kamal Haasan phoned regularly to find out if we intended sticking to our claims. We did. Our agent advised us to carry Amitabh Bachchan on the cover of the premiere issue. He had a point but there were two major hitches. One, we had no Bachchan pictures. Two, Amitabh wasn't talking to the press. We had compiled a desk story, profiling the actor's past, present and future and interviewed Mehmood, Tinnu Anand and Shabana Azmi, but we still needed the picture for the cover.

I asked Shabana Azmi, shooting for *Main Azaad Hoon* those days, to put in a word to Bachchan for me. The appointment was confirmed on J.P. Dutta's set of *Bandhua*. Bachchan was extremely polite and courteous but unwilling to talk. 'I am under a contract where my lawyers have forbidden me to speak. Besides, nobody is really interested in what I say. I'm a boring man,' he drawled. If there was any other way he could help me, he added, he was willing. I asked him for some exclusive pictures. He agreed. I waited for over a week, but there was no sign of the pictures. Then, one exasperated morning, I was passing by his bungalow and decided to make one last attempt. There were just three more days for the magazine to go for printing and we had no cover. I must have been desperate, for I stopped the car and asked the watchman if *saab* was in. He nodded. I hunted in my bag for a piece of paper to scribble a note on. There was none. I found a tissue roll instead. It wasn't appropriate for the occasion but I was too stressed to be logical. I wrote Bachchan a brief note explaining that I wouldn't mind if he didn't give me the pictures, but he had to inform me so that I needn't wait.

The pictures came the next morning, just when I was giving up all hope, in a crisp yellow envelope neatly wrapped with tracing paper. He sent the pictures through Shabana

Azmi. He was horrified but also amused by my outburst the previous evening. 'Can your friend use a better letterhead next time?' he commented to Shabana. I made up for it when I wrote him a thank-you note.

When the Dutt family first discovered that daughter-in-law Richa Sharma was suffering from brain tumour, they were devastated! After Nargis, this was the last straw on their long list of tragedies. Those days Sunil Dutt spoke very highly of Richa. 'She is an asset to the family,' he said. 'Unlike my son, there is pride in her pain. Sanjay is terrified of crises. When he had to go through surgery a few years ago, he brought the whole house down! He'd phone me in the middle of the night from New York to say that he was very scared. He'd ask me again and again if I would make it in time for the operation. On the other hand, my daughter-in-law said, "Don't worry dad, everything is going to be fine."'

At Sloane Kettering Hospital, a few hours before the operation, the doctor, in the presence of the patient and all family members said, 'The tumour is malignant and in all probability it has spread to other parts of the body as well. It may affect her speech and other sensory organs. Do you still want to go ahead with the surgery?' There was a pause while the family exchanged nervous glances. It was Richa who broke the silence with, 'Yes,' then turning to everyone she said, 'Don't worry, I'll emerge a winner.' It was Sanjay who wheeled her into the operation theatre and broke down by her bed. Again, it was Richa who consoled him. 'I'm not going to give up so easily,' she said but the optimism faded as time went by. She put up a brave front, but she knew and so did everyone else, that she was sinking!

This was also the year when Kamal Haasan couldn't stop talking about *Apoorva Sahodarorgal* alias *Appu Raja*. A lot of time and money had been invested into the project. The discussions never stopped in fact—home, office, bedroom, car or the aircraft. Everywhere and always, it was Appu, Appu, Appu. The sets were ready and the dates confirmed. Every room of the Rajkamal International office was stacked with Appu props. Shooting began on schedule, but something was amiss. The unit had two options. To shut shop and rethink the idea or to continue shooting without conviction. Kamal preferred the former. Thus began a long journey to find the answers. There was a delay of weeks. Next time when Kamal returned to the sets, he was well-prepared. It could be because he had endured so much for it that Appu has a special place in Kamal's heart. When the film was released, everyone was keen to know how Kamal had turned himself into a midget. It was a secret he wasn't willing to impart. Except for the fact that foreign engineers worked on the concept, nobody knew the details. And to stop his critics from accusing him of hiding inside dug up ground, Kamal made sure to mostly shoot outdoors and take long shots. A year later, when the actor won the best actor award from the then chief minister MGR, Kamal appeared in his Appu costume. That's when he confessed that it was the most difficult film of his career. That at one point he was diffident, demoralised and that Appu almost didn't happen.

Letter to an unborn child

October 1983, Mumbai

Dear Appu,

The first time I think of you is while shooting for *Saagar*. It's a hot day on the Madh Island set and I'm feeling bored, waiting for my shot. I visualise you as someone resembling Charlie Chaplin. Late at night, when everyone is asleep, I sketch you in my little notebook but because I'm no artist, you resemble an egg.

December 1983, Chennai

Dear Appu,

These days you seem to be my only friend. Whenever I'm sad, under pressure, thoughts of you calm me down. And like a good friend, you always pop up at the oddest moments.

July 1987, Mumbai

Dear Appu,

My shooting is cancelled due to heavy rain and I come home early. I'm sitting on my bed, watching one of Peter Seller's *Pink Panther* movies. There is a brief sequence about a dwarf. Until now I had believed that you were solely mine. I feel a sense of loss. As if a favourite toy has been taken away from me.

January 1988, Chennai

Dear Appu,

I have just realised something. If I want my dreams to come true I cannot work in isolation. If I want you to come out of the closet, I have to share you with a confidante. I do. K. Balachander's assistant and director of *Satya*, Anantakrishnan. They are curious but not convinced. Probably, the fault lies with me. In my excitement, I'm unable to communicate clearly. I need to know you sufficiently to be able to introduce you to strangers.

February 1988, Chennai

Dear Appu,

I cut figures of you out of cardboard and make a video film. Later, I show the video cassette to Balachander. He looks enchanted but unsure. Only one man is optimistic. Anantakrishnan. 'The subject has promise,' he emphasises. 'No matter what the pressures, we mustn't give up the film.'

May 1988, Chennai

Dear Appu,

I have been speaking a lot about you to my director Sangeetam. I have great regards for him. He has a barrage of questions about you—'How come you were born a dwarf? Are your parents and siblings midgets too?' There are many more questions to which I have no answers. Maybe you do.

June 1988, Chennai

Dear Appu,

The endless rounds of coffee and the nerve-racking discussions is making everyone sick! We have been talking for days but there is no progress. Eventually, we bring in a catalyst—a simple story-teller. A writer who has given hit films, who knows the public pulse. No complications. No traps.

June 1988, Chennai

Dear Appu,

It's two months, but the script isn't ready. It will be, I tell myself. In the meanwhile, I'm meeting engineers who are working on turning me into a midget. I have shown them my diagrams and all the funny things I did with you on cardboard. They are optimistic. We perform the *mahurat* and begin shooting. One, two, three days pass without problems. On the surface, everything is moving fine, but deep within me, I know something is terribly wrong. On the seventh day, I drop the bomb! I tell the unit that we will have to stop shooting. Nobody protests, which means everyone agrees. The cameras are shut, reflectors lifted, lights switched off and artistes packed off. Only a group of us stay back—the director, the producer, the cameraman, the writer and myself. We talk till late into the evening, but in the end, we still don't have a solution.

July 1988, Chennai

Dear Appu,

A four lakh set is ready but there is no shooting. To avoid rumours, we put up a 'Visitors not allowed' board. People think we are starting a trend. If only they knew the truth! Weeks later, we meet to watch the projection of the video film. This is our third attempt. At the end of the screening director Arunachalam says, 'Okay. Give me two days and I will get back.' He does. Extracting a crumpled piece of paper from his pocket, he says the beauty of the film is its simplicity. 'Do not give the smaller role to Appu just because he is not handsome. Appu is your hero! And it is Appu who will get the claps.' After this, he reads out the story idea—it's a very common idea—about two brothers separated in childhood. This time, I know instinctively that it's going to work.

November 1988, Chennai

Dear Appu,

To carry the mantle of the first dwarf is exciting, even if the burden is killing. Everytime you feature in the scene, all hell breaks loose! Primarily because of the height problem. Everything, including the camera, has to move on ground level. A standing joke on the sets is, 'When Kamal Haasan comes down, the props go up.' The film is over-budgeted by Rs. 20 lakhs. We shoot the climax in the circus gallery. The only way to avoid accusations is to shoot outdoors.

January 1989, Chennai

Dear Appu,

We have star tantrum on the sets. The dog. The mid-summer heat is driving him mad. We send him for a drive in my A.C. car, feed him an ice-cream. Do you blame us for taking 110 days to complete this film?

February 1989, Chennai

Dear Appu,

It's time to say good-bye. The film is a big, big hit. The kind we never anticipated but with every happy moment, comes a sad one. My parting with you. I've taken care never to get attached to my characters. The affair with an old film is best forgotten. I cannot say that about you. I created you, after all. You will always remain special. That I am your mother will remain a fact neither of us can deny.

g, August 1989

A few months later, distributor Rajan Lall released the Hindi version of *Appu Raja* in Mumbai. A grand premiere was organised at Mumbai's Gaiety theatre. Sarika, Kamal and their daughter Shruti flew down from Chennai for the screening. It was their first public appearance since Sarika had left Mumbai and had the baby. The theatre entrance was done up in flowers and coloured lights. But the surprise packet was the group of midgets brought from the circus. Later, the midgets were called on stage and presented with roses and balloons. It was a great idea but poorly executed. Almost all the bigwigs turned up for the show. The press wasn't invited. Kamal Haasan had not forgiven the journalists for writing all that they had about his wife.

An unknown PRO came to our office one wet afternoon and left behind a packet of publicity pictures. In magazine offices nobody pays much heed to such packets till it is time to clear the trays. The packet, we discovered, contained large colour prints of Dimple and Sunny Deol in romantic poses and some showed them kissing on the mouth. My first reaction was that there had been a mistake. The packet couldn't have been meant for me. So we traced the PRO to confirm if the packet was for *g* magazine. He confirmed it was. As coincidence would have it, Dimple was on our cover that month and we were in fact composing the pages of the interview that very day. We used the pictures with no reference to Sunny Deol but with a caption giving credit to the film. They were scoop pictures and we could have used them on the cover with sensational headlines. Sunny Deol wasn't grateful to us. It was the day of the cyclone. I was at home when Sunny phoned and started hollering. Deol raved and ranted, threatened to flex his muscles and finally banged the phone warning me to never come in his presence ever again.

I wrote a scathing editorial on his behaviour which made him more angry. 'She should have been grateful that I didn't

SUNNY DEOL

Deol raved and ranted on the phone

break her bones,' he told a common friend. It surprised me how he never thought of breaking the producer's bones, without whose permission the pictures could never have travelled to my office. Stars repeatedly do this. They will shoot kissing scenes for a film but when the film is due for release, they develop cold feet. The episode instilled fearlessness in me and Deol unwittingly proved the catalyst.

The year was 1989 and one late evening, a friend who lived in Kalumal Estate, Juhu, phoned to say that Parveen Babi was back! Memories flooded my mind. Jeetendra's outburst with secretary Ved Sharma. Sharma's weak defences to the press, wild stories of Parveen's paranoia, the day she began howling in the middle of a shot and wouldn't stop crying. When shooting for Prakash Mehra's *Jwalamukhi*, she wouldn't come on to the sets because she insisted that the chandeliar was going to fall on her. In the years she was missing, more ugly rumours made the rounds. Some said she was living with a Sheikh, some said she had lost her memory, was penniless and hooked on to drugs and some even said she had been found dead on the streets of Geneva. After all these horror stories, this was indeed happy news. I couldn't believe the news that Parveen was alive, hale and hearty and back where she belonged.

Two hours later, I was at the door of the familiar building. As I waited for the door to open, I felt nostalgic. I remembered my innumerable sphagetti lunches and discussions on J. Krishnamurthy with Parveen. A servant boy opened the door. I gave my name. He asked me to wait, then shut the door. A few minutes later, she emerged. The woman before me was unrecognizable. Plump, with frizzy hair, she was a far cry from the lily in the woods I once knew. She smiled. The old familiar smile, 'Come on in,' she drawled. The accent was unmistakeable. As I followed her down the long passage, part shocked and part in despair, more surprises awaited me. The living-room which had once blossomed with colourful cushions and warm lights looked drab and dilapidated. There were scraped wall paintings, moth-eaten sofas and cobwebs on the ceiling. There was a strong musty, smell typical of a house which has remained closed for a long time. All the air-conditioners, fans and phones had been packed and transferred to her new bungalow. Parveen was using this flat as transit accommodation.

This was truly a new woman. The actress who was once obsessed with her image, didn't care today what impression her house or her face created. She had a project to accomplish and she wasn't going to waste time. The project, one soon discovered was to expose Amitabh Bachchan! She had chalked out his character traits and was going to give elaborate discourses on him. She sat with a thick pad of hand-written foolscap sheets—her story on the man. She also kept a tape-recorder, a diary and a pen by her side and wrote down the name, address and telephone number of every journalist who visited her. Systematically and sticking labels, she changed tapes and recorded every piece of conversation with every member of the fourth estate. In an ill-ventilated room without fans or air conditioners, she talked non-stop for hours, an unconnected, irrelevant bizarre monologue. It was clear that she was obsessed. Obsessed to the point of destruction. How and what Amitabh ate, what he drank, how he sat. She said he manipulated women, was the cause of Jaya's and all his heroine's low self-esteem. All the trade and transport in the country were manoeuvred by him. He controlled the finance, made political decisions in India and had put spies on her. Wherever she travelled, he spoke to her through the television and deliberately put horror films on the cable because he knew it scared her. She wanted to return to films, but he wouldn't let her. The only way she could survive was to stay away from films, be away from India. She showed me a scar on her right cheek (the scar disappeared mysteriously) which was the result of physical abuse by him. 'The last time I went to the hospital, he installed a transmitter inside my ear. This way he can keep tabs on everything I say and to whom.'

The room was packed with journalists and even though everyone enjoyed the madness initially, after a while they couldn't take it. Everyone wanted to return to office to compile the story but Parveen wouldn't stop and so nobody was allowed to budge. It was the funniest encounter of my career—a group of journalists sitting on the carpet, scribbling and passing notes to each other. Four hours later, I thought I'd faint if I didn't leave instantly. I needed some fresh air desperately. On the staircase I met a fresh group of photographers and journalists who were going up for the same story. For the next few weeks, the press only talked about Parveen Babi. It was not so much what she said but what she did that was hysterical. She walked to a xerox shop and sat there for three hours making copies of her 100 page thesis on Bachchan. On another occasion she went to the office of a film magazine in town and sat there all night making more zerox copies of the same thesis. She made sure to distribute the chapters of the unpublished book to various publications. 'I'm the sole copyright holder of my autobiography,' she said. 'I'm a better actress today than when I left, but there will be no way of testing it because he (Bachchan) and his mafia connections will destroy everything I touch. He will put a spoke in the wheel of my new career as an interior designer.'

I had carried her outburst in our sister publication *Chitralekha*, but made no mention of it in *g*. This annoyed her. A year later, I was attending a dance recital at the Nehru Planetarium and met Parveen. She was standing all alone, staring into space looking quite lonely, so I decided to chat with her. She said icily, 'You are a spy of Amitabh Bachchan's and I don't wish to talk to you.' After that I lost all touch with Parveen. From time to time I would read about her progress in interiors, her loss of weight, her change in name and wardrobe and her views on paintings and architecture. She lambasted Mahesh Bhatt for making a film on her life—

Arth. The blitz lasted a year. Then gradually the media lost interest in Parveen Babi. Only one man remained loyal to her, secretary Ved Sharma. All through her career, the good and the bad phases, he stuck by his madam. He faked illnesses for her from ordinary flu to jaundice then allergy and finally nervous breakdown! Not until his madam was out of the country did he let out the true cause of her ailment.

Even when she first returned and it seemed impossible to stage a comeback, the secretary got her plum assignments. The film industry forgave her past crimes, like they had forgiven Vinod Khanna who left films for Rajneesh. But Parveen Babi betrayed her producers once again. A few years ago Ved Sharma, working for actress Gautami now, stopped by our office. Still loyal to madam, he said, 'It's a pity that things ended the way they did. I never expected her to return after so many years and start a tirade against Amitabh Bachchan. That man did so much for her. He got her the maximum films with him and it was because of him that she rose to the top bracket and was considered a top league star. Her success wouldn't have been possible without him but she kicked the same ladder that helped her to climb up. So sad!'

14

g MAGAZINE HAD completed one year. We sent a copy of the annual to Amitabh Bachchan in acknowledgement of his adorning our first cover. It was a gesture I have never regretted. The same evening I received a surprise call from the actor to thank me for the complimentary copy. Since film-folk seldom acknowledge gestures, I appreciated the effort that Bachchan had made. Bachchan's lifting of the ban on the press followed subsequently. Initially, the megastar seemed awkward and ill-at-ease when dealing with the fourth estate. Slowly, however, he became a master at the media game. He met a dozen journalists everyday and they came from Japan to Jhumritalaya. On an average, at least, three interviews appeared daily. He knew all there was to know about journals, journalism and journalists.

Minutely observant, he had interesting insights on the art of interviewing and how journalists conducted them. 'It's not possible for any critic to be completely unbiased. It's not likely that their personal preferences will not interfere with their copy.' He was the first to talk about the media's selective perceptions. And to prove it during the Bofors case. He cited examples to show how the insinuations always came in big headlines on the front page—while the clarifications were given in small print in a remote corner of the third page. Not all observations were as serious though. He was amused and intrigued at how every journalist who visited him was paranoid about the tape-recorder. 'When something is very precious, one is scared of spoiling it.' Objective and accessible, he did not discriminate between the small reporter and the popular columnist. Wife Jaya made wisecracks about her husband's new pastime. She said her husband was so busy giving interviews that he didn't feel the need to return to films.

Nobody will ever know what made Bachchan talk to the press after avoiding it for over a decade. He had taken a risk when he decided to drop his defences. But the outcome was worth the gamble. The truce was more emotional than controversial. When the press confronted him with bottled up queries, they were more sentimental than accusatory. The outburst proved therapeutic for both! He had been their forbidden fruit for fifteen years and they were not going to let him off so easily. In the privacy of their office, journalists put forward different versions of what had led to the ban. The stories have changed so many times over the decade, that one still doesn't know the truth. Editors working at that time have retired, subordinates taken over, but the puzzle continues. Some say that the ban was imposed when troubled stars got together to jointly protest against bedroom journalism. A confidential meeting was called where everyone agreed to the boycott. That same night, somebody from the group leaked the secret to the press. Before the stars could boycott them, the press decided to boycott the stars. Or rather one star. Amitabh Bachchan. Deceived and betrayed by his own colleagues, Amitabh decided that he wouldn't talk to anyone in the media.

Photographers constantly hung around his sets. Magazines used these pictures to tell their side of the story. Then came the famous accident. Amitabh had reported for the shooting of Manmohan Desai's *Coolie* after a gap of six months. There was a large gathering on the set at Film City. Still recovering from the illness, the actor didn't wish to be clicked, but a new photographer, unaware of the history, clicked Bachchan all the same—that too in the middle of a shot. Those present on the sets say that Bachchan didn't say a word to the man. He just snatched away his camera roll. The Photographers Association decided to take the affront personally. An SOS meeting was called at the President,

Umesh Vyas' studio in Andheri and everyone agreed that nobody henceforth would click Bachchan.

Their moment of revenge came when a week later, at a public function, the photographers clicked everyone on the dias, but at the precise moment when Amitabh rose to address the audience, the lensmen shut their cameras! They had succeeded in humiliating the superstar collectively. Or so they thought. At Chandivali studio, 15 years later, it was the same actor and the same photographers. Amitabh stood outside his make-up room facing 15 lensmen standing in a row flashing their cameras non-stop. The film was Shashi Kapoor's *Ajooba*. 'Sir, please look towards your left . . .' 'Sir, towards your right . . .' 'Sir, please smile a little more . . .' they went on and on with their instructions. Amitabh smiled throughout. '*Arrey bas karo, kya karoge itni zyada tasveeron ka?*' he asked them jovially. '*Bahut kaam aayegi—chotti se chotti bik jayegi*,' they laughed. It was Bachchan's moment of triumph, but he preferred to let bygones be bygones. Bachchan's reconciliation with the photographers was even more emotional than it had been with the journalists.

If he suspected betrayal, he never revealed it. He spoke to everyone in the same tone. They asked him the same questions and he gave the same answers. The photographers got the same expression and yet nobody wanted to give up. Almost identical interviews with slight variations in titles and blurbs, appeared first in the dailies, then weeklies, followed by the fortnightlies and finally the monthlies. Everybody read everything and everyone knew all there was to know. And Amitabh wasn't willing to reveal all that much. Editors complained that he was over-exposed. Journalists complained that he made boring copy. Yet, week after week, month after month, journalists visited him and editors put him on their covers. Everyone advised him not to give so many interviews, but no one was willing to call a stop to it! Reason: Amitabh was saleable! If he went through phases when he didn't enjoy talking, he didn't show it. Once in a while, amidst the routine responses, came an odd quote that gave a glimpse of the real man. Most of the time, despite daily interviews, the floodgates of the heart remained neatly locked. After he made up with the press, his first film to be released was Mukul Anand's *Agneepath*. For the first time, all the magazine editors were travelling together for a premiere out of town. The flight to Calcutta was delayed by almost five hours and by the time the plane took off it was late afternoon. Bachchan walked down the aisle to apologise for the inconvenience caused. The gesture evoked mixed reactions and was the beginning of many controversies that followed.

On landing, we discovered that members of the Amitabh Bachchan Fan Club had gatecrashed right upto the tarmac. This annoyed the security. Outside, a crowd waited for the actor to emerge, but Bachchan wasn't allowed to meet them. The bus driving us to the hotel was parked close to the aircraft landing. The police had specific instructions to not let Bachchan travel by the regular route. The Fan Association complained it was an attempt at sabotage. 'They want us fans to go against him. They want his premiere to flop. It's all politics,' screamed the President of the Club. Thousands of fans who'd been waiting hungry and tired for hours had to return home disappointed. They came to see their hero the following morning at the hotel. Bachchan was summoned from his room and personally apologised to them.

The same evening the actor received threatening phone calls warning him against stepping out of the hotel. Producer Yash Johar had no choice but to cancel the party. Guest of honour, chief minister Jyoti Basu didn't turn up for the function, despite prior commitment. An impromptu party was organised in Bachchan's suite.

That was the first time one saw the other side of the actor. Jovial and with his defences down, he made a spirited host, looking after every guest personally. It was by far the most pampered outdoor. Precise to the minutest detail, he had gone to great lengths to make the guests feel special.

From the personalised stationery on the desk to the choco-late, flowers and champagne, it had a touch of class. Typed agendas were slipped into the rooms accompanied by polite reminders on the phone. Everyone travelled together in a bus with security guards trailing behind. The mood persisted till the end of the trip.

A year later followed Romesh Sharma's *Hum*. At the premiere function held in Delhi, Bachchan, put a wine glass in my hand and raising a toast said, 'Cheers'. 'But shouldn't this be had in a slender glass?' I asked. 'That's white wine. Red is always served in a globet,' Bachchan explained. If he was surprised, he didn't show it. I murmured something like an 'Oh' and tried not to look embarrassed.

Why is it that embarrassing moments in retrospect always seem funny? I recall an office party during my tenure at *Super*. It was nearing midnight and I was getting anxious. 'I want to go home just now,' I threw a tantrum. Publishers Namita and Rajiv Gokhale, confused by my behaviour, promptly organised transport. The matter was a topic for discussion for months at the office. This was no way for a professional to behave. Ten years later, in a joyous mood at the International Film Festival in Delhi, I was at producer Ramesh Jhindhal's party, surrounded by friends, when a familiar figure walked in. Our eyes met and we smiled simultaneously. It was Namita Gokhale and she looked visibly surprised. 'You are Bhawana, aren't you?' she asked. I nodded. 'One moment,' she said and excused herself. A minute later, she returned holding husband Rajiv's hand. 'Recognise her?' she said to him. He smiled uncertainly. 'She cried at our party because it was late and she wanted to go home.'

There was warmth and pride in their eyes. It was nice meeting the Gokhales after so many years. I would have hated them to remember me as the weepy reporter. At last, the impression had altered.

Writer-lyricist Javed Akhtar has a favourite anecdote about me. Sometime in the late seventies, Javed and his partner Salim Khan used to be permanent fixtures at Hotel Holiday Inn, Juhu. That's where they wrote their scripts. To stop by and meet Javed on that sunny afternoon was my colleague Pammi Bakshi's idea. Pammi was very friendly with the writer those days and insisted we have a cup of tea with him. We made an odd threesome. Pammi and Javed were in a boisterous mood. This wasn't the man I had imagined writing intense dialogues for Amitabh on screen. The man before me was a bag of tricks. I consoled myself that I had no sense of humour and felt relieved when the waiter arrived with the bill. Since this was our first meeting and Javed was virtually a stranger, I insisted on paying for my coffee. It's something he's never forgotten and rags me about to this day. Had I known that years later he would marry my best friend and repeat the story to every stranger, I'd have been more cautious. 'Remember the five rupee note you sent to my room?' he tells me even now. I do. Moral of the story: Never offer to pay for your coffee. And if you do, make sure the man does not marry your friend.

The only time I saw Boney Kapoor visibly disturbed was when brother Anil Kapoor hurt his foot during shooting. Since he had ruptured his ligament, Anil's shooting schedule went for a six as he was laid in bed for more than a month. Spread on the bed with a blanket over him, initially Anil Kapoor enjoyed himself thoroughly when his writers and directors dropped by. He was in a cheerful mood. The kids played hide and seek around the bedroom and a sentimental Sunita whispered, 'I'd forgotten what it felt like having my husband at home.' But when the holiday stretched from days to weeks and the foot refused to heal, an impatience crept into Anil.

Brother Boney had bigger problems weighing him down. Torn between guilt for producer D. Rama Naidu (*Rakhwala*) and concern for his brother, Boney buckled under the

ANIL KAPOOR
Anil worried endlessly about his delayed shooting

mounting pressures. Nobody mentioned it but there was an underlying tension in the house. And it was aggravated everytime the phone buzzed from Chennai. Everytime D. Rama Naidu's office called, Boney turned ashen-faced. It was the same story with the Mumbai producers. A pall of gloom descended on the house when the visitors left in the evening. Anil worried endlessly about his delayed shooting. So did Boney. It was the first time I saw Sunita make professional decisions. She couldn't understand the hysteria and fear about letting Rama Naidu know that it wouldn't be possible for Anil to report for work so soon. It wasn't as if Anil was being irresponsible or gambling at home. Accidents happen! And filmstars are human beings too!!

It took Anil a long time to drop his anxiety and use his free time constructively. He held story-sessions, saw lots of films, read a lot of books, introspected, reflected, analysed his life and career. Much later, when he was a little better, he hobbled on his crutches for dubbings. His two constant companions those days were the television and the phone, besides his secretary Rakeshnath. It was during this bed-ridden phase that he signed up for Viddhu Vinod Chopra's, *1942: A Love Story*. He watched the vintage films of Ashok Kumar and other actors of the silent era. Yash Chopra's *Lamhe* was also offered to him around the same time.

The idea of shaving his moustache and shedding weight for the early portion was Anil's own. From *Ek Baar Kaho* to *Rajkumar*, Anil earned the reputation of being extremely dedicated. He wasn't ashamed of making suggestions even if this made him unpopular. He wasn't hesitant in asking for a role, if he felt it was worthwhile. An absolutely anti-late night, anti-booze, fitness conscious, achievement oriented actor, he was the first amongst the new breed of stars to take his career seriously.

In the beginning Deepti Naval didn't take the minor dis-cords in her marriage seriously. Married in 1984, disillu-sioned in 1985, heartbroken in 1986, Deepti separated from Prakash Jha in 1987. Year 1988-9 was a turbulent year as Deepti struggled to live on her own. She had to bury memories of shattered dreams and resist fatal attractions. Unable to uproot herself from a soiled relationship and without courage for a new bond, Deepti finally put an end to her trauma by filing divorce papers. Prakash and she met at the Maurya Hotel coffee shop in Delhi. It was their favourite haunt. Many years ago, that's where the romance had blossomed and that's where the two finally said goodbye. Months later she said, 'We agreed on most things. There were no disputes, no arguments and most important, no complaints. Everything was so peaceful. I guess that's what relationships are all about. When you don't have any expect-ations there are no demands.' Deepti and Prakash accepted that their marriage had failed because they had failed. 'It's so strange, but divorce, to my mind, was an ugly word. But with Prakash, I knew it would all be very dignified.'

While Deepti was settling down to her new status as a single woman, the single girl everyone least expected to settle down had got married. In a whirlwind romance Rekha had got involved with industrialist Mukesh Agarwal in Delhi. The marriage was shrouded in mystery from the very beginning. The film industry was curious to the point of cruelty. Even before the bride could return from her honey-moon, the industry predicted doom! Call it irony, but the tragedy occurred three months later. Mukesh Agarwal, com-mitted suicide hanging himself from the ceiling fan with Rekha's *dupatta*. It was a burning scandal in Delhi and Mumbai. The more details one read and heard about the more macabre it seemed. Only a month before the actress had blushingly said, 'It's still too new to sink in, but it feels good. I feel happy. People had given up hopes. My family had begun to despair. But there's something like destiny. I'm the chosen one.'

The mainstream media made the most of it. The scandal justified their assessment of the film industry. For all its feeling of superiority over the film press, the mainstream press never misses an opportunity to cover a film story. Every Sunday supplement or magazine section carries a film column. And no matter what the profile of the paper, the film page is restricted to gossip items. That's how they perceive the entertainment world. It's another matter that everytime their sales dwindle, they put out pictures of glamorous stars to perk up circulation figures. That's what happened with the Rekha-Mukesh story as well. It was the most written about scandal of the decade!

To Hell And Back

3 October 1990. Rekha, on a flight to New York, is unusually quiet. Bhagyashree, one of the artistes accompanying her notices that Rekha has been weeping in her sleep. When she wakes up, Bhagyashree asks her if something is troubling her. 'Nothing,' smiles Rekha and goes back to sleep. By this time, news of Mukesh's demise has reached America but the sponsors do not think it inappropriate to receive the actress with a video team, photographers and press.

Assuming that Rekha and her troupe have heard about the death, the sponsors don't mention a word in the car enroute to the hotel. An hour later, in the privacy of her room, as Rekha is arranging her trunks secretary Farzana walks in. From Farzana's expression Rekha knows that there is bad news in store. But nothing in her wildest imagination could have prepared her for what Farzana has to say. Farzana breaks the news hesitantly. Rekha's first reaction is to hold her head and flop on the sofa. Salman Khan, Bhagyashree and the rest of the unit gather in the room. Rekha is silent for a long time. Her head throbs but she doesn't break down. Not with so many people in the room.

Around the same time, many miles away in Mumbai, a greater drama is unfolding at Rekha's Sea Spring residence in Bandstand. Rekha's old maid is howling on the phone to Farzana's sister Rehana. 'The police are here. They say that they have been sent by the Delhi police. They are threatening to enter the house. They insist that madam is hiding inside. I'm frightened.' Farzana's sister checks the clock. It is 3 a.m. She cannot run to the maid's help, but does so early the next day. She pacifies the servant that all will be well once Rekha returns home. It's not that simple. With every passing day, the atrocities increase. There are crank calls in the middle of the night. The voice on the phone says, 'We'll put her behind bars. Where is the witch?' As days go by the phone rings with more horrifying messages. Journalists, photographers, filmmakers, strangers ask the same questions, 'Where is Rekha? When is she returning? Where is she hiding?' Lensmen wait outside her house for days just in case she arrives at midnight. Magazines carry stories of Rekha holidaying in America, while her husband lies dead.

In America, the sponsors and organisers do not allow her to leave the country, unless she goes on stage. Their motives are clear.

They have sold the show and they want her to fulfil her commit-ments. To ensure that the actress does not run away, they slap a five-million dollar suit on her. No amount of pleas from Rekha or Farzana can make them see reason. 'She had divorced the man. How does his death affect her now?' they ask.

Rekha begs of them to let her go. 'I'll come back next month and we'll sort it out.' But they don't give in. There are heated arguments for days until contracts are signed and legal formalities completed. Finally, on 13 October, Rekha and her troupe leave for India.

g, November 1990

Rekha arrived home five days after her birthday and three days before Diwali. It wasn't a happy homecoming. The house that had been filled every 10 October with flowers, was barren. The garden that had been lit up like a bride on Diwali night was plunged into darkness. A very apt reflec-tion of Rekha's own life. Thank God Rekha didn't play the mourning widow. It was bad enough that she had agreed to settle down in an unequal match. Rekha had paid a heavy price for having gambled her life's most important decision with a stranger who was mentally imbalanced and who loved her obsessively, to the point of destruction.

When I met her weeks after the tragedy, a sentence she kept repeating over and over again was, 'It's a different world. These business families can live and die for their business.' While Mukesh was alive his family drew the maximum mileage out of her celebrity status. When he died, they used her betrayal to wash private linen in public.

The victimisation was more of Rekha than of Mukesh. Despite another woman in his life—his psychiatrist, Akash Bajaj—Mukesh got all the sympathy and Rekha all the condemnation. The actress becomes an easy suspect. After all these years, even today, every time one discusses Guru Dutt's suicide, a question often asked is—Did Waheeda

Rehman have a role to play in the tragedy? At that time it seemed as if the scars would never fade. There was a strong anti-wave against the actress—some called her a witch, some a murderess. Women's organisations even went and painted her film poster of K.C. Bokadia's *Phool Bane Angaarey* black. Fortunately, she wasn't in town to suffer the humiliation.

When she got back, the storm had to be weathered. One will never know how she endured her private hell. What made her survive? Calmpose, consolation, or the shoulders of dear friends, but Rekha came out of the eclipse once again unblemished! Only once and very briefly, I saw the armour drop. It was soon after the tragedy. She decided that she needed to give her side of the story, speak out once and for all. We met at Sea Bird, her old flat turned into an office. A few months ago we had met in the very same room, soon after her honeymoon. Dressed in a *tussar kurta*, her hair tied in a top knot, *maang* full of *sindoor* and arms adorned with gold bangles, she had blushed and played the new bride.

Today, she was in a white kurta and her eyes were vacant. She answered my questions in brief sentences. After half-an-hour of intense interrogation, we were still going around in circles, when suddenly, more out of exhaustion than pain, her eyes filled with tears. Just for a fraction of a second, Rekha broke down! Farzana, Rekha's secretary, who had been hovering in the background, heard the change in madam's voice and sprang into action protectively. Immediately, Rekha regained composure. The vulnerable eyes turned blank again. I'll remember those vacant eyes forever—the dark rings around them had a story to tell that only Rekha knew—now that Mukesh was dead!

When *Phool Bane Angaarey* was to be released, Rekha's popularity was at an all-time low. Her distributors developed cold feet but the fiery climax of Rekha riding on a horse silenced her detractors and revived the producer's faith in her. In a way I admire Rekha for not succumbing to the pressure and staying away from the *Filmfare* awards. Nobody expected her to attend the award ceremony, in the

REKHA

An actress is an easy suspect

wake of the ugly scandal. There was a hushed silence when she strolled in, escorted by Farzana. Days after the episode, spikey actresses discussed her flashy costume and said she was too garishly dressed for a new widow. She retorted that she didn't mourn for public pleasure. During our interview when I'd asked her how she viewed herself—as a widow or as a divorce, she had given me a cold stare and replied, 'As a human being.'

It must have something to do with the celestial stars, but 1991 proved an important year for three actresses in filmdom. Three jinxed romances culminated in marriage. Kiran Joneja, Tina Munim and Sarika. All of a sudden, Raksha, Ramesh Sippy's first wife granted him a divorce. The Ambanis dropped their objection to Tina being a film actress and Kamal Haasan was finally free of his legal and moral responsibilities to tie the nuptial knot. While the Ambanis had a grand affair, only a select few were invited for the Kamal-Sarika wedding. Close relatives and friends flew down to Chennai for the simple ceremony.

To keep up the excitement, Sarika slept in the ladies' room the night before the wedding. *Atti*, Kamal's father, ailing by now was brought on a wheel chair. Sarika was dressed in a *navvari* saree sent by Asha Bhonsle. Carried on a stool by four men, a tradition in Maharashtrian weddings, Sarika was brought to the garden amidst a lot of laughter and cheer. It was when the *pundit* began chanting the *mantras* and Kamal put the yellow thread strung with a *thaali* around her bent neck, that the long controlled tears rolled down. More tears threatened when he put *sindoor* into her *maang*. Suddenly, the dam burst and all the emotions repressed over the years were let loose. As she went through the ritual of touching the feet of the elders, my mind raced back. I remembered the time she told me she was carrying his baby. The time he told her he was marrying her no matter what the repercussions. The time they discovered and confessed love when they were both shooting in Ooty. It was a crazy outdoor. Sarika's unit packed up two days early, but she stayed back all alone in the hotel. Kamal was to arrive two days earlier but his schedule was upset when, due to heavy rains his flight got cancelled. On the second day, Sarika began to feel restless and was contemplating going back, but couldn't manage the tickets. She was lying on the bed, depressed, staring into the stormy night from her window, when there was a knock on the door. Assuming it was room service, she said, 'Come in' without looking. The door opened and a familiar figure entered the room, holding a bag and a coat in his hands. Kamal Haasan had driven all the way from Chennai to Ooty. He knew that she would be terrified to spend another day alone in a hotel. And this proved to be the night for confessions! Amidst fierce lightning and a power failure, Sarika told Kamal about her pregnancy.

Amrita Singh wasn't willing to admit to her marriage and militantly went about denying rumours linking her to Saif Khan. When I phoned to ask her if the reports were true, she said, 'Give me a break. He is so young. I don't understand why people assume it's love. Why is it so difficult to accept friendship?' Those days Saif Khan lived in his parents' home, Rashmi, at Carmichael Road and was not contactable on the phone. Amrita was expecting Saif Khan to drop by that evening at her home. Not realising that it was all stage managed, I walked into the trap when I dropped by to do a joint interview with the two. After an hour of clarifications, denials and more denials, I came home thoroughly confused. Saif Khan dropped me to my doorstep in Amrita's car which was later to drop him in town, or so he said though I had a suspicion that he went right back to Amrita's house.

When I sat down to write the story, I had a nagging suspicion that there was more to it than had met the eye, but suspicions cannot be reasons for mistrust. In the following weeks, eveningers announced the Saif and Amrita marriage. The couple denied it once again. It was 9 a.m. on 10 October. I was getting ready to leave for work, when the telephone rang.

It was Amrita on the line. 'Hi,' she said cheerfully. 'How are things?' Her tone was too casual and and my journalistic instinct warned me that something was in the offing. So without waiting on formalities, I said, 'You've called to say you have got married.' There was a brief silence followed by a giggle. 'That's right. How did you guess?' 'Because,' I told her, 'A star marriage has once again followed the predictable pattern. Always, the stars first deny the news, then confirm it, cleverly packing their interviews with philosophic quotes to cover the confusions. We journalists have learnt to take star contradiction in our stride. We never completely trust them.'

'I guess you are right,' Amrita admitted sheepishly. 'It does feel a bit awkward confirming the story now. But even if it's embarrassing, it has to be done.' Why had she denied the story in the first place? 'At that time we hadn't informed our parents and we wanted them to be the first to know. Now that they do, we don't mind going public.' They got married on 21 September. The ceremony was performed according to Islamic rites, at a common friend's house.

On 22 September they broke the news to their parents. 'Or rather to our moms,' clarified Amrita. 'We were too scared to tell our fathers.' When the mothers knew about it, why did they hide the news for so many days—18 to be precise? 'Our moms were going to tell our dads and they had to go about it in their own way. It needed time. Saif and I decided that until we had sorted it out within the family, it wouldn't be ethical to make statements to the press.'

Didn't they think it unethical to get married without their parents' consent in the first place? 'Our marriage was our personal decision. Something strictly between Saif and me, so it was okay,' Amrita answered. After the news was broken to the fathers, the couple went to Delhi. The families met, talked, planned. 'Everything was okay and not at all trau-matic. Contrary to what we had anticipated, everybody was gracious. In fact, our parents are planning to hold a recep-tion for us in December,' she blushed.

And how does it feel to be a new bride? 'I feel happy but more than anything, I feel relieved that I've confessed to the event.' I asked her if she felt embarrassed by her earlier defensive statements when she had said that she was not a cradle snatcher (Saif is six years younger than her). 'I deliberately said these things to mislead the press. When you are in love nothing matters. If he's younger, so what? He is not successful today, but he is very intelligent. Life isn't over. There is plenty of time and there will be plenty of opportu-nities. And what's most important is that I love him.' Does it matter that they have made a laughing stock of themselves? 'It does,' she admitted. There was a long pause. Where is Saif Khan now? 'If we are newly married, he has to be beside me. Wait, I'll put him on the phone for you.'

A minute later, Saif came on the line and true to his reputation, answered my queries cautiously. 'My mom was to arrive in Mumbai on the 22nd from Delhi. That was the day of our *nikaah* and I went to receive her at the airport after the ceremony. When I felt it was the right time, I broke the news to her. Naturally, she wasn't ready for it, and was shocked. She was slightly hurt too, that we had kept her in the dark but once she got over the initial hurt, she was very sporting.'

Does he agree that their marriage has turned into a joke? 'No,' Saif protested. 'Our marriage isn't a joke. We went through all this in order to save our parents from embarrass-ment. In the bargain, I do agree we have appeared very silly, sounded like liars, but it was a situation that couldn't be helped. Our action has caused a lot of confusion. We apologise for it. What more can I say? People have tried to warn me against Dingy (Amrita). But I don't care for what people say. I don't think Dingy is a problem and if she is, she is a beautiful problem. I will face it.'

Before disconnecting, I spoke to Amrita again. 'My mar-

202 • SALAAM BOLLYWOOD

riage is forever. I should know. I have loved and lost too many times to know what I'm getting into. I'll make it work.' When I put down the phone and sat to pen the Amrita-Saif love story on paper, I couldn't help remembering the *pundit* who, after reading Amrita's *kundali* had predicted that she would marry a *nawab's* son. 'It's in her horoscope and she will not be able to avoid it.'

On the whole it was a controversial year. A weekly column reacting to an April fool joke by a rival magazine brought me more stress than I had bargained for. Amitabh Bachchan look-alike Vijay Saxena of Tulsi Mix advertisement fame was photographed in an intimate pose with Archana Puran Singh. I felt that the idea was in poor taste and wrote about it. The very idea that stars could actively participate in fabricating a scandal was distressing. Is reputation so cheap that one can barter it for a magazine cover? And if that's so, stars deserve the scandals they are beset with. My outburst was more an emotional reaction. Besides, the current trend in journalism encouraged media-postmortems, only I had to pay a heavy price for self-expression. I was subjected to character assassination which caused me heartburn and loss of sleep. Still, I don't regret taking a stand. It was an ugly incident but I'm glad I stood up for my convictions.

Four months later, I walked into another controversy. A scandal involving Anupam Kher and Mamta Kulkarni's younger sister Moulina led to a lot of bad blood between Anupam and the actress. On the sets of Yash Chopra's *Parampara* in Pune, in the presence of the entire unit, Anupam slapped a journalist and the episode blew out of proportion. The controversy became a burning issue when film journalists combined to fight the physical assault and made it a moral issue. Anupam was equally distraught. Sworn to fighting till the end, he systematically instigated a campaign and led morchas to protest against the magazine. But once again, disunity amongst stars worked in favour of the press. One of his colleagues forewarned the magazine and the journalists had sufficient time to get their act together.

To Kher's credit, it must be said that he managed more support from his colleagues than others have ever managed. It's a different matter that a lot of them changed their mind later and a few withdrew half-way. Anupam's well-wishers had predicted all this. 'You will be lonely, alienated, isolated.' But at that time Anupam was too angry to see reason. '*Maine sar pe kafan bandh liya hain, koi saath chale na chale.*' As months passed, however, Anupam lost his anger and patience altered his perception. Nobody was worth so much heartache. That's when Anupam dropped his campaign and conquered his bitterness. 'The episode taught me two lessons,' he told me one day. 'One, that no one walks with you. Two, nothing in the film industry works without vested interests.'

I had interviewed the actor when the controversy was still hot. He wasn't prepared for my uncomfortable questions and reacted sharply. It was a side to his personality I hadn't witnessed earlier. He had similar observations about me. He thought I was professional and made no concessions for a friend. It was an awkward moment for both of us when our professional roles overtook our friendship. Luckily, he was called for a shot at that precise moment and the break diffused the tension. When he got back, he was calmer. Always reflective and analytical, Anupam has interesting insights about himself and others. That's his attraction and also his strength.

Over the same issue, my colleagues looked upon my difference of opinion as a betrayal. I don't know why loyalty is confused with the herd mentality. Just because you are a part of the tribe it does not mean that you share the same sensibilities. I wasn't willing to take sides. In my editorial I attacked the current trend in journalism. In the interview, I attacked Anupam. When the article appeared in print, Anupam withdrew from me completely. It took him a long time and a lot of effort to trust me again. He expected that because he had exposed his vulnerability, I'd protect him. I had stood up for the truth but in the bargain displeased both. The journalists accused me of victimising them. And Anupam of letting him down. 'I don't expect anyone to walk with me for life,' he said to me philosophically, months later. 'That they walked even a few steps, I'm grateful. Eventually everyone is alone. We all have to fight our own battles.'

Those days, Anupam often appeared disillusioned but never totally without hope. 'I may not be the idealistic B.V. Pradhan I once played in *Saaransh*, but I can aspire to be one.' His favourite story was of Mahatma Gandhi getting thrown out of the train by the whites in Africa. He argued that if they hadn't, Karamchand Gandhi would have remained an ordinary barrister. In everyone's life, he said,

15

ONE AFTERNOON Anupam Kher spotted an overturned rickshaw and stopped to help. A lady passenger lay bleeding under the overturned rickshaw on the road. Anupam and his driver carried the lady into the backseat of his car and drove her to the nearest hospital, where they refused to register a case. At the next hospital the formalities took ages. The police wanted to know if Anupam knew the woman personally. The hospital authorities wanted to know if the patient was run over by Anupam's car. The inquiries took quite a while and crowds gathered around the actor. Hours went by and in the meantime, Anupam had to cancel his appointments. The few people he couldn't get in touch with, began phoning his residence. His family was worried, but there was no way of finding out. It was a crazy day. The woman who'd met with the accident was to get.married the following day and wouldn't stop crying. In the given circumstances, the onus of breaking the news fell on Anupam. When Anupam phoned the woman's home and introduced himself, the parents were immediately suspicious. The fiance was confused. There were too many questions, too many fragile emotions to be dealt with.

I became a witness to the incident because I was visiting my ailing aunt in the Breach Candy hospital the same evening. Vinod Khanna was at the hospital too. His grandfather-in-law, wife Kavita Daftary's *dadajee* had suffered a stroke and was admitted to the ICCU on the third floor. The entire Daftary clan was present. An elderly relative remarked that they had to be careful, since it was the night of *amavas*. Anupam and I travelled back together in his car.

It was the night before Diwali and Anupam was on his way home. Outside, the streets were bursting with crackers and *kandeels*. There was festivity in the air but Anupam seemed a broken man. 'It was a normal day and then in just a fraction of a second, I touched so many people's lives. There's so much suffering all around the world and all we are worried about is catching up with time.' And as he said this, a fire cracker fell against our window. Anupam sighed and smiling weakly said, 'Happy Diwali.'

It was a special Diwali for Rajkumar Santoshi. His debut film *Ghayal* had won two National awards and now he was launching his pet project—*Damini*. The film was being seen as Santoshi's autobiography told on celluloid. He was in love and he didn't care to hide it. He told everyone who congratulated him on the day of the *mahurat* that *Damini* was conceived and written specially for Meenakshi Seshadri.

'My film will unfold a volcano of talent,' he said. If Meenakshi was embarrassed, she preferred not to show it. At least, not in the initial stages. In fact, the more vocal Santoshi got, the more reticent she turned. The press, for some strange reason, was critical of Meenakshi and supportive of Santoshi. Their hot and cold vibes on and off the sets kept the gossip-mills churning. They were working together in four films (*Damini, Ghatak, Dil Hai Tumhara* and *Ajay*) and all the time thrown in each other's company. They had frequent arguments. Santoshi objected to Mrs. Seshadri's rude behaviour and constant interference during shootings. The break-up came over something very inconsequential. Meenakshi had injured her foot and cancelled her shooting. On the same day she did a photo-session for a magazine. When the producer got wind of it, he accused the director of promoting unprofessionalism. Humiliated, Santoshi dropped Meenakshi not just from *Damini*, but from the remaining films as well.

This wasn't the first time that a director had fallen in love with his heroine. Nor was it the last time that a heroine had rebuffed her director. What made the Meenakshi-Raj Santoshi story unique was their clashing interests. While Raj's attraction towards Meenakshi was solely personal, Meenakshi's interest in Raj was strictly professional. Raj hoped that in making these four films he would somehow pursue and win over his heroine. Meenakshi, on the other hand, hoped that his attraction for her would induce her to give greater performances. That's not how it happened. Things would have been different had Raj not worn his heart on his sleeve. Or Meenakshi not been as self-righteous. She could have flirted with the filmmaker and then on the completion of the film, dumped him! Instead, Meenakshi preferred to play it straight. Just as Raj preferred to make his suffering public.

The emotional drama soon reached a climax. The press-release announcing Meenakshi's ouster from *Damini* shattered the last vestige of hope. Within a few days of the fiasco, Raveena Tandon was finalised for *Ghatak* and Madhuri Dixit and Sridevi began to be considered for the other two projects while *Damini* was temporarily shelved. Weeks passed without any sign of the Santoshi-Seshadri saga being resolved. Santoshi filed his complaints with the Filmmakers Combine and Film-makers And Directors Association. Meenakshi filed her grievances with the Cine Artistes' Association. Those were tension filled days.

The fate of the film was to be sealed on 9 September 1992, when the heads of the two Associations gathered at Yash Chopra's office to severe the contract. Formalities over, while everyone waited for the draft to be typed, Yash Chopra turned to the two, 'Can nothing be done? Are you sure you want to split? If you feel even slightly inclined to work together don't hesitate to shake hands. Once you are out of this room, you may live to regret the decision.' He had barely finished the sentence when Santoshi and Meenakshi got up simultaneously and shook hands.

This was the first instance when two warring parties had agreed to a patch-up so easily. Obviously, the film mattered

208 • SALAAM BOLLYWOOD

equally to both. Raj had conceived the film for Meenakshi and Meenakshi knew it was the role of a lifetime and therefore deeply hurt when she lost the National Award to Dimple Kapadia for Kalpana Lajmi's *Rudaali*. I remember meeting her the evening the news came. It was at a party hosted by HMV. Meenakshi tried to be in good cheer, but her disappointment was apparent. A fortnight later, when the reviews came out after the release, the wounds multiplied. There was not a single word of praise for the actress or for the film. Meenakshi's fragile but powerful portrayal in a role Nutan had specialised in, went unnoticed. There were other reasons for the film's bad reception.

All media attention had diverted to Sanjay Dutt's arrest under TADA. What made matters worse was the unflattering box-office collection. Her self-esteem at its lowest, Meenakshi went into a shell. But not for long. Within two weeks came the good news of the tax exemption granted to the film and its subsequent pick-up at the theatres. In the coming months, Raj became reconciled to the idea that his heroine wasn't in love with him and would never be. He got engaged to a Bangalore-based girl Manila and Meenakshi had the last word. 'A lot of water has flown under the bridge. Whatever happens, happens for the best.'

Boney and Anil Kapoor tried their best, but *Roop Ki Rani Choron Ka Raja* was a jinxed project and bombed. It had been in the making for over five years but the family rode the crisis with astonishing grace. Everyone knew that the film was heading for disaster. And on the night of the premiere, people discussed the fact openly. Stories of Boney Kapoor pumping in the last earnings of brother Anil into the dream project had been making the rounds for over a year. The grapevine even said that Boney had borrowed heavily from the market and was insolvent. Boney knew deep down that he was flogging a dead horse. The project had been under production for too long to retain magic. One knew he had lost hope when he stopped showing sufficient interest in his wardrobe. Weeks after the film bombed, Boney said that he had had a hunch that the film wouldn't work. When he was getting ready for the premiere, he felt there was something missing. 'A feeling deep down told me that something wasn't right. The spark was not there. The excitement was lacking.'

The excitement was missing at the party too. The guests stayed till early morning but their faces were cold. 'In normal circumstances, I should have received the first phone call by 6 a.m. When there was no ring till 8 a.m. I began to get suspicious. And when the distributors evaded my call at 10 a.m. I was sure! But I needed to hear it. So I began making the calls.' When the finality dawned, Boney shut himself up for a few hours. The next morning, he contacted the distributors on his own. 'I wanted to save them from the embarrassment of asking. The film had bombed but I had all intentions of paying my dues. All I needed was time.'

Anil Kapoor and his wife Sunita looked relatively calm when I met them at a common friend, Naresh Goyal's launch of his new airlines, Jet Airways. Standing next to me at the Santacruz Airport Sunita was, as always, in high spirits. 'The film has bombed and we have finished with the mourning. Some of us cried, some of us screamed but now it's over! Money is transitory. If it's in your destiny nobody can take it away. Our savings of a lifetime have sunk, but we can start all over again. There's still time and God willing, there will be more chances. There are no deprivations. What did Anil have when I married him? We have built this house slowly and steadily. We can put the pieces of our life together again. And if for that we have to let go of a few luxuries for a while, it's no big sacrifice.'

Madhuri Dixit was introduced to the press by Subhash Ghai on the sets of *Ram Lakhan*. When, later in the evening, she sang, 'Number 54. House with the bamboo door,' everyone was impressed. From the very beginning, Madhuri has maintained her distance with the media. No journalist can claim to know her on a personal level. Even though she has done a number of photo-sessions for a number of magazines, the defences have never been lowered. I have seen flashes of anxiety when a favourite film like *Prem Pratigyaa* or *Sangeet* was due for release. She was keen to know what the press thought of her performances. They were performances she was proud of and she wanted the films to do well. Much later, there were moments of vulnerability when travelling to the USA for her shows with Anil Kapoor, she was tired and unwell but was expected to perform within hours of landing. At the Chicago airport, during the immigration, the officer insisted on breaking up the group. Madhuri was on priority for she had a show the same evening, but not her parents. When Madhuri remonstrated, the officer retorted, 'It's only a day and you are not dependent on them, are you?' When, later, I told her that she could have argued that she wasn't but her parents, being old, were dependent on her, she regretted keeping silent. 'I didn't think of it. I'm not used to arguments.'

For the launch of our Hindi edition, it was decided to invite her as our chief guest. Her arrival created a storm in Delhi. After the function, as I was leading her to her room, I felt giddy and nauseous. Even before the elevator could stop on the third floor, I started to throw up. I was rushed into Madhuri's room but before I could make it to the basin, the passage and the toilet area had been soiled. It was a repulsive sight and I felt deeply embarrassed by the mess, but there was genuine sympathy in Madhuri and her mother. At awkward moments like this you miss your own family. Still, the Dixits showed a lot of grace, even though the housekeeping took some time to clear the carpet and the walls.

My family, I noticed, had begun to take the film industry in its stride. They were neither surprised by the occasional visits by stars to my home nor did they question me about

MADHURI DIXIT

Not used to arguments

my visits to their homes. Holi, Christmas and Diwali, which until recently had been strictly family affairs were slowly spilling over into celebrity happenings. Without my having to explain it to them, my family learnt to distinguish between the on-screen images and the off-screen ones. As years went by, they became equally familiar with the jargon and began to understand what were premieres, parties; outdoors, *mahurats* and trial shows. They became as immune to shocks as I was. Their anxiety vis-a-vis me had subsided completely. While earlier the constant line thrown at me had been, 'Who will marry anyone working in films?,' now my job was considered to be artistic expression. Even so, confusion persisted on the domestic front. A lot needed to be resolved with maids and drivers. They assumed I was working in films and expected enormous salaries. Everytime my driver saw Jackie Shroff or Anil Kapoor open the car door for me, he made a mental note to ask me for a raise. A few drivers left the job because they wanted to become heroes. When I told one that I could help him get a job only as a spotboy he said, 'It's hero or nothing.'

My visits to the studios become infrequent as my administrative responsibilities increased. I didn't miss the interaction as I had little in common with the new breed of stars. I'm of the opinion that every fresh crop of journalists must discover a fresh batch of stars to interview. Only then can new insights emerge. It's best that they fight, make-up, trust, grow and influence each other. This prevents cynicism. Once in a while, when the pressures were less and the mood right, I would drive to a neighbouring studio but returned confused. In the new world the stars and their staff, make-up men and dress-designers were too informal. The heroines travelled to studios in *kaftans* and the heroes in shorts. Aamir Khan, who was shooting in my neighbourhood, dropped in at my home wearing shorts, with a briefcase in hand. I was embarrassed introducing him to my 85-year-old mother. 'Is he the neighbour's son?' she asked me through sleepy eyes. A few days later he was shooting outside the building and visited me early in the morning. An hour of heated discussions and three cups of tea later, when he could not control his hunger, Aamir said, 'I'm famished. Aren't you going to offer me breakfast?' Accustomed to eating an early lunch, I told him the family wasn't reared on the breakfast culture, but the maid could cook him some *upma* or *aloo poha*. 'I want eggs.' There are no eggs, I told him. This is a vegetarian home. 'What about toast and butter?' Gujaratis have superior notions about eating bread but we can get you a packet as soon as the shops open. 'In that case, what about some cornflakes?' I shook my head again. 'Forget it. Just give me some milk.' That was the last time Aamir Khan came home. Or I invited him over.

Not all star-scribe encounters were as pleasant. One year after her marriage Amrita Singh, accompanied by husband Saif Ali Khan walked into the *Star & Style* office and attacked its assistant editor. Later, Amrita went to the Santacruz Police Station and admitted to manhandling. 'I don't regret my action and will do it again if she misbehaves,' she complained to the inspector on duty.

A few months later, followed another violent incident. The line of defence offered was provocation. The difference this time being, that cameraman Rakesh Shrestha had the courage to strike back at the truant star, Salman Khan, in the presence of half-a-dozen witnesses on the sets. Perhaps, Salman thought that Rakesh would flee from the scene. But in striking back, Rakesh redefined the star-scribe equation. On another occasion, Shah Rukh Khan chased a reporter off his sets and a month later, Sunny Deol threatened a journalist. Earlier, Gulshan Grover had summoned a journalist to his make-up room and bashed him up!

Looking back, I feel it wasn't fair to single out Anupam Kher. Dharmendra, Farha, Moushumi Chatterjee have all done it before him. It is said that Shanta Apte had stormed into editor Baburao Patel's *Film India* office, carrying a hunter. Anupam erred when he refused to apologise. But then how often do scribes say sorry? While violence under all circumstances should be condemned, it's time to re-evaluate the fire-fighting operations between stars and scribes. For, whether it is the press who exposes the stars or the stars who strangle the scribes, it's the film industry that gets defamed!

Sordid stories revealed by stars going through turbulent times were exploited by the media for sensational headlines. Heroines involved with married men were frequent targets. It happened with Sridevi too. Boney Kapoor thought their problems would end once he publicly declared his marriage. He was wrong. The relationship was open to further debate and discussion. The most vociferous reactions came from star wives. 'Could she not find a bachelor that she's running after a married man? These actresses are home-breakers. Don't they realise that they are bound to be cursed?' I have lost count of the number of times I have heard such state-ments. A woman involved in an extra-marital relationship is crucified, but no charges are levelled against the man. Would it have been possible for Sridevi or for that matter Hema Malini or Vyjayanthimala to get involved in a relationship had their feelings not been reciprocated? All break-ups are painful but to look for poetic justice in the suffering of the 'other' woman is stretching even morality a bit too far.

Sridevi was wooed and swept off her feet from the moment Boney Kapoor set his eyes on her during the filming of *Mr. India* in 1987. *Roop Ki Rani Choron Ka Raja* took years in the making and in the interim, Sridevi lived as a house-guest first at Anil Kapoor's and later at Boney's bungalow Arjun in Versova. A privilege no other Narsimha Enterprise heroine has enjoyed. From then on, in every film Sridevi signed—*Khuda Gawah, Laadla, Mr Bechara*, Boney played a vital role in her life. He was her only support during her mother's illness and innumerable family crises.

Their dependence was mutual and gradually the bond strengthened.

If logic was all we lived our lives by, there would be no love stories. If we expect the 'other' woman to 'think' about her man's family and future, so should the man before leading the woman on with promises of love and passion. Out of the many heroines involved with married men in the volatile seventies, only three culminated in marriage. Only three men had the courage to break off old ties and begin life on a clean slate. Javed Akhtar, Kamal Haasan and film-maker Ramesh Sippy. Mahesh Bhatt preferred to change his religion in order to marry Soni Razdan. Dharmendra is deliberately kept out of the list because after two decades, he leads a life divided between two homes. Hema Malini is still not included in his family functions be it the premiere of *Barsaat* and the wedding celebration's of Bobby Deol.

Second marriages are no beds of roses and Jaya Prada and Smita Patil discovered the bitter truth on their own. The problems multiplied with each passing year. They always do, when the children get older. There have been instances, when the betrayed woman chose to break her silence after the beloved's death. If the relationship was sacroscant while he was alive, why not honour it with dignity in death? Kabir Bedi maintained that there was a fundamental difference in the way men and women handled emotional pain. 'Men stuff it, while women reach out to a network of supporting friends and listeners, and some have the capacity to share their sorrows in print.' Trauma evokes different reactions in people and to view it as a gender issue, is not fair.

In the film industry, tragedy has unfailingly stirred up a hornet's nest. The storm brews, most of the time, at the funeral pyre. Before dust could settle on Amjad Khan's grave, Kalpana Iyer, linked with the actor, made emotional headlines in magazines. A need for self-expression probably, but why after the man's death? When he's not around to defend himself? Even the beautiful Madhabi Mukherjee (*Charulata*) could not resist admitting her liaison with Satyajit

Ray in print after his demise. How come she never confessed to the relationship when he was alive? Then, he would have had the option to clarify. Hollywood actress Ingrid Bergman, in the foreword of her autobiography wrote, 'It was my children who compelled me to write my memoirs. . . . When you are no more, we will not be able to protect you from your critics for we will never know the truth. . . .'

One more foreign unit was in India to make a film about our country. And one more time, condemning everything about it. *City Of Dreams*, an Indo-European-American serial co-produced by London based Spotlight Leisure group and our very own Firoz Nadiadwala. Publicised as the mega-budget, mega-star soap, about Bombay's film industry. 'We are not making a documentary,' emphasised associate producer Victoria Cocks to a weekly tabloid. 'The serial is pure fiction.' Hadn't we heard that earlier? Film-makers projecting distorted versions of events with selective perspectives in the disguise of fiction was dangerous enough. What made one even more suspicious was their round about way of not hiring an Indian script-writer.

Even though ten Indian script-writers were tested all were rejected because they, 'failed to capture the flavour of the colurful, chaotic world.' The flavour, if you please, would come from their foreign author, Bradley Cole, who had never lived in this country. It did not matter that he was unfamiliar with our ethos and culture, our star-system and their idiosyncracies. His excellent research and quality time spent hanging out with directors at studios would compensate for the lack of authenticity!

Director Tim Graham had so far only shot the pilot but was already complaining of the heat and the language barrier. He had problems with star schedules, 'Your stars function differently from what we're used to.' He found the presence of his co-producer on the sets intrusive. 'They are always hovering around, putting in their bit and adding to the escalating confusion.' No such problem with their own people, please note. The patronising attitude prevailed in the entire unit. Cameraman Jonno Smith was surprised that the technicians here still used only rubberband technology while the sound recordist was impatient that people wouldn't maintain absolute quiet once the shot had been called . . .!

To cap it all, associate producer Victoria Cocks maintained that 'The serial was a revelation of what you thought happened behind the closed doors of Bollywood.' Really? How did they know what happened? Or for that matter their writer, cameraman, or director? None of them were born here, or lived here. Perhaps their only reason for making the project India-based was that things are much cheaper here. This was also the time when the distinguished director Warris Hussein (*Intimate Contact, The Passion Joel Delaney*) was in town casting for his new film *Such A long Journey*, about a Parsi family trying to rise above its differences. The director had not made up his mind on the main lead. 'Gustad Noble will most likely be played by an Indian actor.' One wouldn't be surprised if he wasn't. After swallowing the dishonour of watching Ben Kingsley play 'Gandhi', we are used to foreigners discrediting our Indian actors. The only time Hollywood thinks of casting Indian stars is when the role calls for an Asian.

Three years ago, Hollywood director Roland Joffe thought of Shabana Azmi and Om Puri when casting *City of Joy*. The film had its share of controversies. After granting permission for shooting, Calcutta had second thoughts about a foreign unit shooting in the city. Predictably, there were bomb-blasts and bandhs. I was present on location when a reporter from a Bengali newspaper deliberately provoked the unit make-up man (Anoop), and producer (Ian Smith) to initiate an argument.

The incoming finance was in the interest of Calcutta and the country at large. Also, it was too late in the day for the government to suddenly start circulating the film script amongst intellectuals for a second opinion. One wonders how they would feel if our own Raj Kapoor and Satyajit Ray, shooting abroad, had to go through similar scrutiny and censorship? Is it justified to be so paranoid about Calcutta's poverty after seeing it innumerable times in all of Satyajit Ray films?

A few months after Mother Teresa's demise, a TV documentary on the Mother by Channel Four outraged conservative catholics. According to the script-writer, Mother was nothing but the product of a 'profane marriage between tawdry media hype and medieval superstition.' Titled *Hells Angel: Mother Teresa*, the film attacked her for accepting donations from dubious characters and awards from murderous dictators. One part of the mind wanted to dismiss the controversy with, 'Who is the West to pontificate on our dacoits, dons and demigods?' The other part, was more objective.

The donations were an international controversy. It wasn't the first time that Mother had been accused of a cult. What was unfair and mischievous in this case, was the statement of a former British volunteer, who after having served for years at Mother Teresa's chose the opportune moment to comment that the injections weren't sterilised. Probably not. But what attracted the volunteer to come in the first place had not been Mother's scientific acumen but her selfless service!

16

LIFE WAS GETTING to be fairly comfortable and if the growing mediocrity and fall in standards bothered me, I chose
to ignore it. My enthusiasm had waned more than I cared to
admit. Filled with a stubborn indifference and dis-dain,
immunity had become a part of my character now. Seven
film studios and more recording theatres were in
the vicinity, but I seldom visited them. I preferred keeping
tabs on the film world through colour or black and white
pictures brought in by freelance photographers to the office
everyday. The photographers also narrated interesting ane-
cotes of what went on within the studios. Junior reporters
narrated interesting observations on what went on within
the make-up rooms. And film magazines on what went on at
the outdoor locations.

With time, star interviews began to read more like ac-
counts of battles and photo-sessions became, an excuse for
exhibitionism. The one who was ready to scream louder, or
strip faster, won that month's applause. I watched the
changing morality of the new breed of stars dispassionately,
recording the incidents mechanically. Nobody said anything
new, different, original or stimulating. Nobody shocked,
nobody surprised. Nobody bullied or threatened anymore
either.

The equations changed first when I became an editor and
then a columnist. Author and dear friend Shobha De (also
responsible for this book) recommended my name to Anjali
Mathur of *Sunday Observer*. The paper was looking for a
fresh name to do their film page and when editor Chandan

Mitra (currently with *The Pioneer*) met me at the Sea Lounge, Taj Hotel, to discuss details, I wasn't aware that the encounter would mark one more turning point in my career. The pressure of deadlines created its own high and much as I cursed and complained every Wednesday morning, the discipline kept me on my toes. In the years to come I would sail through weekly columns for *The Afternoon, Janmabhoomi Pravasi, Hindustan Times, The Pioneer, The Hindu* and *Newstime*, without feeling persecuted.

Once in a blue moon, when the occasion or the star was special, I broke my rule and strolled inside the studio. The familiar sights and sounds filled me with nostalgia but also a certain inexplicable fear. The new me was more inhibited and less adventurous. Success had taken away my spirit to survive under all circumstances. Cushioned and shielded in the interim, the new me was vulnerable and therefore more selective of the company I chose to spend my time with.

Back home, the magazine everyone had predicted would not last more than a month had completed seven years and was the first Indian magazine to go on the internet. Sitting on the mezzanine floor of my office at Veera Desai Road, Andheri, I would often recall the early days of struggle. Anxiety and doubt would alternate with hope and fear as we stumbled over piles and piles of pictures and galleys, trying desperately to push the artworks to the press. There was the overpowering smell of varnish and the continuous hammering of carpenters on the walls. Sawdust spilling out of our clothes, hair and nostrils, a lot of staffers left before completing their probation period. Another lot refused the job because the location was way out.

I sensed disapproval from my rivals at the launch party. 'Scandal is the spice of Bollywood' said our critics who felt everything was wrong with the magazine—the size, the look, the title. Credibility came with time and the allegations died slowly. The copy travelled from the bathroom to the living-room. Now they say that the magazine holds a mirror to the film industry. Sometimes as a pointer and sometimes as a

SHAH RUKH KHAN
He knows it isn't an ego issue

whiplash to the system, the magazine is unafraid to take up issues.

When Bhagyashree backstabbed us by giving pictures shot exclusively for our magazine to a rival magazine on the pretext of showing them to her husband, we pulled her up for the betrayal. We pulled up Amrita Singh when she invited us all the way to Karjat for a photo-session with her newly-wed husband Saif Khan but on realising that director Hema Malini looked upon this as an intrusion, she did a volte-face. We supported a not-in-the-running Ayesha Jhulka, suffering victimisation during the *Dalal* controversy and had the courage to ban Shah Rukh Khan at the peak of his career at the time of *Baazigar* and *Darr*. Shah Rukh abused us and attempted to assault two of our journalists and threatened to burn the office on more than one occasion. We ignored his threats. The problem can be very easily dismissed as an ego issue. It wasn't. And Shah Rukh knew this.

The trouble with our new breed of stars is that they come into films so young that they treat the studios like the college canteen—now warring, now making up with co-stars and filmmakers. Most of them are not mature enough to handle the pressures of a demanding career. And so everytime stress increases, they throw up their hands in exasperation. In the early days every time Karisma Kapoor bungled her shooting dates or appointments with photographers, she'd burst into tears and shriek, 'I'm only 16.' My argument is, if you are old enough to earn money in lakhs, you are old enough to shoulder responsibilities. They want too much and too soon! They want the perks, not the penalities. Exploding on the screen with their new life-styles and morals, the new breed is an ambitious bunch of go-getters. Their maxim being, 'It's our life and we are going to lead it the way we want to.' It's not as if they do not have their plus-points. They do.

Compared to the stars of the seventies who were entrenched in old patterns, the eighties batch is disciplined and committed. The danger re-emerged in the nineties. Determined about redefining rules, they were unwilling to play the image game. A classic example is Salman Khan.

After Sooraj Barjatya's *Hum Aapke Hain Koun* and Rakesh Roshan's *Karan Arjun*, Salman should have been a hot proposition. Instead, everyone connected with the film benefited, except Salman. While Madhuri Dixit bagged all the awards and appeared on the covers of the film glossies, Salman went unnoticed. Only because Salman was not accessible to the media. After Amitabh Bachchan, he is the only actor to say 'no' to the press and to stick to his word. He believes that an actor should be judged by his work. Unlike his contemporaries, who've made a joke of their now-on, now-off stand on the press, Salman has consistently refused to give interviews, his standard line being, 'Leave me alone. I have nothing to say.'

To give him credit, he has not exuded contradictory signals. Unlike many who deny interviews, but make sure to circulate their pictures through photographers, Salman never sneaked in backdoor stories, never sent feelers even when his career hit a low. There are many instances when he has been denied justice. He has never been nominated for awards, never won them. Whenever a film flopped (*Chand Ka Tukda*, *Veergati*), he has been blamed. Whenever a film clicked (*Maine Pyar Kiya*, *Hum Aapke Hain Koun*), he went unsung. Whenever he did films with two hero roles (*Saajan*, *Andaz Apna Apna*, *Karan Arjun*), the other hero walked away with the praise. Whenever his relationships broke off (with Shaheen, Sangeeta and Somy), the women got the sympathy. On the other hand, instances when Salman Khan has been accused of being unjust are just as many. Directors said he was irreverent and co-stars complained he was high-handed. Journalists said he was violent and uncharitable. He denied some of these accusations and admitted to a few mistakes. 'If they can attack me in print, I'm at liberty to behave as I wish on my home ground.' In a surprise gesture Salman, after months of silence, lowered his defences to give an exclusive interview to my magazine. It was Salman's frankest interview to date. I had gone to meet him with a lot of apprehension, escorted even by a bodyguard (my photographer). But he won me over with charm and honesty.

Around 40 people are always present for lunch and this excludes half-a-dozen servants and the watchman of the building. Friends and friends-of-friends drop by in the afternoon and stay for hours, play Scrabble or just watch a film. We conducted the interview in the balcony at the far end of the living-room. It took longer than expected because Salman, I discovered is a brilliant raconteur and an excellent mimic. He had me in splits and days after our encounter, I continued to think of Salman fondly.

Of the new stars, the only relationship based on a soil of trust is with Aamir Khan. Our encounters are a reservoir of

SALMAN KHAN

No contradictory signals

disagreements. The first slab of endless arguments came in 1986 when Aamir agreed to pen his memoirs of *Qayamat Se Qayamat Tak* for *Movie*. His only condition was that not a single word or line should be altered. I disagreed. It's something he hasn't forgiven me for in all these years. He felt I was being unfair and autocratic because he was a newcomer. I felt he was being preposterous and was an upstart. Time and a healthy respect for each other's work made us drop our defences and change our perspectives about each other. Our arguments continued, nevertheless. If I give in to Aamir more often than I want to, it's less out of conviction and more out of exhaustion! Aamir knows this and rags me. Once, while driving with him to the studio, Aamir asked me all the questions he shouldn't. Or rather, questions well-mannered boys don't ask women. Staring out of the window, he enquired about my age and salary. I told him. He nodded understandingly. When I hit him on the head and revealed I was lying, he nodded again, eyes on the road. 'I was about to tell you, you look much younger.' The three days I spent observing him for our 'Diary' were full of similar pranks. Little wonder I never wanted to spend another day on his sets again.

Aamir Khan—committed to quality

Bhalla's bungalow. It's an evening shift but, as usual, Aamir is amongst the first to arrive. After the customary greetings with the unit hands, the actor disappears into his room for a coffee break. Ashutosh Gowarikar, the director of *Baazi*, joins him and they discuss the scenes they are to shoot. It's only 7 p.m. but the unit is ready with the first shot. 'I will need half an hour,' Aamir warns, sipping his tea. A quick shave, a quick bite, change of clothes and Aamir is ready. Attired in a black T-shirt and jeans, he arrives on the sets almost immediately. 'I play a cop in the film, actually a commando,' he tells you. 'But not the uniform wearing cop, thank

God.' They are shooting a police station scene today. An anonymous caller has phoned to give some important information to Aamir. As they go through the rehearsals, Gowarikar improvises. There is a slight confusion over the placing of the telephone. While Ashutosh wants it on the right side of the desk, Aamir feels it would be better to have the instrument on the left. 'That is precisely the reason,' explains Gowarikar. 'The inconvenient placing will bring about an awkwardness which is essential for the anxiousness required in the scene.' Aamir nods understandingly, his eyes brightening. During the take, as per the instruction, he tries to shift the phone but is unsuccessful because the wire is too short.

One notices that a lot of care is being taken over the minutest details—how the assistant gives the cues, how the junior artistes (*havaldars*) acting as move in the foreground or the background, what they do with their hands, where they stand. 'Ashu's strength as a director is that he gives excellent instructions,' elaborates Aamir. 'If my performance is appreciated in *Baazi*, the credit ought to go to him.' The very next shot proves Aamir's point. It is an ordinary scene but Ashutosh's running commentary from behind the camera does the trick. What follows is a flurry of activity—entirely unselfconscious but effective. One hand holding the phone, Aamir wards off the constable with the other. His eyes searching for the keys in the desk drawer and hand checking the revolver on the belt, he scribbles an address on the paper, to finally grab the jacket off the chair before running to nab the culprit. Cool and level-headed, Aamir, you notice, is a relaxed worker—earnest and not at all high-strung. In fact, he is extremely good humoured.

The next shot involves his reading a file. As he goes through the rehearsal, the critic in him takes over. 'This file looks too limp. Can I have some papers inside it, please?' An assistant aids him by filing in a few full sheets. 'Also, how about a pen that works? This one has no ink.' Again, somebody comes forward to give him a new pen. 'One has to be patient,' he says with a wink, 'The average age in this unit is 25. Can you believe I'm the seniormost in this unit?' Then pointing to an assistant dressed in bermudas, ponytail and one ear-ring, he says, 'Doesn't Avinash look like a hippie? Or better still, a terrorist?'

The atmosphere on the set is informal. There are no *saabs*, no *haan jis*. No MTV culture either, thankfully. Everyone is addressed

The Cannon Group presents
PLACIDO DOMINGO
in a Golan-Globus Production of a Film by
FRANCO ZEFFIRELLI

GIUSEPPE VERDI
ENNIO GUARNIERI
FULVIO LUCISANO
FRANCO ZEFFIRELLI

AAMIR KHAN

I give into him out of exhaustion

by their first names, including Aamir. In fact, Aamir looks different too. 'It's because I have cut my hair shorter than usual. Also, I'm not wearing make-up. I'm seriously considering giving up make-up altogether. I've realised I look better without it.

An hour later, when it's dinner time, the director joins Aamir in his make-up room. Aamir's staff has a way of fussing over their master. They hover around him soundlessly, especially his driver-cum-Man Friday, who is always around even before Aamir can call out to him. A mere expression is sufficient for the man to know whether Aamir should be served water, tea or snacks. At the moment he serves him his bowl of soup. 'Saab loves soup,' he tells you softly. When Aamir has finished with the first bowl, he brings the second one. Aamir usually has two bowls before his meal. Chicken, you soon learn, is Aamir's favourite food but it shouldn't be too oily or spicy. His favourite snack is sandwiches. Club sandwiches being the first choice, failing which they can be either chicken or cheese. His favourite drink is Pepsi. Not because he models for it. 'On the contrary, I agreed to model for Pepsi, because I liked its taste.' He drinks at least six to eight cups of tea during the day and, as far as possible, must munch something with every cup of tea.

When I meet him the following day, he is munching Monaco biscuits and before one knows it, has cleared off the entire plate. He is shooting for *Baazi* again, though at a different venue. Today we are at the Conference Hall of the SNDT College, Santacruz, and the accompanying artistes are Raza Murad, Paresh Rawal, Satish Shah, Avtar Gill and some others.

In between shots, when Aamir is not required, he comes outside to sit in the quadrangle. This is the moment the hostel girls have been waiting for all evening. As soon as he emerges, the girls begin to cheer him loudly. Shouting from their balcony they call out his name and wave at him—some even blow flying kisses. 'Aamir Khan come up,' they shout in chorus. Aamir blushes. 'I'm shooting,' he makes a lame excuse. 'Just for a little while,' they insist. As minutes go by, they become hysterical. When they realise he will not indulge them any further, they throw him a bedsheet that they want him to autograph. They continue to shout instructions and blow flying kisses from the first floor. Embarrassed and blushing beetroot red, Aamir refuses to look up. By this time the *verandah* is packed with faces. Throwing him *dupattas* and scarves, they create a racket! The director is not amused. Distracted, he comes forward to reprimand them but they are too euphoric to be tamed. That's when Aamir rises. Raising both his hands, he requests them to keep quiet. They do so instantly. A hush prevails and Aamir bows down to thank them.

It's Sunday evening and we are at Bella Vista, Aamir's residence in Pali Hill. Reena, with Junaid in a pram, sister Nikhat and cousin Nuzrat are on their way for their evening walk. As soon as they come out, children playing in the compound surround the baby's pram with. 'Aunty, let us see the baby. Can we play with Junaid? He is so cute.' By this time Aamir, who never works on a Sunday, but has to attend an important meeting, comes down. Not finding his car, he joins the rest of the family. The kids, who were until now completely engrossed with Junaid, charge towards Aamir with screams of, 'Aamir *bhaiya*!' Nuzrat, Nikhat and Reena observe this with amusement. 'If he is Aamir *bhaiya*, then how come we are aunties?' The children chuckle and run away. That's when Aamir's Maruti 1000 drives up. His chauffeur gets out to open the car door. Aamir Khan gets inside the car with a brief, 'So boring to have to work on a Sunday.'

g, March 1994

20 April 1993 was a black Tuesday, when Sanjay Dutt was arrested at the Mumbai airport, on arrival from the shooting of *Aatish* in Mauritius. What followed was a round of denials, insinuations, accusations and confessions. There were tears and tantrums. The press took sides and the controversy helped the actor to get bail. The relief was short-lived. Three weeks later, Sanjay was back in the Arthur Road jail and his family back in mourning. The suspense ended on Monday, 4 July, when the order detaining Sanjay was passed. If the public was sympathetic the first time, there was confusion and anger the second time round. On

8 July, 30 activists of the Akhil Bharitya Vidyarthi Parishad (ABVP) staged a demonstration outside the Central Jail in retaliation for the rally led by the Cine Artistes Association in favour of Dutt junior. The activists urged the authorities not to give any special treatment to the jailed film star.

I remember a decorated 58, Pali Hill, on the day Sanjay was granted interim bail for the first time. The family welcomed the erring son home, but the tension was tangible. At the gate, a traditional *arti* was performed by his sisters. Next, Sanjay disappeared upstairs for a private meeting with his father. Downstairs, journalists, photographers, fans and friends shouted 'Victory.' But even when the public protested bitterly and Sanjay's fans prayed feverishly, the Dutts maintained a studied silence! The Dutts knew that the crisis hadn't ended, that the triumph was temporary, that anytime, anywhere, the ghosts of TADA could catch up with them. Sanjay knew it too. Cautious and quiet, he had lost the old cheer and abandon.

The new Sanjay was a harassed, hounded man, nervous and restless with whom his friends could identify no longer. With close associates, Sanjay sometimes dropped his defences and confessed to lack of sleep. 'My recurring nightmare is that they might arrest me again.' Whether he was shooting in Mumbai or out, attending a film party, *mahurat* or social function, his lack of confidence and concentration was unmistakeable. He refused to talk or make statements in public lest he was misquoted. Shielded by escort and secretary Pankaj Kharbanda, Sanjay felt secure only in isolation.

The trauma of being ostracised, the pain of being a suspect, the humiliation of being handcuffed, the helplessness of being frequently summoned to the courts took its toll. Meanwhile, stories about him kept growing. There were rumours that he had been seen dancing in the discos until the wee-hours of the morning. Some said he had been seen drinking in the pub with his friends and some others swore they had seen him driving with girlfriend Rhea Pillai all night on the streets of Mumbai.

There were stories of him having turned into a fanatic. That he visited temples and shrines, fasted on Mondays and Saturdays and even made a trip to a certain Guru who had advised him to abstain from booze, cigarettes and sex on certain days of the week. Insiders said that he indulged in elaborate prayers and spent a major part of his day in religious ceremonies. His sister Priya told me once that there was nothing Sanjay hated more than his visits to the court. As the date of his hearing approached, his tension increased. Sanjay himself admitted to being fed up of the constant shuffling of dates and the constant explanations to his directors on account of his parole. The constant apologies and post-mortems and the constant waiting in a way ended when judge J.N. Patel rejected the filmstar's bail application on 5 July. The court order, though depressing, relieved Sanjay of his trauma. The cloud of uncertainty that hung over him and his family for 15 fear-filled months was at last over! As Alan Paton rightly put it in *Cry The Beloved Country*, 'Fear is a terrible journey. But sorrow is at least an arriving!'

The film star who had driven to the court in his Maruti 1000 in the morning was taken away in a police van, handcuffed, in the afternoon. Those present outside the court premises witnessed a frightened Sanjay Dutt finally break down. He asked to meet his father, whom he first hugged and later touched his feet before the final parting. 'Pray for me,' he pleaded to the throngs of the crowd waiting outside. He tried to smile, but couldn't. Two days earlier, an equally emotional Sanjay, inaugurating the Shraddha Rehabilitation Foundation for Destitutes and Mentally Retarded at Bhayander, had embraced the young and old patients. He said his best wishes would always be with them. 'I will always be there when you need me.' Shying away from making a speech, he was edgy and anxious. But he had been like that for quite some time. Four days ago, on the sets of Jyotin Goel's *Safari* at Mayur Mahal, Sanjay was uncharacteristically reflective and withdrawn. Call it the gloom of intuition or the persecution of a marked man, but the stress was evident. Depressed and desolate, he paced the garden path, expressed incomplete thoughts and lost interest mid-sentence when communicating with the unit.

Like a man possessed, he was awaiting an ominous sentence! The premonition wasn't misplaced. Bold headlines of, 'Sanjay Dutt back in jail—Bail not granted,' flashed in the papers on 5 July. The same evening, Newstrack on television featured a rare and candid interview with the actor conducted sometime ago. 'It was awful,' he said, choosing his words carefully. 'Imagine first one, then a second and finally a third iron gate shut on you while you are all alone in a cell. I would sit by this little window and stare at the busy street outside. All day I spent watching these people passing by, walking into shops, buying things, talking, walking again. At that time I felt that the world was moving by while I was just waiting! There was a *chaiwala* in the prison. He'd come carrying his kettle and cups, pour out a cup of tea, then go into the second and then the third cell. I envied this *chaiwala* his freedom and wanted so badly to exchange places with him.'

Unfortunately, Sanjay's freedom lasted only 15 months. He was detained in the same prison cell again. And this time, indefinitely! The one place he never wanted to go back to, even in his worst nightmare, the one place his father never wanted to see his son in. It is said that Sunil Dutt wasn't allowed inside the court premises initially. Not until he loudly proclaimed that he was an MP. Later, of course a message was sent to let him in. Before going in, Sunil Dutt sent a boy to buy Marlboro cigarettes, toothpaste, soap and Marie biscuits for his son. The rest of the family came to visit him in the evening. And members of the film industry came the following morning. In a bid to show solidarity with Sanjay, the FMC made plans alongwith the CAA to move the Supreme Court to grant Sanjay bail. They drove down to Thane carrying placards of 'We are with you Sanju.'

'We are with him too and feel sorry for him,' said a

SANJAY DUTT

Sanjay was a marked man

woman constable I got a chance to speak to outside the Arthur Road jail. '*Yeh sab rajniti hai,*' said another constable. 'When the father and the son embraced and wept, we felt choked too, but the law isn't in our hands' interrupted the first. 'There was a beautiful girl who came with Sunil Dutt this morning. Was she his daughter?' asked the third. 'Sanjay is allowed food from home. He's alright but lonely and sad. But then that is expected. A jail is after all a jail.'

An hour later, on our return journey, directors who had worked with Sanjay and watched him in more familiar surroundings rambled, 'What must he be doing inside the jail the whole day? How does he spend his time?' Director Bobby Raj, whose film *Zamane Se Kya Darna* starring Sanjay had been released sometime ago was of the opinion that Sanjay was not the reading kind. He wasn't even sure if Sanjay was allowed books inside the prison. 'I think so, but it is difficult to concentrate when you are feeling low,' said Jyotin Goel. 'And Sanju is a hyper guy,' added Bobby. 'He cannot sit still in one place for more than five minutes. He shuffles and shifts all the time.'

The last time he was in prison, Sanjay spent a major part of the day crumbling biscuits and feeding them to the pigeons. And the nights he spent watching the guards taking their rounds. From his cell window all Sanjay could see was the lower half of the guard's legs. On a moonlit night, the walking guard was more like a prop on a film set. Only this time the moon in the background was real, not a cut-out!

17

A NIL KAPOOR AND his family had been receiving threatening calls for sometime and they were scared. Finally, his
brother Boney Kapoor traced the calls to a suburban hotel
only to discover that it was none other than actor Aditya
Pancholi, notorious for his brawls and police records, who
had been threatening the Kapoors. A strong contender for
Sanjay Dutt's role in Subhash Ghai's *Trimurti*, Aditya thought
that it was a golden opportunity to star in a big banner
production and he was going to leave no stone unturned to
get the role. When he discovered that Ghai was considering
Anil he began hounding the actor with vicious phonecalls
threatening him with dire consequences if he accepted the
film. The Kapoors couldn't believe that anyone could stoop
so low and indulge in blackmail and life threating phone
calls for the sake of a role. When arrested by the police,
Aditya pleaded not guilty. What was disappointing was that
the Cine Artistes Association didn't take any action against
the erring actor. Far from penalising him, they even failed to
extract an apology.

Twenty-five years ago, when Nutan had slapped Sanjeev
Kumar on the sets of *Devi*, a ban had been imposed on the
actress by the Artistes Association for misconduct. Producers
were restrained from signing her until she had apologised to
Sanjeev and to the CAA. But discipline doesn't seem to be
sacroscant anymore. Today, the stars, be it an Ayesha Jhulka,
Dimple Kapadia or Anil Kapoor have to beg justice!

The year 1997 will be remembered for the mafia threats
that seemed to have overtaken Bollywood. Character-actress

Urmila Bhatt was murdered under mysterious circumstances. Dara, comedian Guddi Maruti's brother, was shot dead in broad daylight at her residence in Versova. A few days later two unidentified assailants waiting outside producer Mukesh Duggal's office on J.P. Road, killed the producer as he stepped out of the building at 10.45 p.m. The killers, parked inside a Maruti 800, fired 13 rounds into him. Duggal's assistants drove him to the nearest hospital but it was too late. Suffering severe chest and abdominal injuries, Duggal succumbed minutes after being admitted. The police believe that all the three murders were linked with the underworld.

A few months later another producer was being threatened. He had borrowed heavily from one mafia don and then he dared to befriend the don's rival—and Financier Vallabhai Thakker was shot dead in his car at point blank range. Fear gripped Mumbai and the Karnataka film industry, as friends and associates of victims went underground. As many as 22 Kannada film producers were running scared after the brutal killing of Kannada filmmaker Chidambara Shetty. Abducted from his house, Shetty was tortured and assaulted and his body thrown on the road the next morning. The most gruesome was music baron Gulshan Kumar's broad daylight murder. He was praying at a temple in Versova when three unidentified assailants pumped in 15 bullets and killed him on the spot. 'I'm a man of God nobody will harm me,' Gulshan liked to say but he was wrong. Music-director Nadeem of Nadeem-Shravan fame was held as the prime suspect and Ramesh Taurani of Tips, too, was arrested!

On 17 April 1998, a starlet, reportedly also Miss Bombay, landed in Tihar jail under the Immoral Trafficking Prevention Act. The 19-year-old had been arrested by the Delhi crime branch. While she waited for her surety to be furnished by a Mumbai film director, she complained that she had been implicated in a false case by the police. The Mumbai producer has been absconding ever since. Two days later Govinda received vicious calls from an unidentified person. Sensing mischief, Govinda informed the Juhu police and was immediately provided with security. The same evening, came the news of the death of Vijay Sippy son of G.P. Sippy, brother of Ramesh Sippy and producer of *Aatish*, *Hamesha* and co-producer of *Raju Ban Gaya Gentleman* and *Patthar Ke Phool*. The police described Sippy's death as murder!

One wonders what it was about the film industry that attracts scandals. One expected that the Sanjay Dutt episode be a learning experience but it didn't work out that way. TV artiste Harish Patel and his friends were arrested for attempting to murder a security supervisor whom they suspected of having stolen Rs. 55,000. Mamta Kulkarni was attacked by three strangers who had barged into her apartment. In Orissa, Archana Joglekar was assaulted by a group of men who pushed their way into her hotel room and Pooja Batra was attacked by *goondas* on her way home after shooting at Film City.

For sometime the old guards had been complaining of strange businessmen who had infiltrated into the trade. Despite recurring incidents of coercion, of blackmail and backlash, however the film industry had refused to recognise the signals. Soon after the 1993 December riots, the film fraternity managed a show of solidarity and trudged a peace march from Bandra to Juhu. If only peace could be purchased by offering flowers to the statues of Mahatma Gandhi. These peace-mongers-by-day, however, hobnobbed with dubious characters at night. Writers willingly penned scripts and the actors happily starred in projects funded by quest-ionable men. Producers did not hesitate to invite anti-social elements as chief guests and as audience, we lent social legitimacy to release and *mahurat* functions.

Five years ago BJP spokesman L.K. Advani had blamed the film industry for the Ayodhya riots. 'Doesn't the hero of the Hindi films take the gun in his hand in the last reel and seek justice? So why blame the public for doing the same now?' It was an unfair accusation but instead of protesting against it, film-makers agreed on a nine-point charter with the ruling party which they promptly denied the next morning. The late Ramdas Nayak, the then BJP president, angrily remarked, 'Their leaders come running to us with their problems, then as usual, change their minds. The proof is in their joint signatures.'

The Film Makers Combine had agreed to most clauses, except to the one stating that no member of the film fraternity would have any links with the underworld. Affronted, they backed out but the timing was wrong. The film fraternity couldn't afford to talk about credibility, specially when dirty linen was being washed in public.

Six years after Divya Bharti's suicide, her death is still shrouded in mystery. It is alleged that the actress was being threatened by the underworld because her producer husband Sajid Nadiadwala had borrowed heavy sums from the underworld. Divya preferred to end her life rather than succumb to their demands. Soon, the only films being made in Bollywood were about the mafia or other controversial subjects like Sanjay Dutt's arrest and Rajiv Gandhi's assassination. After a bio-pic on Phoolan Devi, *Bandit Queen*, outlaw Veerappan declared that he wouldn't surrender until a similar film was made on him!

According to the Karnataka police, the Mumbai underworld is slowly losing its hold over Bollywood and spreading its dragnet through small operators in Bangalore. At a cassette release function held in Mumbai, many years ago, Deputy Chief Minister Gopinath Munde and Minister of Transport and Cultural Affairs, Pramod Navalkar had announced that the ministry didn't empathise with the film industry's tax problems because more than 50 per cent of the investment came from underworld kingpins. He publicly attacked the film industry for surviving on slush money!

After eight years of steering clear of gossip, *g* magazine was going through a lean phase. The print media was facing stiff competition from the electronic media and the magazine sales had begun to dwindle. The publishers, Maulik Kotak and Bharat Kapadia felt that the time had come to revamp the magazine. After innumerable meetings, brain storming sessions, and expert consultations, we were ready for change. A market survey revealed that readers prefered a magazine that was convenient in size and spicier in content. I wasn't sure if I'd be able to deliver the goods and suggested that we take on a younger team, more familiar with the new breed of stars and their lifestyles. The new policy brought in a new set of adjustments and after some teething problems and some headlines and stories I regret, we struck a balance between the commercial and the cerebral. Soon, film stars got accustomed to our vibrant and assertive stand though there were many who were also disappointed. Change always arouses mixed emotions, and yet change is inevitable.

I was surfing channels when I happened to catch an interview with veteran actor K.N. Singh on Zee TV. Nattily dressed in a yellow shirt and with neatly combed hair, the old-time villain looked at peace with himself. Reminicising about his life and career, Singh appeared cheerful and candid till at the end of the programme, he casually mentioned that he had lost vision in both his eyes. Then how do you spend your time, asked the interviewer. 'Once in a while, old friends drop by to see me. Sometimes, I tell them of my difficult times. They console me and say, "Singh *man ki ankhon se dekho. . . ." Kehna asaan hai, jeena bahut mushkil.* There are so many who suffer bigger tragedies. In comparison, I've been fortunate. Life has been kind to me. *Mujhe talash hain ek aise insaan ki jo sirf itna bata de ki din kaise guzara jata hain/*I'm on the look out for a person who can tell me how to spend my day. . . .' The anguish well-concealed, until then, burst like a bubble. The withered face cracked into a sad smile as the credit titles rolled on the screen. It was a poignant quote and for days, Singh's sad smile haunted me.

It is unfortunate that a number of our senior artistes, who

have seen fame and glory in their prime, are today living in solitary confinement. A lot of them are condemned to penury because they were too foolish to invest their earnings wisely. There are those who are financially secure but doomed to loneliness. Nadira is one such. The film industry has not made adequate financial or medical provisions for its senior artistes. Where so much money is wasted in premieres and parties, nobody thinks of mobilising a support system to rehabilitate the yesteryear stars. Nobody thinks of setting up a recreation club where veterans can meet for coffee and confessions. With government aid, the Association could have set up teams to document the bygone era. Some of our artistes are living legends and very soon they will become history. Why is it that we only cherish people when they are no more?

I remember writing about the poverty-stricken condition in which Leela Chitnis existed after being abandoned by her children. A generous couple in Bangalore read the story and contacted the magazine offering to adopt the ageing actress and look after her till her end, but the proud actress declined the offer. A few months before Lalita Pawar's demise, she was in town for a Marathi Sahitya Sammelan and was invited to appear on television. The old-timer discussed her retired life in Pune with humour. She related an accident about her maid: 'One day my maid asked me what I did for a living. I told her, I acted in films. She asked me if I'd heard about Lalita Pawar. When I told her I was Lalita Pawar, she became furious. She said, "You mean you are the ugly woman who tortured us for so many years?" She dumped the utensils in the sink and walked out of my home refusing to work for me. I was greatly amused by the incident.'

Not all are as fortunate. I've spotted an embarrassed Tun Tun, waiting at a suburban bus stop, unable to handle the attention. Roly-poly Manorama still travels by rickshaws to shootings carrying her own vanity bag. It was only a few years ago that technician Jamal Sen, who had compiled music for Kamal Amrohi's *Daera*, was caught begging at a railway station by a journalist. The examples are innumerable.

Yesteryear actress Mehtab, wife of the renowned actor-director Sohrab Modi and best remembered for her role in *Jhansi Ki Rani*, had a quiet funeral attended by just family members. It is unfortunate how the biggest of them go unsung when their time is out. Meena Kumari's elder sister lashed out at the film industry for not offering the family any help after her sister's demise. One remembers the anguished interviews of Devika Rani's caretaker and from Uttam Kumar's relatives. The Bengal superstar's beautiful resort in Bangonagar, now bought over by Covent Garden, was allegedly being used for illicit dealings.

Leela Chitnis lives in a Home For The Aged. Playback singer Rajkumari runs a tailoring shop from a tiny flat in Versova. Bhagwan Dada, after 66 years in the industry, lives in a chawl and once in a while when he's lucky, is offered wee-bit roles. Comedian Mohan Chhoti, before he died, ran an ordinary *dhaba* named after him. Helen's predecessor, Cuckoo, depended solely on the support of her well-wishers and friends till the very end. So many tragedies. So many heartbreaks.

A fortnight after writing about the plight of senior artistes, I received a threatening letter from the Cine Artistes Association accusing me of abusing the Association. A month later, I received identical typed letters from K.N. Singh and Bhagwan Dada accusing me of distorting facts and defamation. Both insisted that they were healthy, happy and without a worry in the world and if I had the courage, I would reproduce their letters in the magazine. I did.

Through sheer co-incidence, Singh also featured in the vintage section of our magazine, where he discussed the role of the CAA. Two days after the magazine hit the stands, a panic-struck Singh phoned our office to say that he had been misquoted. 'How many people can I go around apologising to at my age?' Out of reverence I visited him the same evening. During the encounter, he made an off-the-cuff comment, *'Pata nahin shabdon aur khayalon mein kahan galat faimi ho gayi/* There has been a misinterpretation of words and intentions, for my intention was not to hurt anyone.'

His helplessness silenced me completely. I didn't have the heart to tell the frail 90-year-old, that there was no chance of his being misquoted because we had the interview on tape. As he was already under a lot of pressure, I didn't want to cause him further stress and therefore dropped the issue. Until one afternoon, Ram Mohan, secretary to the CAA phoned to inquire what was happening about Singh's clarification. 'We warned you the first time and now you've done it again,' he said in an accusatory tone. 'Do you have any proof that the people you have mentioned are living in penury?'

'Do you have the proof that they are not?' I countered. 'We do not believe in making a show about what the Association does for its artistes. The CAA does not indulge in propaganda.' In other words, the CAA does not believe in accountability, I thought to myself. What was so demeaning about suggesting a recreation club for these veterans? Or that recommending the bygone era be documented? Are we so closed that we would rather shun any attempt at experiment than expose our shortcomings?

Ram Mohan demands proof for my 'attacks'. The letter from the Bangalore couple wanting to adopt Leela Chitnis in our office files is the proof! Lalita Pawar's television interview on Doordarshan is the proof! Tun Tun and Manorama spotted on the Versova street as I pass in my car is the proof! Jamal Sen caught begging at a suburban station by a colleague and Parshuram picked up at traffic signal by compere Tabassum on her way to a TV station for recording is the proof!

Ram Mohan has every right to question and yet claim the

privilege to not answer. The CAA has no records for the expenses of 'Hope '86' show in Mumbai. No records for the industry show in America in 1991. Or prior to that, for the industry strike, when huge sums were donated for the benefit of technicians. Do they have an answer for not sending a representative to India's first heroine Devika Rani's funeral in Bangalore? Or not helping actor Raj Kiran, detained in jail for 34 days for barging into the Satya Saibaba Ashram in Bangalore? And in a mental hospital after that? And yet, if Bhagwan Dada after 66 years in films, feels so blissful living in a chawl and Raj Kumari in running a tailoring shop, who are we to question their happiness?

Let us not do this to our elders. Let us not misuse nostalgia. At the 'Aashirwad Awards Nite' held at Hotel Centaur, Juhu, they were felicitating senior artistes. Described as the Navratna Trophy, the nine gems to be honoured were Kedar Sharma, A.K. Hangal, playback singer Rajkumari, Jairaj, Sitara Devi, Naushad, Rajendra Kumar, Shammi and Biswajeet. The artistes turned up on time but the show started two hours late. The stage was uncomfortably high for the seniors to climb up. Imagine a 90-year-old Kedar Sharma lumbering up the narrow steps without support! The volunteers escorting the veterans lacked reverence and grace. Some of them were dressed in obscene costumes with broad slits waist downwards exposing bare thighs.

Once the guests stepped down, the volunteers abandoned all responsibility. Raj Kumari, 80-plus after singing, 'Ghabra ke mar jaye to achcha . . .' to a thunderous applause was indifferently dumped between boisterous Arshad Warsi and Sharad Kapoor who kept exchanging jokes and bubblegum across the older woman. Raj Kumari looked terrified. It was only after desperate announcements by the compere that the singer's escort returned to her seat. Disorganised, shoddily structured and full of glitches, the function lacked basic courtesy. They called out winners at random and distributed trophies callously. Those in a hurry, left early. Those who didn't protest were made to wait. Many unwilling to address the audience, feigned a sore-throat. Everything from the seating arrangement, audio-visual presentation to the microphone system was a disaster. When the show ended, there were no escorts to lead the veterans to the exit. Nobody to make sure that the seniors got to their cars. And if they didn't have their own transport, to organise one for them. It was distressing to watch two old people hail a cab on their own. It made me wonder what makes our senior artistes endure such functions. It cannot be just nostalgia. And if not, it has to be social deprivation. And if that's so, haven't we all failed somewhere?

Epilogue

M ONTHS ROLL INTO years and years into decades. Actors
have turned businessmen. Actresses have become directors. Directors have turned producers. Producers have
expanded into distribution. Co-ordinators have become
designers. Journalists have become editors. Strugglers have
become TV stars and TV stars have opened software
companies. The fifties stars have retired, turned into sepia
memories. Once in a while you bump into Ashok Kumar and
Dilip Kumar at public functions and they talk about sunsets
and siestas. Dev Anand is still announcing new films and
Lalita Pawar has died only recently. The sixties stars have
mellowed, become grandparents. Shammi and Shashi Kapoor
and Sharmila Tagore have gained weight and wisdom.
Dharmendra and Jeetendra are active no more. The seventies stars are stable and branching out. With grown up kids,
they are into their second innings. Shatrughan Sinha, Raj
Babbar and Rajesh Khanna have got into politics. Vinod
Khanna has launched his son and Rakesh Roshan is in the
process of doing so. Amitabh Bachchan is the sole survivor
of his generation, still playing lead roles.

Shabana Azmi is a respected Rajya Sabha member. Rekha,
Dimple, Jaya Bachchan and Hema Malini do only selective
films. Zeenat Aman has turned producer and Neetu Singh is
still evading offers of a comeback. The eighties stars have
gone through their cycle of hits and flops, had their share of
big and small controversies, purchased property and reared
babies. Anil Kapoor, Sunny Deol, Jackie Shroff and Sanjay
Dutt are all proud *papas*. Madhuri Dixit has ventured into a
partnership with M.F. Husain and Juhi Chawla with Jai

Mehta. The nineties stars are calling the shots. Shah Rukh, Salman, Saif, Kajol, Karisma and Raveena blow hot and cold each day. Manisha Koirala and Tabu, though reflecting old world charm, have their share of controversies. Now snatching lovers, now stealing roles, they fight and make up and fight and defame. They are used to scorn, blasphemy and mud-slinging. So are the readers. I cannot say I know the new breed as well. Ajay Devgan is appealing, Sunil Shetty chivalrous and Akshay Kumar intriguing. They are informal and inconsistent. I prefer watching them on screen to meeting them. I seldom interview the current crop and am not familiar with what they think or feel. I remember Kajol as a little girl when I went to interview her mother Tanuja, at their Santacruz home. The three-year-old had flashed the same sunny smile, and, with a broom in hand, exclaimed with childlike candour, *'jhadu lagata hai'*.

I remember Karisma Kapoor during a photosession with her father. Sitting on Randhir Kapoor's lap she announced to a roomful of people, *'Papa, I want to wear a bikini.'* I remember an absolutely dream child, Pooja Bhatt, skipping the playground of her building and my colleague and I treating her to an ice-cream.

I remember a very fat Bobby Deol wheeling a toy electric train in his father's van at Film City, as a weighed down Dharmendra rambled on about the stressful phase he was going through. Married to Hema Malini a few weeks ago, Dharmendra spoke about their future. I remember a shy boy with intelligent eyes waiting outside Dimple theatre as I rushed past him without a second glance to make it on time for Nasir Hussain's, *Qayamat Se Qayamat Tak*. The shy boy, Aamir Khan, was later introduced to me as the hero of the film. I remember a very special, gentle, girl dropping by at my office carrying her black and white pictures. 'Go away,' I told Juhi Chawla, then known as Miss India, 'You don't need to do this. You are going to be a major star!'

I remember the trusting face of Govinda. 'I'm Nirmala Devi's son,' he announced proudly. In a yellow *banian* and a *kada* on his arm, there was promise in his smile. He still has it. I remember Sunny Deol at his first photosession, nervous and eager, embarrassed by his aggressive co-star Amrita Singh. I remember Akshay Kumar pushing my car, stuck on Juhu road in torrential rain. The boy from Bangkok, then new in Mumbai, would assist our staff photographer Jayesh Sheth at studios and star homes. Shy and reticent, nobody knew that the handsome hunk was keen on films till he asked Jayesh to prepare his portfolio. Raj Sippy liked what he saw and gave him a break in *Saugandh*. I remember Ajay Devgan as cinematographer Sameer Arya's friend. Ajay and his four friends hung outside the Juhu *gully* every evening, self-sufficient and happy in each others' company.

I remember Tabu as the girl from Hyderabad. Yash Chopra had confirmed elder sister Farha for *Faasle* and she was feeling left out. A week later, Dev Anand dropped by at Chetan Anand's home for lunch, saw Tabu and signed her for *Hum Naujawan*. I remember Urmila Matondkar and Jugal Hansraj on the sets of Devi Dutt's *Masoom*. I remember Shekhar Kapur spending quality time with his child artistes. I remember Twinkle Khanna as a spoilt brat. Twinkle would exasperate her mother, making her change her frock three times and hair band twice before she would be satisfied with her appearance. The same brat turned divine in adolescence. The sensitive girl would sit rivetted at her mother's story-sessions. I remember Sanjay and Chimpoo Kapoor, the boys from Chembur. They were knee-high when I met them at a friend's party, but I remember Chimpoo winking at me and Sanjay chuckling at his friend's private joke. I remember Raveena Tandon playing on the sets of Ravi Tandon's *Khel Khel Mein* and Pratibha Roy clinging to her mother's *pallu* at a relative's wedding in Delhi. I remember a naughty Saif Khan ragging his mother Sharmila Tagore in the middle of an interview. I remember Bosky stamping her foot, demanding a Smash T-shirt from father Gulzar. I remember a trusting child, reverentially folding his hands into a 'namaste' assuming that I was a friend of the family because I was with his mother. The following afternoon, when he discovered my identity during a family cover shoot, Abhishek Bachchan was withdrawn and reticent.

Memories of the past mingle with memories of the present. Vivid in the mind is the night villain Mahesh Anand's car ran over and killed innocent people sleeping on the road. The time filmmaker Raj Kumar Santoshi declared his love for Meenakshi Seshadri from the roof-tops. The time Bachchan's *'Jhumma chumma . . .'* and Sanjay Dutt's *'Tamma tamma . . .'* controversy got bigger and bigger, involving choreographers, music companies, film-makers and stars. The time debutant, Bhagyashree star of *Maine Pyar Kiya* cold-shouldered hero Salman Khan saying she wasn't interested in films. Two years later, she returned to launch husband Himalay.

The time Zeenat Aman delivered a baby boy and introduced him to visitors with, 'We have a gentleman amidst us.' The time Mithun Chakraborty decided he was going to be a full-fledged businessman. The controversial time after *Bombay* when director Mani Ratnam's house was bombed. The time Akshay Kumar ditched Pooja Batra, then Raveena Tandon. The time Raveena couldn't decide if Akshay was her co-star, friend or lover. In between she even claimed, 'Akki who?' The time Pooja Bhatt ditched Bobby Deol, and Bobby ditched Neelam, and Neelam ditched Govinda. The time Govinda abused Anil Kapoor, then shook hands with him over a photosession. The time Anil Kapoor recommended Jackie Shroff and Jackie publicly thanked Anil.

The time Boney Kapoor's *Roop Ki Rani Choron Ka Raja* bombed and director Satish Kaushik went into a deep depression. The time *Prem* flopped and one was scared that Satish might commit suicide. The time he lost his one-year-old son and everyone was sure that he would do something drastic. The time Naseeruddin Shah wrote us an angry letter for delaying the publication of his fashion pictures. The time close friends and work associates, producer Pamela Chopra and writer Honey Irani split over the screen play credit of Aditya Chopra's debut film *Dilwale Dulhaniya Le Jayenge*. The time colleagues Aamir Khan and director Ram Gopal Varma split over conflict in ideologies after *Rangeela*. The time Sanjay Dutt was admitted handcuffed to a hospital and a guard sat with a machine gun watching over him and a humiliated Sunil Dutt said, 'They treat us worse than animals.' The time Amjad Khan compared the film industry to *kadipattas*. 'The government exploits us as long as we retain the flavour. Once dry, they throw us out of the plate, lest the taste turn bitter.' When filmmaker Roland Joffe compared the city of Calcutta to a beautiful woman obsessed with her bad nose.

The time Amitabh was crucified for winning the National Award for *Agneepath* and the parallel cinema called it an undeserving honour. The time Boney married Sridevi and Sattee Shourie, his former wife's mother assaulted Sridevi in a five-star lobby on New Year's night. The time Shekhar Kapur raved and ranted about his problems with the censors over *Bandit Queen*. The time newspapers reported that Rishi Kapoor had abused his wife and the couple denyed the police statement.

The time Karisma Kapoor had to scream she was 'ordinary' since being 'sexy' was a crime. The time Ajay Devgan said he'd prove himself and did. The time Saif Ali Khan was dropped, picked up and dropped again until Yash Chopra gambled with *Parampara* and immortalised him in, 'Ole Ole.' The time Sridevi took over from Dimple, Jaya Prada and Meenakshi Seshadri. The time Madhuri Dixit took over from Sridevi and Boney Kapoor took over from everybody by marrying Sridevi and the time Subhash Ghai became successful, then power-generating, and finally unpopular over his bitter battle with protege Mahima Chaudhary in *Pardes*. The time Mumtaz and Reena Roy returned to arc lights and the time Divya Bharati jumped off the balcony and what's worse, predicted it. The time Juhi Chawla denied, then ignored and finally accepted Jai Mehta in public. The time one fell in love with Simran of *Dilwale Dulhania Le Jayenge* and baffled when one met Kajol.

The time Information and Broadcasting Minister Sushma Swaraj granted the status of industry to the film world. The time Aamir Khan promised he'd never work in a violent film but did just that. There were dreams and disillusionment, turbulence and tears. One accepted Bachchan's beard, Raj Kumar's wig, Dharmendra's second marriage, Sanjay Dutt's imprisonment and Neena Gupta's out-of-wedlock baby. 'Your morals are mixed up,' said an older sibling when I related certain astounding incidents. To my friends and family, I'm answerable for the whacky world I'm associated with. With them I'm the out-sider. Left open mouthed personally by the savagery of the stars, I find myself defending the celluloid world in their absence. My behaviour puzzles my loved ones. Some feel alienated but these are fleeting phases. 'Do you believe in the world you work in? In the people you write about?' they often ask me. I do. But it's not that simple to explain. There is another side to stardom. The better side—of creativity and compassion, of glory and generosity. Of sacrifice and sustenance, of warmth and wisdom that an outsider will never know. Inaccessibility prevents identification.

It's simpler for me to smile and change the topic. Today, when someone asks me the question, 'How does it feel to be a film journalist?' I look at the person asking. Is it worth reacting? Strongly? I'm not sure.